Reader's Guide
to
ELIZABETH BARRETT BROWNING

Reader's Guide
to
ELIZABETH BARRETT BROWNING

Rudolf Eisler

CENTRUM PRESS
NEW DELHI-110002 (INDIA)

CENTRUM PRESS
H.O.: 4360/4, Ansari Road, Daryaganj,
New Delhi-110 002 (India)
Ph.: 23278000, 23261597

B.O.: No. 1015, Ist Main Road, BSK IIIrd Stage
IIIrd Phase, IIIrd Block,
Bangalore - 560 085 (India)
Tel.: 080-41723429
Visit us at: www.centrumpress.com

Reader's Guide to Elizabeth Barrett Browning

First Edition, 2009

ISBN 978-93-80106-51-9

PRINTED IN INDIA

Printed at Salasar Imaging Systems, Delhi-110035 (India)

Contents

Preface

Elizabeth Barrett Moulton Barrett was born on 6 March 1806 at Coxhoe Hall, County Durham, England, the daughter of Mary Graham Clarke (d.1828) and Edward Moulton Barrett (d.1857), who amassed great wealth from his Jamaican sugar plantations. Three years after Elizabeth was born, he bought the 500 acre estate `Hope End' in Hertfordshire. Empathetic due to her own lifelong physical sufferings but evocative of profound intellectual thought, Browning's poems are considered among the greatest contributions to English poetry for the nineteenth century.

Through her pen, she was passionately outspoken on issues of social injustice like slavery, child labor, and oppression of women, and later in life expressed her political opinions of the struggle in Italy with Austria. She had a lasting influence on future American poet Emily Dickinson (1830-1886) and English author Virginia Woolf (1882-1941) who praised her works, which are still widely read in the twenty-first century. Just over a year later, on 29 June, 1861, Elizabeth Barrett Browning died in her husband's arms. She is buried in an elaborate Cararra marble tomb designed by Lord Leighton in the English Cemetery in Piazzale Donatello, Florence, Italy. Her husband survived her by twenty-eight years

Author

Chapter 1

Introduction

Elizabeth Barrett Browning (March 6, 1806 – June 29, 1861) was one of the most respected poets of the Victorian era. Elizabeth Barrett, an English poet of the Romantic Movement, was born in 1806 at Coxhoe Hall, Durham, England. The oldest of twelve children, Elizabeth was the first in her family born in England in over two hundred years. For centuries, the Barrett family, who were part Creole, had lived in Jamaica, where they owned sugar plantations and relied on slave labour. Elizabeth's father, Edward Barrett Moulton Barrett, chose to raise his family in England, while his fortune grew in Jamaica. Educated at home, Elizabeth apparently had read passages from *Paradise Lost* and a number of Shakespearean plays, among other great works, before the age of ten. By her twelfth year she had written her first "epic" poem, which consisted of four books of rhyming couplets. Two years later, Elizabeth developed a lung ailment that plagued her for the rest of her life.

Doctors began treating her with morphine, which she would take until her death. While saddling a pony when she was fifteen, Elizabeth also suffered a spinal injury. Despite her ailments, her education continued to flourish. Throughout her teenage years, Elizabeth taught herself Hebrew so that she could read the Old Testament; her interests later turned to Greek studies. Accompanying her appetite for the classics was a passionate enthusiasm for her Christian faith. She became active in the Bible and Missionary Societies of her church. In 1826 Elizabeth anonymously published her collection *An Essay on Mind and Other Poems.* Two years later, her mother passed away. The slow abolition of slavery in England and mismanagement of the plantations depleted the Barrett's income, and in 1832, Elizabeth's father sold his rural estate at a public auction. He moved his family to a coastal town and rented cottages for the next three years, before settling permanently in London. While living on the sea coast, Elizabeth published her translation of *Prometheus Bound* (1833), by the Greek dramatist Aeschylus.

Gaining notoriety for her work in the 1830's, Elizabeth continued to live in her father's London house under his tyrannical rule. He began sending Elizabeth's younger siblings to Jamaica to help with the family's estates. Elizabeth bitterly opposed slavery and did not want her siblings sent away. During this time, she wrote *The Seraphim and Other Poems* (1838), expressing Christian sentiments in the form of classical Greek tragedy. Due to her weakening disposition she was forced to spend a year at the sea of Torquay accompanied by her brother Edward, whom she referred to as "Bro." He drowned later that year while sailing at Torquay and Elizabeth returned home emotionally broken, becoming an invalid and a recluse. She spent the next five years in her bedroom at her father's home. She continued writing, however, and in 1844 produced a collection entitled simply *Poems*. This volume gained the attention of poet Robert Browning, whose work Elizabeth had praised in one of her poems, and he wrote her a letter.

Elizabeth and Robert, who was six years her junior, exchanged 574 letters over the next twenty months. Immortalized in 1930 in the play *The Barretts of Wimpole Street*, by Rudolf Besier (1878-1942), their romance was bitterly opposed by her father, who did not want any of his children to marry. In 1846, the couple eloped and settled in Florence, Italy, where Elizabeth's health improved and she bore a son, Robert Wideman Browning. Her father never spoke to her again. Elizabeth's *Sonnets from the Portuguese*, dedicated to her husband and written in secret before her marriage, was published in 1850. Critics generally consider the *Sonnets*—one of the most widely known collections of love lyrics in English—

to be her best work. Admirers have compared her imagery to Shakespeare and her use of the Italian form to Petrarch.

Political and social themes embody Elizabeth's later work. She expressed her intense sympathy for the struggle for the unification of Italy in *Casa Guidi Windows* (1848-51) and *Poems Before Congress* (1860). In 1857 Browning published her verse novel *Aurora Leigh,* which portrays male domination of a woman. In her poetry she also addressed the oppression of the Italians by the Austrians, the child labour mines and mills of England, and slavery, among other social injustices. Although this decreased her popularity, Elizabeth was heard and recognized around Europe. Elizabeth Barrett Browning died in Florence on June 29, 1861.

FAMILY BACKGROUND

The Barrett family had been associated with Jamaica for generations. As a boy, Elizabeth's father Edward Moulton Barrett emigrated to England with his brother and sister Sarah. Sarah is the subject of the painting "Pinkie" in the Huntington Museum. Edward and his wife, Mary Graham-Clarke, were parents of twelve children, of whom Elizabeth was the eldest.

BIRTH AND YOUTH

Elizabeth Barrett Moulton-Barrett was born March 6, 1806 in Coxhoe Hall, Durham, England. In 1809, her father Edward, having made most of his considerable fortune from Jamaican sugar plantations which he inherited, bought Hope End, a 500-acre (2.0 km) estate near the Malvern Hills in Ledbury, Herefordshire, England. Elizabeth was educated at home and attended lessons with her brother's tutor and was thus well-educated for a girl of that time. She was an accomplished child, having read a number of Shakespearian plays, parts of Pope's Homeric translations, passages from Paradise Lost, and the histories of England, Greece, and Rome before the age of ten.

She was self-taught in almost every respect. The first poem we have a record of is from the age of six or eight, the manuscript of which is currently in the Berg Collection of the New York Public Library (the exact date is in question because the 2 in the date 1812 is written over something else that is scratched out). A long Homeric poem titled *The Battle of Marathon* was published when she was fourteen, her father underwriting its cost. Although frail, she apparently had no health problems until 1821, when Dr. Coker prescribed opium for a nervous disorder.

When in her early teens, she contracted a lung complaint, possibly tuberculosis, although the exact nature of her illness has been the subject of speculation. She was subsequently regarded as an invalid by her family. During her teen years she read the principal Greek and Latin authors and Dante's *Inferno* — all texts in the original languages. Her voracious appetite for knowledge compelled her to learn enough Hebrew to read the Old Testament from beginning to end. Her enjoyment of the works and subject matter of Paine, Voltaire, Rousseau, and Wollstonecraft was later expressed by her concern for human rights in her own letters and poems. By the age of twelve she had written an "epic" poem consisting of four books of rhyming couplets. Barrett later referred to her first literary attempt as, "Pope's Homer done over again, or rather undone."

ADULTHOOD

In 1826, she published her first collection of poems, *An Essay on Mind and Other Poems*. Its publication drew the attention of a blind scholar of the Greek language, Hugh Stuart Boyd, and another Greek scholar, Uvedale Price, with both of whom she maintained a scholarly correspondence. At Boyd's suggestion, she translated Aeschylus's *Prometheus Bound* (published in 1833; retranslated in 1850). During their friendship Barrett absorbed an astonishing amount of Greek literature — Homer, Pindar, Aristophanes, etc. — but after a few years Barrett's fondness for Boyd diminished. From 1822 on, Elizabeth Barrett's interests tended more and more to the scholarly and literary.

Her intellectual fascination with the classics and metaphysics was balanced by a religious obsession which she later described as "not the deep persuasion of the mild

Christian but the wild visions of an enthusiast." Her family attended services at the nearest Dissenting chapel, and Mr. Barrett was active in Bible and Missionary societies. Her mother died when she was 22, and critics mark signs of this loss in *Aurora Leigh.* The abolition of slavery in the early 30's, a cause which she supported, considerably reduced Mr. Barrett's means. His financial losses in the early 30s forced him to sell Hope End, and although never poor, the family moved three times between 1832 and 1837, first to Sidmouth and afterwards to London, finally settling at 50 Wimpole Street.

After the move to London, Elizabeth continued to write, contributing to various periodicals *The Romaunt of Margaret, The Romaunt of the Page, The Poet's Vow,* and other pieces, and corresponded with literary figures of the time, including Mary Russell Mitford. In 1838, The Seraphim and Other Poems appeared, the first volume of Elizabeth's mature poetry to appear under her own name. That same year her health forced her to move to Torquay, on the Devonshire coast. Her favourite brother Edward went along with her. The subsequent death of her brother, Edward, who drowned in a sailing accident at Torquay in 1840, had a serious effect on her already fragile health. When she returned to Wimpole Street, she became an invalid and a recluse, spending most of the next five years in her bedroom, seeing only one or two people other than her immediate family.

Eventually, however, she regained strength, and meanwhile her fame was growing. The publication in 1843 of *The Cry of the Children* gave it a great impulse, and about the same time she contributed some critical papers in prose to Richard Henry Horne's *A New Spirit of the Age.* In 1844 she published two volumes of Poems, which included *A Drama of Exile, A Vision of Poets,* and *Lady Geraldine's Courtship.*

MARRIAGE

During Elizabeth's confinement at Wimpole Street, one of the only people besides her immediate family whom she saw was John Kenyon, a wealthy and convivial friend of the arts. Her 1844 *Poems* made her one of the most popular writers in the land, and inspired Robert Browning to write to her, telling her how much he loved her poems. Kenyon arranged for Browning to meet her in May 1845, and so began one of the most famous courtships in literature. Their courtship and marriage, owing to her delicate health and the extraordinary objections made by Mr. Barrett to the marriage of any of his children, were carried out secretly. Six years his elder and an invalid, she could not believe that the vigorous and worldly Browning really loved her as much as he professed to, and her doubts are expressed in the *Sonnets from the Portuguese* which she wrote over the next two years.

Love conquered all, however, and after a private marriage at St. Marylebone Parish Church Browning imitated his hero Shelley by spiriting his beloved off to Italy in August 1846, which became her home almost continuously until her death. Elizabeth's loyal nurse, Wilson, who witnessed the marriage at the church, accompanied the couple to Italy and became at service to them. Mr. Barrett disinherited Elizabeth, as he did each one of his children who eventually married without his permission—and he never even gave his permission at all. Unlike her brothers and sisters, Elizabeth had inherited some money of her own, so the Brownings were reasonably comfortable in Italy.

The union proved a happy one. In her new circumstances Elizabeth's strength greatly increased. In 1849, at the age of 43, she gave birth to a son, Robert Wiedemann Barrett Browning, called Pen. He later married but had no children, so there are no direct descendants of the poets. At her husband's insistence, the second edition of her *Poems* included her love sonnets. They helped increase her popularity and the high critical regard in which the Victorians held their favourite poetess. On Wordsworth's death in 1850, she was seriously considered for the Laureateship, which went to Tennyson.

The Brownings settled in Florence, where she wrote *Casa Guidi Windows* (1851) under the inspiration of the Tuscan struggle for liberty, with which she and her husband were in sympathy. In Florence she became close friend of British-born poets Isabella Blagden and Theodosia Garrow Trollope. The verse-novel *Aurora Leigh,* her most ambitious, and perhaps the most popular of her longer poems, appeared in 1856. It is the story of a woman writer making her way in life, balancing work and love. Among Barrett Browning's best known lyrics is *Sonnets from the Portuguese* (1850) - the 'Portuguese' being her husband's petname for her. The title also refers to the series of sonnets of the 16th-century Portuguese poet Luis de Camões; in all these poems she used rhyme schemes typical of the Portuguese sonnets.

DEATH

In 1860 she issued a small volume of political poems titled *Poems before Congress.* Her health underwent a change for the worse; she gradually lost strength, and died on June 29, 1861. She was buried in the English Cemetery, Florence. Elizabeth Barrett Browning was a woman of singular nobility and charm. Mary Russell Mitford described her as a young woman: "A slight, delicate figure, with a shower of dark curls falling on each side of a most expressive face; large, tender eyes, richly fringed by dark eyelashes, and a smile like a sunbeam." Anne Thackeray Ritchie described her as: "Very small and brown" with big, exotic eyes and an overgenerous mouth.

It is still unclear what sort of affliction Elizabeth Barrett Browning had, although medical and literary scholars have enjoyed speculating. Whatever it was, the opium which was repeatedly prescribed probably made it worse; and Robert Browning almost certainly lengthened her life by taking her south and by his solicitous attention.

INFLUENCE

No female poet was held in higher esteem among cultured readers in both the United States and England than Elizabeth Barrett Browning during the nineteenth century. Barrett's poetry had an immense impact on the works of Emily Dickinson who admired her as woman of achievement. Barrett's treatment of social injustice (the slave trade in America, the oppression of the Italians by the Austrians, the labour of children in the mines and the mills of England, and the restrictions placed upon women) is manifested in many of her poems. Two of her poems, *Casa Guidi Windows* and *Poems Before Congress,* dealt directly with the Italian fight for independence. The first half of *Casa Guidi Windows* (1851) was filled with hope that the newly awakened liberal movements were moving toward unification and freedom in the Italian states.

The second half of the poem, written after the movement of liberalism had been crushed in Italy, is dominated by her disillusionment. After a decade of truce, Italians once again began to struggle for their freedom, but were forced to agree to an armistice that would leave Venice under Austrian control.

Barrett Browning's *Poems Before Congress* (1860) responded to these events by criticizing the English government for not providing aid. One of the poems in this collection, *A Curse For a Nation,* which attacked slavery, had been previously published in an abolitionist journal in Boston. *Aurora Leigh* also dealt with social injustice, but its subject was the subjugation of women to the dominating male. It also commented on the role of a woman as a woman and poet.

Barrett's popularity waned after her death, and late-Victorian critics argued that although much of her writing would be forgotten, she would be remembered for *The Cry of the Children, Isobel's Child, Bertha in the Lane,* and most of all the Sonnets from the Portuguese. Virginia Woolf argued that the heroine in *Aurora Leigh,* "with her passionate interest in the social questions, her conflict as artist and woman, her longing for knowledge and freedom, is the true daughter of her age." Woolf's praise of that work predated the modern critical reevaluation of Elizabeth Barrett Browning, and today it attracts more attention than the rest of her poetry.

Chapter 2

Her Early Years at Hope End

Some Time during the winter of 1794-95 Mr. and Mrs. Edward Barrett, their ward, their daughter, and their three grandchildren left their comfortable plantation home in the British West Indies to undertake the tedious passage to England. They left behind them both wealth and influence. Ever since Hersey Barrett had landed in Jamaica in 1655 with the British expedition of Admiral Penn and General Venables which wrested control of the island from the Spanish, the Barrett family fortunes had improved.

The period of their most rapid expansion was the second half of the eighteenth century, when Edward Barrett and his brothers were buying estates along the western portion of the Northside, in the precincts of St. James and Trelawny, from Montego Bay eastward to Palmetto Point, which later became Falmouth. By the 1790's Barrett prestige was at its peak, the family being ranked among the leading planters of the island. But in 1794-95 Edward Barrett and his family said goodbye to their relatives and friends at Cinnamon Hill Great House and made their way to the port of Falmouth, ten miles along the shore to the east, to embark for England.

The grandparents looked forward to visiting a brother and sisters in London before returning to Jamaica, while the younger members of the party, Miss Trepsack and Elizabeth and her children, were planning to remain in England. Mary Trepsack (Trippy) was an orphan whose father, an impoverished Jamaica planter, had died suddenly and left her without means for her support. She had been accepted as a member of the family by Samuel Barrett, and after he died in 1782 by his brother Edward.

The Barretts' daughter Elizabeth, accompanied by her three children, was leaving the only home she had known and the birthplace of herself and of at least two of her children, Edward and Sam, who were then about ten and eight years old respectively. Her twelve-year-old daughter Sarah and, very likely, the tutor of the children, Francis Murphy, completed the group.

Elizabeth's reason for transplanting her family in England was that they might receive an English education and an English upbringing. And when the education of these rich children should be completed and they should in turn have established homes for themselves, the family plan was to allow them to remain in England, receiving rents as absentee owners of their vast and profitable Jamaica estates. Elizabeth's husband, Charles Moulton, was not present and in fact had not been within the family circle for several years.

The marriage had not been successful, and soon after Sam's birth in 1787 he had wandered off-to New York for the slave sales, and to England, where he fathered several children by various mistresses—never again to return to his wife and legitimate offspring. It may have been before Edward Barrett's departure from Jamaica that he leased for his daughter Coxhoe Hall in Durham County, through the good offices of a business acquaintance, John Graham-Clarke, a wealthy merchant of Newcastle and the future father-in-law of young Edward Barrett Moulton—though after their arrival in England the Barretts seem to have lived for several months with their London relatives.

It was during this interval that Sir Thomas Lawrence painted the now famous portrait of Sarah Goodin Moulton (Pinkie), who died on April 23, 1795, shortly after the canvas was finished. Coxhoe Hall, which became in the spring of 1795 the home of Elizabeth Barrett Moulton, of her life-long companion Mary Trepsack, and of the two remaining Moulton children, is six miles south of Durham. It is a large stone castellated building of three stories set in the middle of a beautiful wooded estate of more than a thousand acres. The hall had been built about 1725 by John Burdon, who is said to have imported Italian workers to make the interior decorations, which were handsome and ornate.

The large and elaborate fireplace in the drawing room was of carved wood with figures of floral wreaths and shells. On the ground floor were three reception rooms and a billiard room, and upstairs about twenty bedrooms, many of which had fireplaces decorated with colored marble. As one looks at the estate today, he needs an effort of the imagination to visualize what it must have been like toward the end of the eighteenth century.

At that time no village of Coxhoe had yet come into being; about one hundred people lived in scattered cottages in the outlying districts. In all directions from the mansion one would have seen only woodland and pasture and low hills in the distance, with everything rural and unspoiled. Now only the shell of Coxhoe Hall remains, for prisoners of war billeted there during the conflict of 1939-45 completed the ruin of the interior. Since then the building has been allowed by its present owners, the National Coal Board, to fall into even greater disrepair. Huge slagheaps from coal-mining operations disfigure the landscape, and much of the original estate has become an ugly modern town, with rows of cheaply built brick houses all looking much alike.

Mrs. Moulton in her magnificent palace decided that her eldest son should be educated in a style appropriate to a future country gentleman who would inherit much of the Barrett property. Young Edward Barrett Moulton was indeed fortunate.

According to the principle of primogeniture he would some day be the chief proprietor of his grandfather's extensive Jamaica plantations. By 1797, when Edward Barrett Moulton entered Harrow, his grandfather Edward Barrett had buried all three of his sons. His eldest, George Goodin, had died a bachelor and had bequeathed £30,000 and other wealth to nephew Edward Barrett Moulton. Another son, Henry, was survived by one daughter, Elizabeth; and the youngest son, Samuel, left four children by an illicit union with a second cousin, Elizabeth Barrett Waite Williams. So shortly before his death in 1798, Edward Barrett made his will in favour of the sons of his daughter Elizabeth, with the provision that the sons adopt the surname of Barrett.

Once again John GrahamClarke acted as intermediary for Edward Barrett and secured in 1798 permission from the King for the change. The full names of Mrs. Moulton's sons were now Edward Barrett Moulton Barrett and Samuel Barrett Moulton Barrett. (In later years the first "Barrett" was usually dropped by both brothers.)

How long the twelve-year-old Edward remained at Harrow is not known. He seems to have entered in October 1797, and may have remained only a few months. Oddly enough, in none of her correspondence did his famous daughter in later years ever refer to her father's education or to his activities during the period he would normally have spent at school and the university. Long after his wife's death, Robert Browning wrote that Edward Moulton Barrett received at Harrow "so savage a punishment for a supposed offence ('burning the toast') by the youth whose 'fag' he had become, that he was withdrawn from the school by his mother, and the delinquent was expelled."

Whether or not that old family legend has any basis of truth, it was unfortunate for Edward that his indulgent mother allowed him to remain away from school. Evidence suggests that even as a boy he was permitted to live in a dream world of his own, so that he never had to discipline himself by academic studies or to learn how to get along with other people in the give-and-take of school or college life.

The guardian of the Barrett brothers was James Scarlett, later Lord Abinger, one of the most brilliant lawyers of his time, who had originally come from an estate near Cinnamon Hill, Jamaica. No family records tell whether he took the place of the missing father or whether he was too much occupied with his own practice and his personal affairs to have time to supervise very closely the upbringing of the late Edward

Barrett's heirs. Although in October 1801 Edward Moulton Barrett entered Trinity College, Cambridge, as a fellow-commoner at the early age of sixteen, it would be fruitless to speculate upon the influence his tutor Thomas Jones and other teachers may have had upon him, for there is in fact no proof that he ever resided at Cambridge.

From 1798, when he was removed from Harrow at the age of twelve or thirteen, until his early marriage, he apparently had very little formal schooling, except perhaps for some desultory tutoring at home. Free from external pressures and restraints and relieved of the necessity of assuming responsibilities, he no doubt was becoming more and more self-willed, isolated, and insensitive to the feelings of those around him.

The large, coarse handwriting and the manner of expression and subject matter of the letters of his mature years reveal him as a man who probably did not often put down his thoughts on paper and one whose mind had a practical bent far removed from the intellectual and artistic interests of his daughter. His younger brother Samuel, who was to become "more than uncle" to Elizabeth Barrett, had a more attractive, more outgoing personality and evidently more facility in self expression, since he was for several years a member of Parliament.

On May 14, 1805, Edward Moulton Barrett married Mary Graham-Clarke of Newcastle—he not yet twenty, she some four years older. It would have been very natural for Mrs. Moulton and her sons to visit John Graham-Clarke and his family, for Newcastle is not far from Durham and he had been for many years an adviser and friend of the Barretts in Jamaica. Edward's bride was of a family as wealthy as his own. Her father was one of the first citizens of Newcastle; he took an interest in civic affairs, and had a fleet of ships sailing between England and the West Indies, as well as sugar plantations in Jamaica, and diversified business investments in his home city. Edward brought his bride to Coxhoe Hall, where they lived with Mrs. Moulton, Trippy, and Sam, and where two of their children were born.

While the mansion was large enough to accommodate several families, Edward and Mary, like many young couples who have to live for a while with their parents, must have been hoping they would soon have a house of their own. Their first child was born on March 6, 1806, and was named after Mrs. Moulton; hence the full name was Elizabeth Barrett Moulton Barrett.

With her oval face and slightly receding chin, she looked more like her father than her mother. About a year later a son and heir was born whose features had a remarkable resemblance to those of his older sister. The second child was named Edward Barrett Moulton Barrett, after his father and grandfather.

The two children were baptized together at nearby Kelloe Church on February 10, 1808. The owner of Kelloe Manor, which is a mile or two from Coxhoe Hall, was Sir Henry Vane Tempest, whose wife was the proprietor of an estate of about five hundred acres called Hope End (meaning "a closed valley") in the eastern part of Herefordshire. On September 6, 1809, Edward Moulton Barrett wrote his three-yearold daughter, who was staying with Mrs.

Moulton at her home in Surrey, that he and several other men were examining Hope End, and he added, "The more I see of the property the more I like it and the more I think I shall have it in my power to make yourself, Brother and Sister and dear Mamma happy." Accordingly, later in the year, several months after the birth of Henrietta, the third child, Edward Barrett bought Hope End and built for himself and his growing family a "Turkish house," as Elizabeth later wrote Robert Browning, "crowded with minarets and domes, and crowned with metal spires and crescents."

It is probable that his daughter's words are not literally true; he may have been responsible only for the pseudo-Eastern excrescences of the house Lady Tempest had owned. Ledbury is approximately in the centre of a triangle formed by the three cathedral cities of Hereford, Gloucester, and Worcester. It is an old market town, and many of its buildings, which date from the sixteenth and seventeenth centuries, are in the black and white half-timbered, half-brick style characteristic of the region.

In the early nineteenth century the town and its environs must have looked much as they do today. The surrounding countryside is gently rolling and covered with forests, pastures for sheep and cattle grazing, apple orchards, hopyards, and fields of wheat and barley. The Hope End estate, which is three miles from Ledbury, is on the northern edge of a range of hills running north and south immediately to the east of the town. To the south of Hope End is the small village of Wellington Heath; to the east, Barton Court, which was the home of the Peytons, friends of the Barretts; to the northeast, the estate of Old Colwall, where Mr. and Mrs. James Martin lived, also close friends of the Barretts; and to the northwest, the low-lying parishes of Bosbury and Coddington.

The highest land in the vicinity, running north and south about two miles to the east of Hope End and Ledbury, is the range of the Malvern Hills, on the sharp eastern slopes of which are Great Malvern and Malvern Wells. It is fortunate that the lovely Hope End estate, with its great forest trees of oak, beech, cedar, and cypress, has been preserved almost as it was when the Barretts lived there.

The only important difference is that Mr. Barrett's dwelling was torn down about 1872 and a new house of more conventional design erected on an eminence overlooking the hollow where the older building had stood. Nothing remains of the earlier structure except some of its foundations. The walls which enclosed the courtyard in the rear and the archway and clock turret (though not the clock) have recently been reconstructed, and on the site of the old mansion the present owner of Hope End has just built a guest house. Neither the suburban areas of Great Malvern nor those of Ledbury have encroached upon Hope End and its neighbouring farms and estates, all of which still retain their rural qualities. However bizarre Edward Barrett's architectural tastes may have been, his mansion was as luxurious as the one he had left in the north. Like Coxhoe Hall, it had twenty bedrooms, many of them with elaborately carved marble fireplaces.

Over the main hall, on the ground floor, and the great stone staircase with its mahogany handrail and brass balustrade was a large glass dome. The folding doors between the various drawing rooms were of mahogany, inlaid with pearl and filled with stained glass. From the windows of the reception rooms one could see pheasants parading their plumage on the lawn, beautiful flower gardens and shrubbery, and a small artificial pond.

The house was unfortunately situated in a vale, so that the higher land around it obstructed the views of the Malvern Hills and of Eastnor Castle. When Frederic G. Kenyon edited Mrs. Browning's letters in 1897, he included only three from the Hope End period, because at that time almost no others were available.

He was not sure how many had been preserved; more than two hundred letters written during her early years have been saved, however, most of them from Elizabeth to her eccentric and scholarly neighbour Hugh Stuart Boyd but many from members of her own family to her. Furthermore, almost every scrap of paper upon which she placed her childish pen has been piously rescued from oblivion even though most of the material has little biographical significance and no poetical merit.

Today one may see in various public and private collections Elizabeth's schoolroom exercises, a succession of birthday epistles in verse to her family, excerpts from plays performed, descriptions of games and entertainments of the Barrett family and their cousins, summaries of her reading, and solemn estimates of her own character and personality, all of them in the open, flowing hand of her teens and even of earlier years.

The impression one gains from reading the letters and other documents of the Hope End period is that Elizabeth was a shy, intensely studious, precocious child, yet cheerful, affectionate, and lovable. She was not so much of a recluse as she later believed she had been, for she took delight in planning charades and composing and taking part in plays with her brother Edward and her sisters as fellow actors. The estate of Hope End and its surrounding hills provided a beautiful and peaceful setting, a "paradise" she always called it in later years.

"Beautiful, beautiful hills, they are!" she wrote of the Malvern Hills; and in the same letter to Richard Hengist Horne, viewing in retrospect her life at Hope End and the countryside of Herefordshire, she spoke of "a retirement scarcely broken to me except by books and my own thoughts, and it is a beautiful country, and was a retirement happy in many ways, although the very peace of it troubles the heart as it looks back."

And in writing to Boyd in the summer of 1846 at the moment a new happiness was entering her life, she confessed that "looking back to that early time, the hours spent with you, appear to me some of the happiest of my life." Mr. and Mrs. Barrett had brought with them to Hope End their three children, Elizabeth, Edward, and Henrietta. Between 1810 and 1824 the patient mother bore nine more, and all grew to maturity, except Mary, who died in 1814 at the age of three. Elizabeth's early verse and letters and her mother's letters to her paint a vivid picture of the daily routine of the large household. Mr. Barrett occupied himself with landscape gardening on his estate and with the supervising of his farms.

He was elected sheriff of the county in 1812 and again in 1814 and took an active part in the meetings of the Bible and missionary societies at Ledbury and Malvern. Before Elizabeth's long and serious illness at the age of fifteen she often went with him to church services. "I used to go with my father always," she later wrote Browning, "when I was able, to the nearest dissenting chapel of the Congregationalists." Edward (Bro) and Elizabeth (Ba—from the first syllable of "baby" and pronounced as though spelled "bah") studied together their French, Greek, and Latin.

The sisters Henrietta (Addles) and Arabella practiced on the piano and played duets with their mother or with their governess Mrs. Orme. The younger brothers Sam and Charles John (Stormie) were often busy copying out French and Latin paradigms.

In the afternoons, when school- work was finished, brothers and sisters, except Elizabeth who was too frail, sometimes went "on some fanciful chase over the hills," in Mrs. Barrett's words, and in the evenings they would often read together. "Books and dreams were what I lived in—and domestic life only seemed to buzz gently around, like bees about the grass," Elizabeth said many years later. The list of books she read is formidable.

At four and a half her "great delight was poring over fairy phenomenons and the actions of necromancers—and The Seven Champions of Christendom in 'Popular Tales' has beguiled many a weary hour." Then she wept over Mrs. Amelia Opie moral tales The Father and Daughter, Temper, and Valentine's Eve. Soon afterward she was absorbed in the histories of Greece, Rome, and England and in Pope Homer, Paradise Lost, and Shakespeare. At the age of twelve the study of metaphysics was her "highest delight." After reading Locke, she "not only felt edified but exalted," and for a time she kept a copy of Hooker's works under her pillow that she might study them at the earliest light of dawn.

Her father had told her not to read Gibbon and Tom Jones "and none of the books on this side, mind!" So she was "very obedient and never touched the books on that side, and only read instead Tom Paine 'Age of Reason,' and Voltaire 'Philosophical Dictionary,' and Hume 'Essays,' and Werther, and Rousseau, and Mary Wollstonecraft." When she was thirteen, she "perused all modern authors who have any claim to superior merit and poetic excellence," but she did not particularize.

She was overserious in her religious devotion. Her religion at the age of twelve, she wrote four years later in an autobiographical sketch unpublished in her lifetime, was "not the deep persuasion of the mild Christian but the wild visions of an enthusiast." One evening her "whole mind was tortured" after she remembered having accidentally forgotten a prayer. "The next morning I renewed with tenfold ardour my agonising prayers," she wrote. "My God, My God, why hast thou forsaken me I repeated in a tone of anguish."

It is no surprise that such a high-strung and bookish child should have made verses from her infancy. "I used to write of virtue with a large 'V,' and 'Oh Muse' with a harp, and things of that sort," she later told Browning. "At nine years old I wrote what I called 'an epic'—and at ten various tragedies, French and English, which we used to act in the nursery." One which escaped destruction was her drama called "Regulus," in French rhymed verse.

Bro took the part of the noble Roman. Elizabeth as his daughter and Henrietta as his wife Marcia both perish from despair at the end when they see the tragic hero leave Rome for his death in Carthage. When she was about twelve, a Mr. MacSwiney came to Hope End to tutor Bro in the subjects required for entrance to Charterhouse. Elizabeth eagerly availed herself of the opportunity for instruction, and for two or three years before Bro's departure for the school in 1820 the two of them studied together Greek, Latin, French, and probably some Italian.

The type of book which interested her may be seen from her casual remark in a letter to her uncle Sam, written when she was twelve, that she had been reading John Bigland An Historical Display of the Effects of Physical and Moral Causes on the Character and Circumstances of Nations, Frederic S. N. Douglas' An Essay on Certain Points of Resemblance between the Ancient and Modern Greeks, Madame de Sévigné Letters (on which Elizabeth commented, "The French is excellent."), and the last canto of Childe Harold's Pilgrimage. Her schoolroom translations and paraphrases written during this early period give evidence of an acquaintance with at least Homer, Plato, Bion, Anacreon, Horace, Claudian, and Dante; and she was also familiar with Xenophon, Ovid, the Aeneid, and several plays by Racine and Molière.

The time when she "read Greek as hard under the trees as some of your Oxonians in the Bodleian" was not to begin until seven or eight years later, after she had been encouraged by H. S. Boyd to renew her Greek studies. "My learning Greek was a child's fancy achieved for Homer's sake," she later wrote to Miss Mitford, and she confessed to Boyd that her reading

Greek with MacSwiney "was rather guessing and stammering and tottering through parts of Homer and extracts from Xenophon than reading."

Her first volume of verse is the product of her early Hellenic enthusiasm. The Battle of Marathon, an "epic" in four book-"Pope's Homer done over again, or rather undone," she later described it—was written in 1817 or 1818 but did not appear until early in 1820, for the inscription in the copy sent to "dearest Grandmama from her affectionate child" was dated March 6 of that year. Just as Elizabeth was beginning her career, several writers of an earlier generation were extending their reputations in 1820.

Washington Irving produced his The Sketch Book, Scott his The Monastery and its sequel The Abbot, Shelley his Prometheus Unbound, and Byron a portion of Don Juan. Elizabeth's book was issued, without any wrappers and with the leaves merely stitched together, under the imprint of W. Lindsell, 87 Wimpole Street, Cavendish Square. On the title page are several verses from Akenside and Byron and the author's name. All of her later publications were to be anonymous until the volume of The Seraphim of 1838. No reviews or publishers' notices announced the slight volume, for it was not published but privately printed by her father in an edition of fifty copies.

Of more interest than the childish, imitative verse are the dedication and the preface. It is significant that it was not to her mother that she dedicated the book, but "to the father, whose never-failing kindness, whose unwearied affection I never can repay." The tone of the preface is oversolemn and self-conscious, but it shows an appreciation of literature which is extraordinary in a child of eleven or twelve. She first praises Homer and Virgil, "those grand and solitary specimens of ancient poetic excellence."

Then she asks, "Who, unsophisticated by prejudice, can peruse those inspired pages emitted from the soul of Byron, or who can be dazzled by the gems sparkling from the rich mine of the imagination of Moore, or captivated by scenes glowing in the descriptive powers of Scott, without a proud consciousness that our day may boast the exuberance of true poetic genius?" In the following year, 1821, when Elizabeth was only fifteen, she had the satisfaction of making her first public appearance as a poet. Thomas Campbell, who had just undertaken the editorship of the New Monthly Magazine, published in that periodical two of her poems, both of them lamenting the present loss of freedom in Greece, in the light of its "glorious" past.

Apparently she had no letter of introduction to Campbell but forwarded her verses to him in the hope he might accept them even though they were from an unknown writer. She was so gratified at his response that she sent him a long poem dedicated to him and asked for his opinion of the work. If it had been favorable, she had evidently planned to have it printed as her second volume of verse, for her dedication and preface were ready for publication and have been saved, whereas the poem itself seems to have been destroyed after she received Campbell's adverse comments.

Though his reply, dated August 28, 1822, was mainly unfavorable, he assuaged her wounded feelings by telling her that the poem "bespeaks an amiable heart and an elegant mind." In general, he objected to the "lyric intermixtures" which he thought were "the most difficult of all gems to set in a Narrative poem and should always be of the first water." Not long afterward she asked for his opinion of another manuscript, and this time he replied in a much shorter letter that it was impossible for him to "admit of renewed applications for criticisms on the works of young authors however promising they may be."

He did not intend to discourage her versifying; nor was she discouraged, since she continued to compose the usual birthday epistles and even attempted several more ambitious pieces, fragments of which were preserved. On June 30, 1824, one of the leading newspapers in London, the Globe and Traveller, printed her "Stanzas on the Death of Lord Byron," with no signature or initials. Mr. and Mrs. Barrett's pride in Elizabeth's accomplishment may be seen in a letter her mother wrote her from Hope End when she was visiting her grandmother, Mrs. Graham-Clarke, and her Aunt Arabella (Bummy) at their home in Cheltenham. "As Papa took up the paper in the Dining Room," Mrs. Barrett wrote, a glance satisfied me whence they [the verses] came, but I said nothing till he came into the Drawing Room, when taking the paper with a becoming carelessness of air, I asked him what he thought of those lines.

He said, "They are very beautiful indeed.""I cannot help thinking," replied I, "that we know something of the Author.""They cannot be Ba's," said he, taking the paper from me to read them again, "tho certainly when I first read them they reminded me greatly of her style. Have you any idea if they are hers?""I have a conviction of it," said the conceited Mother, pouring out the tea with an air that threatened to overflow the tea tray.

Two years later, when Elizabeth's next volume was published, she was staying with her other grandmother, Mrs. Moulton, at Hastings. Mrs. Barrett wrote Elizabeth of the arrival of the books and of the eagerness with which she and Mr. Barrett read her poems once again: "The news ran like lightning last night thro' the nursery to me that a brown paper parcel was come for Papa from Worcester 'which felt very much like books,'. and vain the temptations of our 'rich repast' till I had peeped into those pieces which had not yet delighted our eyes, nor did Papa taste anything, till he had found the paper cutter, so that between every two or three mouthfuls, we had Riga's dying strain."

She added with pride: "I wish, my beloved Ba, that I could tell you all Papa said in commendation of this wondrous little book. The preface he says is equal to anything he ever read, and would do honour to any man... There never was any circumstance in the existence of your dearest Father or my own that could afford us the same gratified feelings, as this strong evidence that our beloved child, has so well applied and cultivated the talents with which she is gifted." The book which thus pleased Mr. and Mrs. Barrett was An Essay on Mind, with Other Poems, a slender duodecimo volume published in London March 25, 1826, by James Duncan, 37 Paternoster-Row.

On the title page was a line from Tasso but no indication of authorship. Neither her name nor her initials appeared on the title page or after the preface. Many years afterward in a letter to the American critic Cornelius Mathews Elizabeth wrote that the book was "a girl's exercise.. nothing more nor less!—not at all known to the public," and she called the work "the black-letter offence of my early youth... an imitation poem (after Pope and Campbell) as all young poems are apt to be... so pert.. so unamiable."

Yet if family records are to be trusted, the volume enjoyed a brisk sale in at least one city. About two weeks after its publication Mrs. Barrett wrote Elizabeth that "Granny" (Mrs. Graham-Clarke) had reported that the book had "caused quite a sensation in the North," that nearly fifty copies had been sold in Newcastle, and that more had been ordered. Perhaps the letter which most pleased Elizabeth was one from her future benefactor John Kenyon, who wrote her from Malvern Wells of his approval of the volume. He said that he had heard that she did not spare herself enough, and he asked her to remember that at her age "all need not be done in a day."

The poem for which the book was named bravely attempted in some 88 pages to survey from classical Greece to the present the fields of history, science, metaphysics, and poetry. To the text of the poem were appended eighteen pages of notes in prose on such diverse writers as Plutarch, Condillac, Cicero, Bacon, Herodotus, and Tyrtaeus. The notice of her volume in the Eclectic Review was mainly unfavorable. It objected to the obscurity of language, to the "barren and dazzling themes," and to the choice of subject, to succeed in which she should have adopted "a style far more remote from the sparkling, crackling style of Pope, with his sardonic grin and ever-recurring antithesis, or from the tinsel and affectation of Darwin."

The reference to Darwin she thought an example of hasty and stupid reviewing, the recollection of which irritated her for many years; she always maintained that she had never read the author of The Botanic Garden before she wrote the "Essay." The Literary Gazette was more condescending and less sharp in its criticism. Since its editor, William Jerdan, had a year before published her short lyric "The Rose and Zephyr," he may have known who she was.

For "the production of a young lady," he wrote, "it certainly displays a much more extraordinary degree of philosophical, we might say, metaphysical acumen, than could be expected either from the youth or sex of the writer." He ended his review with the admonition to "the fair author" that she "address herself more to nature, and undress herself from the deep blue in which she is now attired."

The "Stanzas on the Death of Lord Byron" reappeared in An Essay on Mind, with Other Poems, and in the same volume was a poem with the cumbersome title, "Stanzas occasioned by a passage in Mr. Emerson's Journal, which states, that on the mention of Lord Byron's name, Captain Demetrius, an old Roumeliot, burst into tears." Throughout her life Elizabeth was again and again to be seized with spasms of uncritical hero worship—"My organ of veneration is as large as a Welsh mountain," she once wrote. "I could kiss the footsteps of a great man." —and Byron was one of her earliest heroes.

When she was only a child, she had longed to escape from the nursery, dress up in men's clothes, and become Byron's page. At some time in her teens she read The Corsair, which, she reported to her father, was "exquisitely beautiful," and she wrote in imitation of it a poem called "Leila," which told of the tragic fates of Otho the Corsair in his island home, of his beautiful daughter, of a wan and meek minstrel, and of the captive in the dungeon. And it was under the spell of Byron that she had written her early poems on Greece in the New Monthly Magazine.

One of the personal poems in the volume of 1826, the "Verses to My Brother," recalls the happy times she spent with Bro, their games and their literary pursuits. Now that her "belov'd and best" is continuing his studies away at school, she wonders whether he has "dreams of me and home"; and as she reads Homer alone, her thoughts "often stray" in search of Bro. In the spring of 1826 (although the poem was probably written several years before) Edward Barrett, who was now within a few months of his nineteenth birthday, was at Charterhouse. His leaving Hope End to go to the school six years earlier had caused Elizabeth great anguish. "My beloved Bro and I have parted on the plain of life," she had written in 1821. "The last farewell is agony, for alas our pursuits will now no longer be the same.... I may ascend the delightful hill of classical learning, but he who has added pleasure to every cherished object is no longer with me."

Brother and sister had "fagged at the grammar, wept over the torn dictionary." She continued melodramatically, "Let cold reason scoff but let those who have pursued together the Roman and Greek classics, and who have together resisted difficulties of style and language decide whether or not our attachment be founded on folly." After Bro left Hope End, the separation between brother and sister was only partial.

He was with her some of the time during the year she was in Gloucester in 1821 and 1822. Her mother had written her from Hope End in August 1821 that someone had been sent "to bring dear Bro to pay us a visit, for such it must be, while his dearest Ba is at G." He must have been with Elizabeth at Hope End during his vacations; and when she was visiting Mrs. Moulton at Hastings for a year in 1825 and 1826, Bro was with her for several months, before he returned to school. From 1820, his first year at Charterhouse, to 1826, he had advanced from the ninth to the third form.

"How rejoiced we are to hear dearest Sam is in another form!" Mrs. Barrett wrote Elizabeth in April 1826 of her second son, also at Charterhouse. "Would that we had similar good news of Bro. I am every day more anxious about those dear boys, as time advances when they must be more actively occupied and how? That is the question." Long after Mrs. Barrett's death the question was still being asked, with the answer no less uncertain. At all events Bro was withdrawn from Charterhouse in 1826 before he had completed the last two forms, and there is no evidence that he ever again received any formal education.

In sending to Richard Hengist Horne a few paragraphs about herself for A New Spirit of the Age, Elizabeth wrote in

1843, "As to stories, my story amounts to the knife-grinder's, with nothing at all for a catastrophe. A bird in a cage would have as good a story." Perhaps she had in mind the restricted existence which ill health had imposed upon her during the preceding six or seven years.

During the Hope End period, however, even though she "had no social opportunities" and had her "heart in books and poetry," she nevertheless took trips around England and to the Continent more than many persons could hope to do in an age when travel was slow and expensive. At one time she seems to have lived for seven months with some of her family at Boulogne "for masters, which are excellent there, and for the acquirement of that habit of talking French, which comes at a call," as she later wrote.

More is known about her trip to Paris with her father and mother in October and November 1815, for her "Notes" on the journey have a vividness of phrase and fullness of detail which are remarkable for a child of nine.

Her belief in the superiority of English domestic comforts was to be altered many years later after she had acquired a taste for living arrangements on the Continent. "At length Dover Castle rose as from the sea, to our view," she wrote, "and we rejoiced to find ourselves by a good comfortable English fireside, which, even foreigners must allow, is preferable to all the luxuries in the world."

Among her various trips in England, she went with her parents, Bro, and Henrietta in June 1814, to Carlton Hall, between Richmond and Darlington in Yorkshire, the beautiful home of her father's brother, Samuel Moulton Barrett, who was living there with his mother and Mary Trepsack. During the following July, August, and September they stayed with Mrs.

Barrett's parents, the Graham-Clarkes, at their dignified and spacious residence, Fenham Hall, in Newcastle. There Elizabeth head Madame Catalani sing at the Grand Musical Festival, of which John Graham-Clarke was one of the patrons. Several times she visited at Cheltenham her Aunt Arabella Graham-Clarke, with whom Mrs. Graham-Clarke lived after the death of her husband in 1818.

During the early part of the summer of 1819 she stayed with relatives at Worthing, and she lived with Mrs. Moulton and Miss Trepsack at Hastings from June 1825 until late in May or early in June of the following year. Also she must have visited from time to time her Uncle John Altham Graham-Clarke and his wife in their Elizabethan house called Kinnersley Castle in Hereford. Another long period away from home was from July 1821 to the spring or summer of 1822. She was suffering from such a serious illness that she had to be taken from Hope End to the Spa Hotel, Gloucester, where more adequate medical treatment may have been available than at Ledbury.

Dr. William Coker had written to Dr. G. B. Nuttall on June 24, 1821, about "the case of Miss Barrett, that prodigy in intellectual powers and acquirements!" The symptoms he described, the headaches, the pain and weakness in various parts of the body, the paroxysms and convulsions of the muscles, suggest some kind of nervous disorder, from which she was never to be completely free. She had been treated with many medicines, including opium, Dr. Coker said, and none had proved helpful. As one might suppose, when she was away from home Elizabeth regularly received letters from her mother rather than from her father.

Though only a few of the family letters at this period have been preserved, Mrs. Barrett tried to write or to have her husband or one of her children write Elizabeth almost every day. Likewise when Elizabeth's parents were visiting friends and relatives, she was asked as the eldest child to send messages from Hope End that all was well. One such letter was saved, written by Elizabeth when she was about eighteen or nineteen, to her mother, who was at Hereford with Mr. Barrett.

Her message could hardly have put them at ease, though they may have understood that she was accustomed to exaggerate her illnesses. After commenting on the greatly improved health of her brothers and sisters, she continued, "As for myself the violent cough that I had when you were last here has not left me and I fear will accompany me to the end of my life. My constitution and my appetite is as bad as ever! But do not be uneasy for you know that natural ill health generally continues to death so it is nothing outrée. And have you really the assurance to suppose that in this short period of separation buried as we are amidst hills rocks and woods that we have any news or even scandal to regale your ear?"

Mrs. Barrett's letters from Hope End to Elizabeth and Henrietta, while chiefly filled with domestic details and neighbourhood gossip, are nevertheless of great interest in their revelation of the kind of difficulty she encountered with her husband. Years after her mother's death Elizabeth described her as "very tender... of a nature harrowed up into some furrows by the pressure of circumstances... A sweet, gentle nature, which the thunder a little turned from its sweetness."

Mrs. Barrett, it is clear, was not necessarily consulted when her husband made his household decisions, nor was she always informed of his plans. Therefore she had to resort to indirect means of learning about the arrangements made for her own children. For example, when Elizabeth and Bro were visiting their grandmother in the winter of 1825-26, Mrs. Barrett wrote her daughter on November 25, "I am full of anxiety to hear whether dearest Papa's letter was intended to prevent Bro's going to school, or whether he was gone before it arrived."

Bro had not yet departed, and the letter evidently did prevent him from leaving for school at that moment, for Mrs. Barrett wrote Elizabeth again on December 30 that before long the day would come "when Ba must leave dearest Granny... and from a hint of Papa's yesterday, I have felt an apprehension that it may come too suddenly to admit of your going to Walthamstow [the home of Elizabeth's uncle Sam, near London], which I should dread Sam would consider unkind as they took you from hence... I know not how to suggest any escape from this danger, as it is only a surmise of my own (tho a very strong one) that Papa's cogitations run upon Bro's being your escort home, before he goes to C. House."

Mrs. Barrett then suggested that Elizabeth write her father to express her wish of spending at least a week with Uncle Sam on her return from Hastings, and then she appended conspiratorially, "Say nothing of all this when you write, further than any allusion you may think right to Walthamstow." The strong surmise proved incorrect, for Mr. Barrett arranged for Bro's return to school but made no provision for that of Elizabeth and Henrietta. "How little did I think when I saw you drive away in Mary's barouche," Mrs. Barrett wrote Henrietta on April 11, "that I was not to see those dear faces again for ten long months... and yet no certain means arranged for your return!" Mrs. Barrett's frustration in the whole episode is clear enough.

Yet it would be an oversimplification to conceive of Mr. Barrett merely as a despot exercising his power upon a defenseless household. In the commonly held view of him which has persisted since the time of Elizabeth's marriage, he was "one of those tyrannical, arbitrary, puritanical rascals who go sleekly about the world, canting Calvinism abroad, and acting despotism at home."

This judgment is not altogether fair because it overlooks a more attractive aspect of his personality: "his elastic spirit and merry laugh," in Elizabeth's words—his boyish high spirits, humour, and charm. The evidence in many unpublished letters of Elizabeth and other members of the Barrett family confirms the impression that he was indeed a tyrant; but if he had been no more than that, Elizabeth would never have loved him as she did until the day of his death; nor would his family, at least in the earlier years, have received so much pleasure from his presence. A letter from Mrs. Barrett to Elizabeth which tells of her going out of the house to watch two old apple trees being cut down refers to "Papa's wit" and "the approving laugh of the delighted and busy audience."

In a few lines of doggerel which Elizabeth wrote describing a trip she and her family had made early in the summer of 1814 to the caverns of Matlock in Derbyshire, she mentioned "Papa's laugh," which echoed through the caves. And later in the summer, when she was visiting her grandparents Mr. and Mrs. Graham-Clarke at Newcastle-on-Tyne, she wrote in her "Epistle to Dearest Papa in London" that she wished he would return, because in his absence the house seemed "dull." While Bro was away at Charterhouse, Elizabeth "studied hard" by herself.

The titles of many of the books she read and her opinions on them may be found in an unpublished pocket notebook which was recently given to the Wellesley College Library. In this small volume of 230 pages bound in diced Russia calf she commented on about fifty different works to which she had devoted herself for the three years 1823-25. Although she had earlier shown much interest in the classics and was later to become absorbed once again in Greek studies under the influence of her neighbour H. S. Boyd, the only classical work she criticized was the Ajax of Sophocles.

Most of her comments were in the fields of biography, memoirs, letters, and travel diaries. She read about men and women in many different countries and periods of history. For example, she went through Thomas Roscoe translation of the Memoirs of Benvenuto Cellini, Lord Holland's biographies of Lope de Vega and of Guillen de Castro, a translation of Madame Campan's memoirs of Marie Antoinette, a translation in eight volumes of the memoirs of the Countess de Genlis, a journal of Napoleon at Saint Helena (also in translation) by Las Cases, and another book which also dealt largely with Napoleon: a translation of Madame de Staël's history of the French revolution.

In addition to these works on Continental figures, Elizabeth commented on many books of memoirs of her compatriots. She read three volumes of anecdotes and gossip on Garrick, Dr. Johnson, Horace Walpole, and others of the period, compiled by Laetitia Matilda Hawkins; James Boaden's biography of John Philip Kemble, which also told about many other actors of the time; two different books on Charles James Fox; and the memoirs of Richard Edgeworth (the father of Maria), of the younger William Pitt, and of Byron, who was still living in 1824, when Egerton Brydges' volume on him was published.

Among books of travel Elizabeth was chiefly attracted to recent works on Italy and Greece. She found a "sprightliness of style and a freshness of observation" in the anonymous Diary of an Ennuyée, in which Anna Murphy (later Mrs. Jameson, who was to accompany the Brownings on their wedding trip to Italy) told of her travels through Italy as a governess.

Also Elizabeth was much interested in the three volumes of travel sketches entitled The English in Italy and in two newly published books on the Greek Revolution. The only novels which she discussed in her notebook were Lockhart Matthew Wald and Cooper The Pilot, both of which appeared in 1824. Of all the books upon which she commented, none seems to have pleased her more than an "annual" called The Literary Souvenir; or, Cabinet of Poetry and Romance for 1826. She wrote that it was "an elegant little book" with "beautiful type" and "pretty graphic illustrations" and was "well worth the 12 good shillings" it cost her.

Among the two contributions in this volume which impressed her the most was a sentimental poem by Miss Landon called "The Forsaken," which represented the lament of a country girl whose lover had left her to look for city pleasures. Elizabeth thought the verses were "beautiful and pathetic." She was also much affected by a poem by Mrs. Hemans—it "goes to the heart," she wrote—describing the death of a mother and her baby in a shipwreck.

The longest criticism in the notebook of any one work is the sixteen closely written pages which analyse Locke An Essay Concerning Human Understanding. She also wrote summaries of the philosophical systems of Kant, Berkeley, and Hume and discussed George Campbell The Philosophy of Rhetoric, Southey The Book of the Church, and Jacques Saint-Pierre Harmonies of Nature, which she read in translation. The French writer seemed to her "touchingly amiable"; yet before she dipped into his third volume, she had grown "more than half tired of soli-lunar and luni-solar harmonies." The second longest comment in the notebook is a summary of John Dunlop The History of Fiction; for eleven pages Elizabeth wrote a précis of the author's remarks on Greek and Latin romances, Italian tales, and French and English novels.

Her expressions of approval or of disapproval show her forth right manner of expression. For example, she thought that part of Samuel Parr Characters of the Late Charles James Fox was as "sinewy as Tacitus and graceful as Tully," and she added, "I never read with more admiration, or ceased reading with more regret." She was, however, not impressed with the Recollections of Foreign Travel by Egerton Brydges, who, she wrote, "seems to think that by declaring and insinuating on every other page that his genius was first-rate, he might at least make his readers believe so.

He certainly has not succeeded with me." The dates of the inscriptions in Elizabeth's books indicate that in addition to the works upon which she commented in her notebook, she at this time also came into possession of a copy of the Works of Horace, Milton Prose Works, Percy Reliques, Burns' Works, and a Spanish grammar (although no evidence exists that she ever became proficient in that language). Her copies of the two volumes of Milton's prose, which are now in the Turnbull Library in Wellington, New Zealand, have many markings and marginal comments. Elizabeth was particularly interested in "The Reason of Church Government" and "An Apology for Smectymnuus," but she did not accept uncritically everything Milton wrote.

For instance, she commented in the margin of the treatise "Of True Religion," that it would have been "more admirable and more amiable, had the great author extended to the Papist the same leniency with which he greeted the Socinian." Milton wrote that popery, "as far as it is idolatrous" could be tolerated neither publicly nor privately. "Nothing can excuse this," Elizabeth protested. "Milton was in my opinion a great bigot. When it suits his purpose he is for liberty, as the sacrifice of a King.

If however, any of his preconceived ideas be violated, any of his 'conscientious' notions called into question, then it is a 'great offence to God,' an 'insufferable scandal.'" Since Elizabeth was apparently never able to visit a bookshop and her father seems to have had little interest in literature, how was she able to buy or have the use of so many volumes? I think that she may have regularly received copies of the Literary Gazette or a similar publication, in which she read advertisements and reviews of recent works and thereupon ordered from a London bookseller. Also she probably borrowed books from Mr. Best's lending library, to which Henrietta frequently went in Malvern.

Elizabeth's analyses in her notebook and her many references in the text and in the prose footnotes of the "Essay on Mind" to philosophers such as Burke, Leibniz, Condillac, Locke, and Berkeley are not necessarily proof that she read widely in all of these writers.

It is likely that some of her knowledge of French and English philosophy was derived from Dugald Stewart Philosophical Essays, which deals with the works of Locke, Berkeley, Burke, and Uvedale Price, and the influence of Locke upon French philosophers in the late eighteenth century. Likewise her information on the ancient and modern drama and on the lives of many English and Continental writers came partly from intermediate sources.

For example, in the 1820's, or possibly a little later, she read carefully and made voluminous notes, both in French and in English, on the French translation of A. W. Schlegel's course of lectures on dramatic art and literature. Her comments and summaries were mostly on Greek tragedy and on the English drama, but she paid some attention to the theaters of Rome, Italy, France, Spain, and Germany. In her remarks on the French drama in her "Essay on Mind" she may have been indebted to Schlegel's book.

Elizabeth's footnotes on Bentley, Descartes, and Newton tell several episodes about their lives which were drawn respectively from Isaac Disraeli Curiosities of Literature, his Literary Character, and Spence Anecdotes. But I do not wish to give the impression that Elizabeth was not well informed in the subjects she treated, or that she attempted to pass off second-hand information as her own so that she might appear more erudite than she was. Quite the contrary: her command of languages and her wide acquaintance with literature, philosophy, and history were remarkable accomplishments for a girl who was isolated in the country and was without either the resources of a large public library or the stimulus of sympathetic minds engaged in similar pursuits. Like many of us, she derived some of her knowledge from a close study of the original texts and some from a rapid reading of commentaries, histories, compendia, and other books about books.

During the years when Bro was at Charterhouse and before she knew Boyd, Elizabeth had no mentor; she did, however, receive encouragement from Uvedale Price (later Sir Uvedale), who lived on his estate at Foxley, about ten miles northwest of Hereford. He was a cultured country gentleman, who was a warm friend of Charles James Fox, Samuel Rogers, and Wordsworth.

Among his many interests were the classics, Italian poetry and art, and landscape gardening. In the Lawrence portrait, now at the Boston Museum of Fine Arts, the features of Sir Uvedale in his later years are those of a studious and sensitive man. By the time Elizabeth knew him he had published a translation from the Greek of Pausanias and had written An Essay on the Picturesque as Compared with the Sublime and the Beautiful.

Precisely when she first met him is not known, but in 1826, shortly before her return home from Hastings, she received from him a letter of praise for her Essay on Mind. Soon afterward she wrote a commentary on the proof sheets of his Essay on the Modern Pronunciation of the Greek and Latin Languages, and for the following two years they corresponded on the subjects of classical meters and pronunciation and translations of the classics. A particular reason for Elizabeth's gratitude is that unlike her father he did not discourage her after she had labored for six months on a long poem called "The Development of Genius."

According to her autobiographical notes she gave part of her work on February 3, 1827, to her father, who ridiculed it as "a lamentable waste of time" and brusquely told her: "I would not read over again what I have read for fifty pounds... I advise you to burn the wretched thing." Elizabeth did not describe the form in which Sir Uvedale's encouragement expressed itself, but apparently his criticism was more constructive than her father's. In her record of the interview in which Mr. Barrett had contemptuously dismissed her verses, she added significantly, "Mr. Price's friendship has given me more continual happiness than any single circumstance ever did—and I pray for him, as the grateful pray." Her poem (which remained unpublished in her lifetime) to Price on his eightieth birthday in the following month expresses her thankfulness to him for his sympathy and help. She may have continued to see him occasionally until his death in September 1829, but a year and a half before that event she had found a new guide and ally much closer to her in years and interests than the kind-hearted master of Foxley.

Chapter 3

Her Loss of Hope End

Hugh Stuart Boyd moved to Great Malvern in 1824 or 1825. His interest in Greek studies made it likely that he and Elizabeth would eventually be attracted to each other, and he evidently wrote to her soon after the publication of her Essay on Mind. It is unfortunate that of the hundreds of letters which he must have sent her during the next twenty years, only a handful have survived, for the relationship between them and the resulting tensions within his family and within Elizabeth's must necessarily be viewed only through her eyes. Her letters show that the friendship had a much deeper emotional content for her than for Boyd, that Mr. Barrett was irritated and possibly jealous because of her frequent visits to Malvern, and that Boyd strongly disapproved of Mr. Barrett's possessive and autocratic attitude toward his children.

Also it seems that at times there may have been a lack of sympathy between Elizabeth and the two women of Boyd's household, his wife and his daughter. In Elizabeth's letters to him, she wrote not only of Homer and Ossian, of St. Gregory and St. Chrysostom, of neighbourhood gossip and the domestic routine, but—more important to her biographer—she revealed her hopes, ambitions, conflicts, and frustrations more intimately than to any other correspondent until she began writing to Miss Mitford in 1836.

"Have you ever observed this in me," she wrote Boyd, "that tho' I can restrain myself and mask myself as well as anybody else, in conversation, yet as soon as I begin to write,—out everything comes... ?" Since for six or seven years Elizabeth was closer to Boyd than to anyone else outside her immediate family, it is disappointing that the details of his biography are so meager. His father, Hugh Macauley Boyd, had been a handsome, socially brilliant Irishman well known in several London circles and a friend of Goldsmith and Garrick.

In 1781 he left a wife, a daughter, and a son only a few months old, and went off to repair his dwindling fortune in India, where he died suddenly in 1794, apparently without accomplishing his aim. His son Hugh was admitted to Pembroke College, Cambridge, in 1799, but he was not serious about his university career and failed to take a degree. All his life he was to remain a dilettante. His first published work was a frigid tragedy in blank verse, Luceria, which according to the preface had been submitted to the manager of the Drury Lane Theater and "upon examination it was pronounced to be deficient in interest and effort."

In the following twenty-nine years he published several translations of the Greek Fathers—chiefly St. Chrysostom, St. Gregory Nazianzen, and St. Basil—a number of religious tracts, and a dull prose translation of the Agamemnon of Aeschylus. Inasmuch as not one of his books could have paid for itself and he never held any salaried post, he must have had independent means.

There was never any suggestion of want, and he was free to move himself and his family to a new home every few years. In May 1826 he was living at Morrison's Hotel, Great Malvern, and the following year he was at Ruby Cottage in Malvern Wells, which was his home when Elizabeth first saw him. Some time in May 1828 he and his family moved to Woodland Lodge in Great Malvern, where they stayed until about May 1831. Then they returned to Ruby Cottage for a year before leaving that part of England forever.

At the age of thirty he had become totally blind, after which he had his favourite Greek authors read to him so that he might commit their works to memory. In May 1832, according to a note in Elizabeth's handwriting, he could repeat from memory more than 2,000 lines from Gregory Nazianzen, 1,800 from Aeschylus, and 1,310 from the hymns of Synesius; altogether almost 8,000 lines of Greek verse and prose.

Elizabeth later wrote to Browning that Boyd's memory was "merely the mechanical faculty.

The associative, which makes the other a high power, he wants." She thought Boyd"a very peculiar person... in all possible ways," and in the same letter she showed she was not unaware of his defects. "He talks like a man of slow mind, which he is,.. and with a child's way of looking at things... He cares for me perhaps more than he cares for any one else.. far more than for his own only daughter; but he is not a man of deep sensibility, and, if he heard of my death, would merely sleep a little sounder the next night."

The first letter from Elizabeth to Boyd which has been saved is dated March 11, 1827. In it she referred to a previous note in which she had thanked him for sending her his works, and then she acknowledged his invitation to visit him. Although she had recently celebrated her twenty-first birthday, that event seems not to have conferred upon her any measure of independence. "I very seldom have it in my power to leave home," she said, "and the first time I am able to do so, must visit some friends to whom I am under a long engagement."

As for walking across the fields and over the hill from Hope End to Malvern Wells, that would be out of the question: "My health... is not bad, but deficiency in strength makes me quite incapable of much exercise." During the spring, summer, and fall letters were sent back and forth, and the possibility of her visiting him was still no less remote.

On November 3 she wrote him that he should not feel hurt at her failure to see him because, "My Father has represented to me, that, whatever gratification and improvement I might receive from a personal intercourse with you, yet, as a female, and a young female, I could not pay such a first visit as the one you proposed to me, without overstepping the established observances of society."

Elizabeth and Boyd continued to correspond without seeing each other, and she discussed her reading of Greek and Latin, Uvedale Price's recent book on ancient pronunciation, and Boyd's translations. Perhaps several years might have passed without their meeting each other if a pathetic appeal from Boyd to Elizabeth had not wrung from her father the necessary permission.

On Thursday, March 13, 1828, Elizabeth went in the Barretts' phaeton to Great Malvern to visit a cousin of hers, Mrs. Trant. Within a hundred yards of Mrs. Trant's house, she passed Mr. and Mrs. Boyd in the street. "My first impulse was to stop the carriage—but my courage gave way! I COULD not introduce myself then!" she wrote her grandmother Moulton. The next morning she received from Boyd a long letter dated "Thursday morning," in which he said, "I suppose it was you who passed me this morning... Whether it was you or not, it awakened within me feelings and reflections which for several months have been somewhat repressed! Mrs. Boyd is tired of this place and wishes to leave it.

If I should do so, I shall probably write you a letter the day before, to tell you more fully what I think and feel! I am now nearly forty seven, but, if I recollect right, this is the longest letter I ever wrote in my life." The letter made her feel so "pained and uncomfortable" that she took it to her father and secured his consent, as she wrote, "to do as I liked."

So on Monday Elizabeth undertook the journey with Bro, Henrietta, and Arabel. On the part of the road which descends steeply into Great Malvern the carriage got out of control, and all were thrown upon the bank. Bro then fastened the pony to a tree and after placing Elizabeth in the carriage, dragged it himself into the town.

The first people they saw there were Mr. and Mrs. Boyd. Trembling with fright, Elizabeth went toward him, held out her hand, but could not speak. Mrs. Boyd said, "Miss Barrett"; Boyd and Elizabeth, however, shook hands in silence. She thought him "a rather young looking man than otherwise, moderately tall, and slightly formed. His features are good—his face very pale, with an expression of placidity and mildness." He enquired from Elizabeth whether she had been hurt, and Mrs. Boyd asked if "Miss Barrett would allow them to take charge of her."

She declined since she wished to rejoin Henrietta, who

had been slightly hurt in the accident and had gone ahead to Mrs. Trant's house in the coach. They walked along in silence, broken only by Boyd's saying, "I cannot help thinking that I was the cause" and "this is ominous, Miss Barrett." She, however, "was too frightened and nervous for conversation." They finally reached Mrs. Trant's house, where Boyd said to Elizabeth, "God bless you."

Thus ended "this extraordinary interview" and began one of the most important friendships of her life. In a blank page of his copy of Elizabeth An Essay on Mind Boyd wrote that she did him the honour of paying him a first visit on Wednesday, April 16, 1828, and that on Friday, May 16, she came again and read the opening of the Oedipus Tyrannus. For the next four years she frequently saw him at his house, occasionally paying visits of a week or more, during which she read widely with him in the Greek classics and the Greek patristic writings.

He was not her formal tutor; but if she had never had his encouragement, his suggestions of different authors and texts to read, and at times his instruction, it is doubtful if she would have been so devoted to Greek studies. As for the Greek Fathers, she later wrote to Boyd that they "would probably have remained in their sepulchres, as far as my reading them was concerned." Only a very rapid reader of that language could have gone through so much material. Although a few years before her death she wrote a friend that she did not consider herself "well-grounded by any manner of means" in her knowledge of Greek, she believed that she had "read over a wider surface than most scholars perhaps." In the same letter she also wrote that in her youth she had read through "nearly every word extant in Greek" and that "for years" she did "nothing else."

Her marginal comments in one of her volumes of Euripides testify to the speed with which she read the language. After each of the ten plays in the book she made a short critical evaluation and entered the date when she finished it. She read all of the Rhesus (which seemed to her as a whole "very heavy and uninteresting and cold" in spite of "several beautiful passages"), the first of the dramas in the edition, in January 1832, and by the end of June she had gone through all the plays. She spent a week each in reading the Bacchae and the Heraclidae and about a fortnight upon the Hercules furens (which delighted her more than any other drama in the volume because "few things in real life are so affecting as to see a man shed tears"). Boyd's manuscript notes of what Elizabeth read at his house in the summer and fall of 1830 are also evidence of her rapid reading. The usual stint of a morning's visit at that time was somewhat more than one hundred lines from the Agamemnon, although occasionally she read two hundred in one day. Boyd mentioned at least twice that she did the translation "extremely well."

When she stayed at the Boyds' for some two weeks late in the summer, she read more than one thousand verses from the Agamemnon and about twelve hundred lines from Chrysostom, Gregory, and Basil. At times she must have been studying several Greek texts concomitantly. For example, she wrote to Boyd in an undated letter that she had just finished Longinus'work and the Rhesus of Euripides and had been reading Chrysostom's commentaries on the Epistles to the Co-inthians.

If she found a text hard to understand, she did not hesitate to acknowledge her perplexity. For example she wrote to Boyd in 1829 that she was reading a little of Longinus' De sublimitate every day and that she hoped he was considered difficult, for she had to look at the Latin every five minutes. On the back of the frontispiece of her copy of Longinus she scribbled a short critical estimate of that author and explained that she had found the Greek hard because of "technicalities in the phraseology" and "the involutions of the style."

All her time was spent in reading and writing, as she said to Boyd quite truthfully. But the writing was mostly of long letters to him and a few other correspondents, for she was not composing much poetry. Between the publication of her volume of 1826 and that of 1833, a few of her juvenilia, all of them imitative and without distinction, appeared in the Literary Gazette, the Jewish Expositor and Friend of Israel, and

The Times. Her energies were chiefly directed to her reading, which as in earlier years was mainly in the classics and in modern literature.

Before she left Hope End at the age of twenty-six, she had read one or two books of the Old Testament in the Hebrew, some of the New Testament in Greek, possibly all of Aeschylus, and most of Euripides. The marginal annotations in her two volumes of Sophocles show that either at this time or a little later she went through all the plays with the possible exception of the Trachiniae, the only one upon which she failed to comment.

She also studied the Phaedo of Plato, the orations and letters of Isocrates, and the Memorabilia and Cyropaedia of Xenophon; and she no doubt continued with Homer and Pindar. As for the Greek Christian Fathers, she read hundreds of pages in the closely printed folios and quartos of Gregory, Chrysostom, Basil, and Synesius, for all of whom Boyd had published translations.

The list of the texts with which she became familiar among the Greek writers of the Roman era includes the Enchiridion a treatise on classical prosody by Hephaestion; the Manual of the Stoic philosopher Epictetus; the Aethiopica, a romantic novel in Greek by Heliodorus; and Longinus' De sublimitate. She also devoted some attention to Latin writers; but since Boyd was not particularly interested in Latin literature, she made only a few references to the subject in her letters to him, which are almost the only source of biographical information during these years. It is certain, however, that she finished the Pharsalia of Lucan, whom she described as "an ardent poet," and at this period or possibly somewhat later she read Virgil's Eclogues, the Georgics, and parts of the Aeneid; a number of plays by Terence; some of Lucretius' De rerum natura; and selections from Livy, Catullus, Horace, Aulus Gellius, and Erasmus.

In addition to the Greek and Latin she read Adam Clarke's commentaries on the Bible and several volumes of sermons and theological treatises, and she continued her study of French literature. In 1828, when she was writing to Uvedale

Price on classical meters and was also reading Sophocles with Boyd, she began what she later called in a letter to Miss Mitford a "lengthy" correspondence with Edmund Henry Barker of Thetford, Norfolk.

Because of common interests Barker was an acquaintance of both Price and Boyd, but it was probably the latter who introduced Barker to Elizabeth. At the time of their correspondence Barker was an industrious and productive classical scholar who had edited Lemprière Classical Dictionary and had helped in the production of a Greek thesaurus and a Latin thesaurus. But within a few years he was destined to be financially ruined, placed in the Fleet prison, and die in a shabby London boarding house.

It was evidently Barker, not Elizabeth, who initiated and wished to maintain the correspondence. "To tell you the truth," she wrote him on May 12, 1829, "you a little surprised me by proposing to correspond regularly with me; for, having heard a good deal of your extensive correspondences... I did not venture to conjecture that you could have any time to throw away. You resemble a Chinese waterman, who, while he conducts the oars with his feet, and regulates the sail with his hands, is able nevertheless to smoke his pipe all the while. I hope I need not say that I am gratified by your promising to smoke a pipe now and then for my benefit."

Elizabeth thought him a rather silly man. In her letters to Boyd she made fun of Barker's books for children, several of which he had sent her, and she ridiculed his edition of Cicero," with its mixture of English and Latin notes. The volume contained the orations against Catiline, a dialogue by Tacitus, and "several beautiful extracts from English authors, with a suggestion to the conductors of classical schools to devote one day in the week to the study of English literature."

Elizabeth might well have hesitated to thank Barker and to have wondered how she could fill a letter about "such a mere compilation" when she saw the titles and authors of some of the passages: for example, a "Description of a Christian Family Spending the Sabbath" from the Rev. Joshua Gilpin's Monument of Parental Affection to a Dear and Only Son. A year before the edition of Cicero was published in 1829 Barker issued in two thick volumes his "Parriana: or, Notices of the Rev. Samuel Parr", L.L.D. (1828-29). The work is a compendium of illassorted material, much of which has only a tenuous connection with the life of Parr. Elizabeth struggled through the volumes in the summer of 1828 and presumably at Boyd's request made a list of the passages she thought would interest him.

At about this time Mrs. Barrett, who had been in poor health for a year or two, was encouraged by her physician, Dr. Carden, to go to Cheltenham, where, everyone hoped, she might recover her strength.

When she left Hope End late in September with her sister Arabella (Bummy) and possibly Henrietta, no one knew how critically ill she was. From Tewkesbury on the first of October, Mrs. Barrett wrote back to Elizabeth, "My beloved Ba's tearful eyes as I parted with her yesterday have hung somewhat heavily on my heart."

On the back of the letter Elizabeth wrote, "The very last I ever received from her. One week after it was written, we possessed her no longer. It has been wet with more bitter tears than were those the recollection of which hung heavily on her tender heart, but may the Lord's will be done." She died at Cheltenham on the seventh of October, 1828, and was buried beside her daughter Mary in the Parish Church of St. Michael and All Angels in Ledbury.

Mr. Barrett, who was neither at his wife's bedside at the time of her death nor at home, wrote Elizabeth on a scrap of paper with no indication of address or date a message which appears to have been scribbled hastily:

This morning has the afflicting dispensation of our Heavenly Father been made known to me in two hours I shall be on my way to Cheltenham, where I will have this put with the Post for you. I cannot say what I feel, for I scarcely can define my sensations, the blow is too recent... I would say Lord not my will but thine be done, thou knowest best, teach us to submit patiently to all thy excitations... She is, I am persuaded... now in the presence of him to whom she belongs as a purchased one, and a redeemed one by the pouring out of his precious blood.

Both now and in later years Edward Moulton Barrett was essentially inarticulate, and he bottled up within himself his grief and disappointments, so that no one around him ever knew his feelings. The language of the letter is that of a man who appears never to have had religious doubts and who was, as Elizabeth said of him, "strong in the consolation which is of God."

However much Mrs. Barrett may have been overshadowed by her husband, the ties between Elizabeth and her mother had always been close. In spite of the fact that Mrs. Barrett had been unwell when she left home, her death was for Elizabeth, as she wrote Boyd immediately after the event, an "unforeseen and unexpected" blow, which for a time took away from her the power of thinking.

Her agony was the more severe because she had been "denied the consolation" of being with her mother at the end. It seemed to her that she had perhaps had too much natural affection for her mother and that God had thus "reproved" her. In her next letter to Boyd some weeks or possibly months later, she again wrote of her grief: "I never can forget what I have lost. Her voice is still sounding in my ears—her image is in my heart —and they are to be loved, however unreal they may be!"

Upon Mr. Barrett now devolved the sole responsibility for bringing up the eleven children, who ranged from the twentytwo-year-old Elizabeth to the four-year-old Octavius. It was an obligation which a greatly reduced income was to render increasingly burdensome. Two or three years before his wife's death he had suffered the first of a series of financial losses which were eventually to alter his way of life and even his personality.

The basis of the trouble had been a long-standing dispute over some of the Jamaica properties. After Edward Barrett of Cinnamon Hill, Jamaica, died in 1798, the Moulton-Barretts were the principal inheritors of his Northside estates; they remained absentee owners and entrusted their plantations to resident managers who ran the estates for their own interests rather than for those of the owners. Their cousins, the Goodin-Barretts, instituted a law suit against them in 1801 to recover some property willed them by Edward Barrett, and the case remained in litigation for more than twenty years. In 1824 the court decided in favour of the Goodin-Barretts, and several parcels of the slaves of the Moulton-Barretts were handed over to Richard Barrett as receiver.

The Moulton-Barretts then had to hire the slaves back from their cousin Richard and also pay large interest charges which had accrued during the past years when the slaves had been held by them illegally, according to the decision. Richard Barrett was one of the most brilliant lawyers and politicians of Jamaica and was speaker of the House of Assembly in 1830. Elizabeth in a letter to Miss Mitford later described him as "a man of talent and violence and some malice, who did what he could, at one time, to trample poor Papa down.. did trample him at one moment when he felt him under his feet." So in 1825 Edward Moulton Barrett and his brother Sam must have realized that if they were to salvage a portion of their Jamaica investments, they could not both remain in England as rentiers. Which of the two would have to pull up stakes and go to Jamaica to run the Northside estates?

Some of the reasons why the choice fell upon Sam are obvious enough. Edward had a large family whose removal to Jamaica would have been very expensive, while Sam had no children. On the other hand Sam must have been very reluctant to live in Jamaica because his wife, whom he had married in 1822, was in such poor health that the harsh climate of the island would hasten her death (as it did four years after her arrival).

Furthermore, he had been a member of Parliament since 1820, representing the Borough of Richmond. The brothers seemingly had at one time a serious quarrel which Elizabeth, who was her uncle's favourite niece, may have succeeded in healing. On July 5, 1824, Mrs. Barrett wrote Elizabeth in Cheltenham that she was sending a letter from "Sam offering thro you the olive branch to Papa, and... expressing Mary's desire to know Papa and his own that the past should be buried in oblivion." It seems curious that although Mary Clementina Cay-Adams had been married to Sam for two years, she had never met his brother. Several enigmatic references in Elizabeth's letters suggest that Sam's going to Jamaica, or his remaining there, may have been an act of despair after the failure of everything in England. In all ways he seems to have been in contrast to his inflexible, unimaginative older brother.

He was a brilliant conversationalist, "a bright, gifted being," at one time "a man of large fortune." After he had been "talked into the new South sea bubbles of some years ago," failures came, and he "found himself responsible for companies to whom he had simply given his name." Unlike his brother, he had no gift "for battling with adversity"; and leaving "a situation full of perplexity and distress," he "went to the West—and so ended all!"

In 1827 he resigned his seat in Parliament and left with his ailing wife for Jamaica; apparently neither saw England again. Although the change was less drastic than it had been for Sam, Edward Moulton Barrett also had to sacrifice many of his accustomed pleasures in his effort to retain the Hope End estate and prevent any diminution of the capital he hoped to bequeath to his children. From 1827 until the Barretts left Hope End in the summer of 1832, he no longer was able to spend most of his time at home, enjoying the pleasures and performing the duties of a country squire but for business reasons had to live in London during a large part of each year.

Because of either poor judgment or bad luck, or a combination of both, he found his financial resources were dwindling so rapidly that it would soon be necessary for him to dispose of his large estate and to live in greatly reduced circumstances. The education of Bro and of Sam at Charterhouse had to be interrupted before either could complete his course.

Bro, who had advanced from the ninth form in 1820 to the third in 1826, did not return in 1827. Sam went from the twelfth form in 1822 to the sixth in 1828, which was his last year at that school or any other. None of the other six brothers ever went to a public school. It was evidently in the spring of 1831 that the mortgaged Hope End property, which was then valued at about £50,000, was seized from Mr. Barrett and put up for sale to satisfy the creditors. The great slave insurrection in Jamaica of December 1831-January 1832, with its widespread destruction on the Barrett plantations, increased his difficulties as he tried to find the money to redeem Hope End. At first Elizabeth had no inkling of her father's changed fortunes. She was absorbed in her friendship with Boyd, riding on her donkey back and forth across the Malvern Hills to read Greek with him. Before long she cared for him far more than she ever had for Uvedale Price.

She was attracted to his "unworldliness and enthusiasm" and felt he provided for her the mental companionship and sympathy she could not find at home, except possibly from Bro. In January 1831 when the news reached her of the death of her grandmother Moulton, who had been a second mother to the Barrett children and especially to Elizabeth, she became so ill she could not leave home for several weeks. But she wrote Boyd that even though she could not go to his house, she wished him to know she still cared for him, that "there never were or could be any, out of my own immediate family, towards whom I have felt as I have and must ever feel towards you." Her father seems to have been jealous of Boyd for his friendship with Elizabeth. She often wrote to Boyd of her reluctance to ask her father for permission to see him, for fear he might be irritated by her importuning him too often on the subject. Once she said, "He was not pleased on Monday at my having left home on such a day, and told me that I would certainly kill myself—and then I might be satisfied."

Oddly enough it is likely that Mr. Barrett never visited and hardly ever spoke to the man whose friendship meant so much to his daughter. Although she would have liked her father to call upon Boyd and was distressed at his omission, she never asked him to do so because, as she explained, "from my knowledge of his habits and usual inclinations, there appeared to me no kind of probability of hearing any other than a negative answer." In the spring of 1831 Elizabeth began to hear rumors that her beloved home might be sold and that the Barrett family would have to move away, though no one knew where, and for the next year she was constantly preoccupied with "THE subject," as she called it. Fantastic backstairs gossip and neighbourhood talk came to her that her father was so ill he was not expected to live much longer, or that all the servants but one had been discharged be cause they would not move to the West Indies with the Barretts. She was terrified at the prospect of their going to one of the family's plantations in Jamaica.

Since Mr. Barrett never informed his children of the plans he had made for them, it was useless to question him. She had been present when he had received a letter telling him of the loss of his fortune "not down to the point of 'elegant competence' but very far below it!" Several years later she described the scene to Miss Mitford: "He was surrounded by his family—and they, so young—and not educated,—and with not one prospect amongst them. And the letter came—and just one shadow past on his face while he read it (I marked it at the moment) and then he broke away from the melancholy, and threw himself into the jests and laughter of his innocent boys." He bravely faced the misfortune without complaint and was usually able to hide his feelings behind "a thick mask of high spirits." Owing to his "extraordinary power of self-command," she could guess nothing from his expression and manner.

One day Elizabeth and Henrietta were discussing in the presence of their father the question whether their aunt Arabella had left her home and was now in London. Mr. Barrett remained "perfectly silent" during the conversation, but the next morning he sent a letter to Arabella Graham-Clarke addressed to her hotel on Albemarle Street. "So you see," Elizabeth wrote Boyd, "he knew all about it, all the time. There is nothing but mysteries!" It was from Mr. Curzon, the minister of the Independent Chapel in Ledbury, that Elizabeth finally learned of the certainty that Hope End would be sold, though he was not sure how much more time the Barretts would be able to remain there.

In April or May of 1831, about the time Elizabeth first heard the rumors concerning Hope End, she also learned that Boyd was planning to move away, possibly to Bath. She was much disturbed at the prospect and immediately suggested in her letters to Boyd many reasons why he should remain: the salubrious climate of Malvern, its social advantages for Mrs. Boyd, and the many temptations and harmful influences at Bath for a young girl like Annie.

In the highly emotional language with which she usually expressed her feelings she wrote him that she had lately been suffering such "distress of mind" that her body could scarcely endure any further struggle, and she added, "I would give up all the pleasure and advantage I have derived from your society, for this—that you had gone away three years ago instead of now." Boyd's wife and daughter would have preferred to leave immediately, but he persuaded them to remain, took a year's lease on a house in Malvern Wells, and did not move away until May 1832.

In her letters to him that year, and probably in their many conversations, she traced the fluctuations of her hope and despair as she learned now good news, now bad, about the fate of Hope End. Once she was so happy she could hardly write and rushed to her room, where she added a few words to a letter she had begun earlier in the morning to Boyd: "Promise me," she wrote in great excitement, "that you will not to any one person, say one word of what I am now going to tell you,—and now listen!!"

She had been told by her aunt Arabella that Mr. Barrett believed he could retain his home, but Elizabeth, Henrietta, and Bro were warned not to change their expressions before Mr. Barrett, because if he suspected Miss Graham-Clarke had revealed to them any of his communications, "they would cease from that moment." A "fat gentleman with the rings" came from London and was reported to have said, "The place is to be sold," that he had been appointed to take possession in the meanwhile, and that he had asked a neighbouring farmer to plow the Hope End hopyard.

According to the rumors from some land surveyors, as

Elizabeth told the episode to Boyd, the farmer went to Mr. Barrett for his permission, and since his reply, "Do as you please," was considered too ambiguous, "the fat gentleman's intended ploughing is still unperformed." Another time her father's having a number of his own men work in the Hope End hopyard was interpreted by some as a favorable omen, Elizabeth heard, and by others as without meaning, since he was gathering the crops which already belonged to him. She was particularly distressed at the loss of privacy in having to put up with visitors at Hope End who came ostensibly to consider the purchase of the property. But some of them, she suspected, were there only to gloat over the misfortunes of her family and to snoop around the grounds and the interior of the house that they might have the perverse pleasure of seeing the Barretts in the luxurious surroundings they no longer could call their own.

One afternoon in August 1831 the vicar of the Priory at Great Malvern, Dr. Henry Card, together with his wife and three friends, all five of whom were acquaintances of Elizabeth, "made a party of pleasure" to her home. The ticket of admission which they had secured from a real estate agent in Worcester was invalid, and they were not permitted to go beyond the dining room. Mr. Barrett was not at home. Bro became so angry at the intrusion that he told the butler in a voice loud enough for the unwelcome guests to hear that if he did not show them out of the house immediately, he would do so himself.

They left and walked around the grounds, peering into the windows to look at Miss GrahamClarke in the drawing room. All the time they were laughing and chattering and seemed "satisfied and pleased." And only a short while ago one of the group, a Miss Wall, had written to Eliza Cliffe, a friend of Elizabeth's, of her strong feeling of "compassion" for "those poor girls."

Years later, as Elizabeth looked back upon that "miserable time," she told Miss Mitford that they "had to hide, even away from our own private rooms, where we used to be safe from all the world,—and to hear in our hidingplace the trampling and the voices of strangers through the passages everywhere, and in the chambers which had been shut up for years from our own steps, sacred to death and love." In spite of their unsettled domestic arrangements during their last year at Hope End, Mr.

Barrett, Elizabeth, and Bro were very much interested in the debates over the proposed Reform Bill. Late in May 1831 Bro dined at Ledbury in honour of the victory of the reform candidate, a Mr. Hoskins. When Mr. Barrett was not away in London, he used to read to his children in the evenings the reports in the newspapers of the struggles over the bill and to express his own liberal-whig principles. Elizabeth, who always had a propensity for dividing the world into saints and sinners, thought the language of the anti-reform lords was "disgusting" and that Lord Grey's position was "morally sublime."

After the bill had passed early in June 1832 she wrote Boyd that the event would be celebrated in Ledbury by a procession, a great dinner, and a giving away of food to the poor. Her father contributed "a very large cow" worth £20. In the middle of May the Boyds had moved to Somersetshire, eventually to Bathampton.

Their alleged reason for going was that the health of their daughter would be endangered by further residence in Malvern, but Elizabeth thought Annie was well enough and that Boyd was yielding to the pressures of his wife and daughter, both of whom considered Malvern a dull town and hoped for a more lively social atmosphere in Bath. His departure was a severe blow which, together with the trouble about Hope End, brought on an emotional upset from which Elizabeth did not recover until several months later, after her arrival in Sidmouth. For the three or four years previous he had been the only person outside her own family whom she had cared to see regularly.

A day or two after he left she sent him a letter in which she again expressed her sense of guilt, as she had at the time of her mother's death. She wrote that a recent letter from him had been read by her "with many tears" and that perhaps she deserved the agony of their separation, "because when under the pressure of those heavy afflictions with which God has been pleased to afflict me since the commencement of our intimacy,—I often looked too much for comfort to you—instead of looking higher than you."

She begged him to write her frequently and told him that while he might become acquainted with many persons who were in many ways superior to her, "yet you will never never have another friend whose regard for you can be stronger or truer or more incapable of change than mine." She had for this blind, middle-aged, limited, ineffectual, and rather helpless man an extraordinary attachment. But within one or two years the bonds of the relationship were to be loosened at the very moment she was forming a close friendship in Sidmouth with a man who had many similar qualities.

Boyd apparently wrote Elizabeth that he hoped she would visit him at Bath. Her nerves were tense from the conflict in loyalties and from her dread of having to move away from the only home she could remember. She could not go to see Boyd, for her father would neither allow her to remain as a guest in his house nor settle his family near Bath. When he apparently wrote her that she lacked the "spirit and resolution" to secure her father's permission, she replied that she had no desire to give pain to "the person, who loves me better than any person in the world loves me, for the sake of visiting you for a week or two!!"

All her energy, she said, was "expended in bearing up against the different deprivations under which I suffer." Such language bears little relationship to the outward circumstances of her life, for she was suffering no physical hardships in the summer of 1832. The Barrett fortune, although greatly diminished, had not disappeared, and her father was still in a position to provide for all of them a comfortable, if less luxurious, home. The threatened loss of Hope End, the absence of Boyd, and his misunderstanding of her position all depressed her spirits.

Her letters to him during her last months in Herefordshire are filled with references to her mental suffering and her belief that she was near the breaking point. A passage from her letter to him in July 1832 is typical of many: "I sometimes feel that for the rest of my life, I would barter almost every kind of pleasure for the loss of every kind of pain, and consent to be only tranquil instead of pleased. For a long time my powers of feeling pleasure and pain have been clashing against each other—and neither my body nor mind can bear it any longer." As a distraction against her anxieties and despondency she absorbed herself in the world of books.

With the aid of John Parkhurst's An Hebrew and English Lexicon [with] an Hebrew and a Chaldee Grammar she read her two quarto volumes of the Hebrew Bible "from Genesis to Malachi, right through, and was never stopped by the Chaldee." After the following winter she gave up Hebrew studies and never resumed them.

She also went through the whole of the Aeneid except for two books she was already familiar with; two plays of Euripides, the Alcestis and the Troades, each for the second time; and two novels in Italian. Furthermore she finished for the third time, and admired more than ever, Madame de Staël Corinne, upon which in the maturity of her career she was to draw for some of the characterization and plot of Aurora Leigh. During their last few months at Hope End Elizabeth felt that rather than endure any longer the uncertainty, she would prefer to have the place disposed of and to be far away from her beloved home.

Eventually Mr. Barrett heard it had been sold, and he left immediately to spend a week in Devonshire looking for a new home. He went away so suddenly, without telling anyone his plans or his reasons for the trip that Elizabeth did not know five minutes before his departure that he intended to go anywhere, and she could only guess at the nature of his errand from the trembling in his voice as he said goodbye.

The friends and neighbours of the Barretts, Lady Margaret Cocks, the Cliffes, the Peytons, the Martins, and the Commelines, were all distressed at their leaving Hope End. In the last letters she wrote to Boyd before going to Sidmouth, Elizabeth described all the details of her family's misfortune and confessed that she gained even "a certain pleasure in saying them." She wrote to him with unconscious understatement, "You will think I dare say, that I am apt to be out of spirits and to look at the gloomy side of everything." One woman was in such an agony of grief that she fell down in what appeared to be a fit after blessing "every hair of Master's head, and all his children from the biggest to the least."

Some of the people upon whom Henrietta called in their cottages in Wellington Heath burst into tears and expressed their pity. In contrast to the present, Elizabeth recalled the pleasant time she had spent several years before in France, when she was always joking and in high spirits.

Once when smoke from a wood fire had made her weep, an acquaintance was astonished to "have seen the tears in Mademoiselle Barrett's eyes." But recently a number of "desolating changes" had come to her, and now the loss of Hope End was "the last stroke." She hated to think that strangers would soon be living in her home, that they would be laughing and talking in the rooms "too painfully dear" to her, where her mother had lived and where no one of the family had entered since her death. At the beginning of August workmen came to pack up the furniture to be stored away in Ledbury and the plate to be sent to the bank in London until the Barretts should have another permanent home, and the sound of their hammering and walking about echoed all day long in the empty rooms and halls.

Elizabeth was grieved at the sight of "dear Hope End looking so unlike the happy Hope End it used to be," and she would sit at the window and wonder whether it was all a dream. With the assistance of his sons Mr. Barrett dusted the books and wrapped them up in bundles, also to be placed in safe deposit.

Of Elizabeth's own library two folios of St. Chrysostom and two quartos of Adam Clarke's commentary on the Bible were put in the warehouse. She sent ahead to Sidmouth her folio of Gregory Nazianzen, Wolf's Homer, the first volume of C. G. Heyne's edition of the Iliad and the first volume of his Pindar, possibly her three volumes of the Odyssey, two plays of Aeschylus, the complete works of Sophocles and Euripides, a few small Latin books, her Hebrew and Greek Bibles, Boyd Select Passages, and his Agamemnon of Aeschylus. Mr. Barrett's pride was so hurt by having to forfeit his home that he shrank from old friends and many of his customary activities.

To his children he never referred to the subject, and "he could play at cricket with the boys on the very last evening." Early in the morning of Thursday, August 23, 1832, two carriages left Hope End for the house Mr. Barrett had rented for his family in Sidmouth, Devonshire, 130 miles away. Fifteen were in the party: nine Barrett children (all but Bro and Septimus, both of whom came later with their father), their aunt Arabella, and several servants.

Although most of the Barretts often returned to the neighbourhood of Hope End in later years to visit relatives and friends, Elizabeth was never again to set foot in Herefordshire. They spent the night at the York Hotel in Bath, which she thought, "take it altogether, marble and mountains, is the most beautiful town I ever looked upon." She was so tired and out of health from her long drive that she could scarcely stand and had to be content with the view of Bath from her bedroom window. To have visited Boyd at Bathampton was out of the question. Early the next morning they set out toward Sidmouth; and since it was dark when they arrived, they had trouble at first in finding their new home.

Chapter 4

Epilogue: A Century of Criticism

Although after his mother's death Pen had been staying with Isa Blagden, Browning remained alone at Casa Guidi until the day after the funeral, when he suddenly became so ill with grief that he left the empty apartment and walked up to Miss Blagden's villa. Until his departure from Florence a month later, he went to the villa every night, returning to his own rooms in the daytime.

He realized that in spite of his love for Florence, he could not remain in that city because the associations would have been too painful. So he immediately decided to go to London and there to devote himself to his poetry and to the education of Pen. "Life must now be begun anew," he said to Story; "all the old cast off and the new one put on. I shall go away, break up everything, go to England and live and work and write." Likewise he wrote to his sister Sarianna, "I shall never again 'keep house,' nor live but in the simplest manner, but always with reference to Pen."

The boy who in Browning's opinion had become too Italian in his costume and manners was to receive an English education and upbringing. "Of course Pen is and will be English as I am English and as his Mother was pure English...," Browning maintained to John Forster. Only four days after the funeral Browning wrote his sister that, "Pen, the golden curls and fantastic dress, is gone just as Ba is gone: he has short hair, worn boy-wise, long trousers, is a common boy all at once." After having sold some of his possessions and placed the rest in storage, Browning left for Paris, together with Pen and Isa Blagden, on August 1.

He was never again to see the city where he had spent the happiest years of his life. At Paris, Isa left Browning and Pen and went to England, where she lived for a year, part of the time near the bereaved poet, before returning to her Florentine home. After spending most of August and September at St. Enogat on the coast of France with his father, his sister, and his son, Browning went with Pen to London in the autumn. He eventually settled at ig Warwick Crescent in order to be near Arabel Barrett, who was living in the same neighbourhood at Delamere Terrace.

In the long, busy years ahead Browning's "heart was buried in Florence," as he himself said; he never remarried. After the death of his father in 1866, his sister came to live with him in London and thereafter was his constant companion. The child upon whom so much care had been lavished by a devoted mother was equally spoiled by the father. Pen was not sent away from home to a private or to a public school and was educated in such a haphazard manner that he failed in several examinations for entrance to Baliol. For a year or two he was enrolled at Christ Church, Oxford, but was interested primarily in rowing and in billiards. Later he became a sculptor and a painter, without achieving much success in either field, and eventually made his home in Italy.

Robert Browning gained belated recognition as one of England's greatest poets after the publication in 1868-69 of The Ring and the Book and received honorary degrees from Oxford, Cambridge, and Edinburgh. In later years volume after volume came from his prolific pen, but much of his poetry was less creative, less dramatic, and more analytical and reflective. He not only continued to publish with unflagging energy, but also was a prominent figure in London society, attending countless dinner parties, concerts, art exhibitions, and receptions.

It was not until 1878, after an absence of seventeen years, that Browning again saw the country where he had lived during his marriage. For all but three years afterward he returned late in the summer to northern Italy. It was during one of these annual visits that he died at Venice in his son's home, the magnificent Palazzo Rezzonico, at the age of seventy-seven—twenty-eight years after his wife's death.

Although Mrs. Browning's poetical reputation in England had suffered during the last two or three years of her life because of her political poems, the writers of obituary notices in the leading critical journals rescued her from the disfavor into which she had fallen. They were shocked to learn of her untimely death, which in their opinion prevented her genius from reaching its fullest development. For example, the Saturday Review, which had ridiculed Aurora Leigh and attacked Poems before Congress because of her "un-English" point of view, said, "In English literature, as well as in Italian society, her premature death will leave a visible and melancholy blank."

Most of the announcements of her death reviewed her career almost from the beginning. The unanimous opinion was that in spite of her many offenses against poetic taste and her isolation, which hindered her from observing life in its fullness and complexity, she was the greatest woman poet in English literature—in the judgment of several writers, the greatest in the history of the world. The Spectator said that she had been "one of the very few truly creative minds of whom England could still boast—one who in poetic gifts ranked far above all her countrywomen" and that she was the only English woman who deserved a place among "our genuine poets."

Although the Edinburgh Review found a sense of unreality in much of her verse because of her confinement to a sick chamber, it nevertheless asserted that her equal could not be found in the literary history of any country: "Such a combination of the finest genius and the choicest results of cultivation and wide-ranging studies has never been seen before in any woman, nor is the world likely soon to see the same again."

It was probably her old friend Chorley who wrote the article in the Athenaeum, which announced with regret the death of "the greatest of English poetesses of any time." He traced her career from the time when he first saw her anonymous "The Romaunt of Margret" in the New Monthly

Magazine in 1836 and had been struck by its "daring and deep originality." Chorley had stabbed her in the back when he harshly criticized her Poems before Congress, but he tried to make amends by writing of her literary skill, her intellectual ability, her absence of pretension, her fearlessness in treating unpopular subjects, and the affection and loyalty she had always shown to relatives and friends.

Among the American notices, Kate Field in the Atlantic Monthly and George William Curtis in Harper's Magazine both described Mrs. Browning as they had remembered her and told of her appearance, personality, and surroundings. Curtis, who had seen the Brownings in Florence early in their years together and had joined them in a trip to Vallombrosa, ranked her "among the chief English poets of this century" and believed that she was unusual among poets in that she was "not only a singer but a hearty, active worker in her way, understanding her time, and trying, as she could, to help it." He thought that since the Vita nuova and the sonnets of Shakespeare and Petrarch, almost no one had written poems on the subject of love "so true and sweet and subtle" as the author of the "Sonnets from the Portuguese."

Perhaps the highest praise in any American periodical came from the Southern Literary Messenger, which called her "the Shakespeare among her sex" and was convinced that among all the poems written by women of all eras and nations, there was "absolutely nothing which deserves to be compared for a moment with the marvellous effusions of this poetess."

The writer placed her among the four or five greatest authors since the beginning of civilization: "Mrs. Browning has planted her feet on the mountains of Immortality, and stands glorified with Homer, Dante, Shakespeare, Milton, Goethe, and Shelley,—that august circle of laurelled bards, whose names will go down in music through the echoing aisles of the future." It is clear that immediately after her death she was at the pinnacle of her poetic reputation both in England and in America. On March 20, 1862, Chapman and Hall brought out her Last Poems, which had been collected by Browning. It was a slender octavo volume composed mostly of translations she had made before her marriage for a classical album which had never appeared and of the Italian pieces written after Poems before Congress. The reviews mostly commented on and quoted from such poems as "De Profundis" and "A Musical Instrument," which they preferred to the Italian lyrics. Besides discussing the recent volume, most of the notices considered her entire poetic career, of which they spoke no less warmly than when they had announced her death in the preceding summer.

The Dublin University Magazine expressed the prevailing judgment when it said that she was "one whom many will doubtless rank as the greatest poetess the world has ever known." Once again Chorley in the Athenaeum recalled the delight he had experienced when he came upon her first published poems, reaffirmed his belief that her name would live among the first rank of English poets, and declared that "in sweep of thought, in richness of culture, in pertinence of language" she was the greatest of all English woman poets. The volume of Last Poems which was published in New York simultaneously with the English edition contained a preface, or "Memorial" as it was called, of more than seventy pages written by Theodore Tilton, editor of the Independent.

In his opinion Mrs. Browning had both a wider range of subjects and more readers than her husband. Much of her work, he believed, was the finest since Shakespeare and Milton. He thought that her greatness lay in her eloquent expressions of human hopes, fears, joys, and sorrows and in the profound religious quality of her verses, which brought comfort and inspiration to her readers. As a religious poet she was "more devout than George Herbert, more fervid than Charles Wesley."

The fifth edition of her Poems, which was a reprint of the fourth edition of 1856, was also issued in 1862 and received even more critical attention than the Last Poems. Except for the unfavorable notice in the Saturday Review," the other influential journals were extravagant in their praise. The Christian Examiner l wrote that Mrs. Browning's career was unique in the history of distinguished women, for "the lives of women of genius have been so frequently sullied by sin, as well as darkened by sorrow, that it has been accepted almost as an axiom, that their intellectual gifts are a curse rather than a blessing." Mrs. Browning, however, had been "pure and lovely" in her private life and "noble and dignified" in her authorship.

The writer thought that "In Memoriam" and "Aurora Leigh" were the two greatest poems of the age, just as "A Blot in the 'Scutcheon" was its greatest drama. Furthermore, he believed that Tennyson was the most finished artist of the trio, that Browning had the greatest dramatic power, and that Elizabeth excelled in nobility and in strength of thought. It seemed to him that there were no finer love poems in English than the "Sonnets from the Portuguese.""Such purity, sweet humility, lofty self-abnegation, and impassioned tenderness have never before found utterance in verse," he continued. "Shakespeare's son nets, beautiful as they are, cannot be compared with them, and Petrarch's seem commonplace beside them."

Similar expressions appear in almost all the notices. The North American Review called her "the queen of song" and said that although she was not another Shakespeare, "she came nearest to being Shakespeare's counterpart." The North British Review believed that if a "poetess" like Sappho could see the wealth of poetry produced by Mrs. Browning, she "would shrink from her own fame."

It seemed to the reviewer that "in passionate tenderness, capaciousness of imagination, freshness of feeling, vigour of thought, wealth of ideas, and loftiness of soul," her poetry stood alone among all that had been written by women. The Eclectic Review was also convinced that she was "universally now crowned chief woman-poet of any age or time" and that among the greatest writers of world literature including Homer, Shakespeare, and Milton, "with the exception of Dante, not one had, as she had, entered into the scenery, the mystery, the majesty, the sorrow and glory of the higher life." Blackwood's was certain that her place among the immortals was secure and that however much she might be criticized in the future for her faults of style, "the final result will still leave her immovable on her high pedestal."

According to the writer, she was almost unique in that she had both exquisite sensibility and unusual intellectual activity, with each intensifying and aiding the other. In general, the reviews of the fifth edition of the Poems preferred the "Sonnets from the Portuguese" and such poems as "The Cry of the Children" and "Cowper's Grave" and considered that her political poems were a misdirected effort and that Aurora Leigh contained a mixture of both her best and her worst qualities.

In 1863 Browning issued under the imprint of Chapman and Hall The Greek Christian Poets and the English Poets, the text of which was based on his wife's essays as they had appeared originally in the Athenaeum in 1842. He said in the preface that his reason for publishing the book was that his wife had always had it in mind eventually to make additions and corrections to the essays, which had been all but forgotten by the public, and to bring them together in a new volume. The enthusiastic response from almost all professional critics must have gratified Browning. The Athenaeum asserted that the work was "one of remarkable and abiding interest" and that Mrs. Browning's prose was "from first to last always the richer for her poetry."

A new periodical in London entitled the Reader thought that the book contained "a wonderful amount of sound criticism and valuable thought." Among the American reviews the Knickerbocker Monthly welcomed the volume for the "elasticity and exuberance" of its prose and for the "exquisite" translations. The review in the Christian Examiner was probably by Kate Field, who called Mrs. Browning a true scholar (for she had seen the poet's Hebrew Bible with her marginal notes in Greek), a consummate artist, and a perfect woman.

IT was not until 1877 that the public had an opportunity to see some of Mrs. Browning's correspondence. Her letters to R. H. Horne, who had received permission to publish from Browning, were edited by S. R. Townshend Mayer and issued in London in two volumes by Richard Bentley and Son. The correspondence, which was most active between 1840 and 1846, dealt largely with such literary projects as The Poems of Geoffrey Chaucer, Modernized, A New Spirit of the Age, and the projected drama "Psyche Apocalypt."

In the memoir which served as an introduction to the New York edition of the letters, the American critic and poet Richard Henry Stoddard told of Mrs. Browning's life and writings. He said that although sixteen years had passed since her death, no biography had yet been written, that less was known of her than of any other English woman of genius, and that the sum of the present knowledge about her consisted of the dates of the publications of her writings and a few facts about her life found in the published reminiscences of travelers and in the recently issued correspondence of Miss Mitford.

The letters to Horne were well received both in England and in the United States. The critical notices were in agreement that the tone of her correspondence was natural and spontaneous and that it had more gayety than a reader of her poetry would have expected. The New York Nation, for example, said that the letters were charming and that they offered "a peculiarly pleasing mixture of the ladylike and the highly-intelligent." The impression they left upon the reviewer was "somewhat akin to that of an agreeable woman's voice—soft, substantial, and expressive."

The Literary World of Boston referred to her as "true woman and true poet" and believed that many people had "not yet unlearned their reverence for her womanhood nor their love for her pure and noble verse." It was apparently the fresh interest in Mrs. Browning's life and works which stimulated the writing of an article in Lippincott's Magazine in 1878.

The author coupled Mrs. Browning with Shakespeare, both of whom had "a lavish spontaneity, a swift, uncontrollable impulse of emotional force, a daring freedom of utterance." He added that the greater were her faults of style, "the more her transcendent genius shines in them and through them and over them." Late Victorian criticism of Mrs.

Browning placed great emphasis upon the ethical and religious values of her poetry.

It was especially in America that writers dwelt on this aspect of her work. For example, an article published in 1887 in the Andover Review, which was edited by the professors of the Andover Theological Seminary in Massachusetts, said that such "pure and sympathetic" poems of her early career as "Isobel's Child," "Bertha in the Lane," or "Lady Geraldine's Courtship" could not fail to stir the depths of the reader's conscience or to arouse his spiritual energies.

The writer was convinced that her triumph both in her writings and in her life was "of a distinctively Christian order." In the following grandiloquent passage he was apparently referring to her humanitarian poems: "She descended from the Mount of Transfiguration, where the glory of the Christ had been revealed; but, unlike the useless disciples, she brought with her the mountain splendor and the mountain power to confront and drive away the sin and suffering in the plains of humanity."

A few years later Theodore W. Hunt published in the Presbyterian and Reformed Review of Philadelphia an article with a similar theme. Hunt, who was a professor of English literature at Princeton University and an ordained Presbyterian cleryman, believed that through her teaching, English womanhood had become "a more sacred thing than ever." In his opinion everything she wrote "was suffused and surcharged with the very essence of piety; clean and chaste and white as the snow of heaven."

He felt that although Mrs. Browning's verse was not widely popular, it was best appreciated by the few readers in every country who look for "character" in literature, and he added, "So intensely transforming is this illuminating presence, that at times it assumes a kind of beatific charm and makes it impossible for any mind within the area of its influence to think of anything but God and goodness and truth and virtue."

It was not only in America that critics wrote thus. In 1896, the year of Hunt's publication, an article entitled "The Ethical

Impulse of Mrs. Browning's Poetry" appeared in the Westminster Review. The writer had nothing but praise for her work because it had a deeper spiritual content than any other poetry of the century. In his vague expression, her verses were "largely charged with the sensitive vibration of the spiritual transports of our inmost consciousness."

A notice of her Poetical Works in the Boston Literary World in 1885 was somewhat more realistic in its estimate of her reputation, which the reviewer believed had lessened since her death. He suggested that the reason for this apathy was that the present age had little interest in poetry, and he complained that the spirit of the times was scientific, materialistic, and utilitarian.

It seemed to him that no one in America wrote or discussed poetry except a small literary class and that the general reading public was devoted to mechanical contrivances and to superficial amusements. He thought, however, that Mrs. Browning was a true poet, that her faults were trivial, since she often gained in spontaneity whatever she might have lost in carelessness of expression. In his opinion, the "Sonnets from the Portuguese" were both the finest sonnets and the greatest love poems in English literature. It was his prediction that one hundred years hence her fame would be much greater.

After the appearance of the letters to Horne in 1877, the next important date when the literary world focused its attention upon Mrs. Browning's life and work was 1888, the year in which John H. Ingram issued the first full-length biography of her for his "Eminent Women Series." Ingram had applied to Browning for permission to draw upon some of her unpublished correspondence, but Browning, who was out of sympathy with the project, did not grant the request.

Therefore Ingram had no new material to pre sent and had to fall back on published reminiscences which had long been familiar. Furthermore he was inaccurate in several of his statements. For example, he asserted that his researches had proved without doubt that Mrs. Browning was born in London in 1809, and he rejected as impossible Browning's recent statement that the date was 1806. The book had an unhappy reception from almost all critics, who deplored the dispute and felt that if the poet had not wished a full-dress biography of his wife to appear during his lifetime, his feelings should have been respected. In addition to its dearth of new biographical information, the volume was also censured for its long quotations of hackneyed poems and for its stale and meaningless criticism.

On the other hand, most of the notices of the biography spoke respectfully of Mrs. Browning's verse. The London Quarterly Review believed that her poems furnished "the most astonishing and beautiful contrast to the heart-chilling and melancholy pessimism" which was becoming fashionable. In protest against the agnostic spirit of the age, the reviewer asked God to have mercy "on these erring poet-souls" but gave thanks for the work of Elizabeth Browning.

Arthur Christopher Benson in his review of Ingram's book entered a minority report with his acknowledgment that he could no longer read with pleasure much of Mrs. Browning's verse. Yet he liked her romantic ballads and thought she would be remembered for these, for her simpler lyrics, and most of all for the "Sonnets from the Portuguese."

As long as Browning was alive there was no possibility of the publication either of an adequate biography of his wife or of a comprehensive selection of her correspondence. Eight years after the poet's death in 1889, Frederic G. Kenyon helped to supply one of these two needs by editing a large collection of Mrs.

Browning's letters. The publication of the two volumes by Smith, Elder, and Company in October 1897 was one of the most important literary events of the season. The letters were mostly addressed to her life-long friends Mrs. Martin, Miss Mitford, Boyd, Mrs. Jameson, Kenyon, Sarianna Browning, Isa Blagden, and Fanny Haworth. A comparison of Kenyon's text with the holographs, most of which are in the Wellesley College Library, shows that he omitted remarks about her pregnancies, her use of morphine, other medical details about herself and her friends, family gossip, and uncomplimentary or equivocal references to persons who were still alive in 1897.

Her correspondence is unusually repetitious because she often wrote almost identical letters to four or five different persons. By skillful selection Kenyon eliminated much of this overlapping material. His most serious omissions were the hundreds of letters both to Boyd and to Miss Mitford before Mrs. Browning's marriage and the many intimate letters to Henrietta and to Arabel, but all these portions of the correspondence were not yet available.

The reviews were almost unanimous in their feeling that Kenyon had edited the letters with good taste, and they approved of his supplementing the correspondence with biographical information. Many critics wondered how a person whose health was so fragile could have had the strength to produce such a mass of letters, little realizing that the two volumes contained only a small proportion of her total correspondence. In general, the writers of the notices in the newspapers and journals were especially interested in the first 300 pages which came from the pen of Miss Barrett, since the story of her married life had been somewhat familiar after the publication of Mrs. Orr's biography in 1891.

Several of the reviews regretted the iteration of her faith in spiritualism and in Napoleon III, and they were surprised that she made so few references to serious intellectual pursuits after her marriage. The consensus of the reviews was that her poetical reputation was lower than it had been and that in another generation much of her writing would be forgotten, or else, in the words of the Spectator, "her best work will have shaken itself free of the dross and superfluity, and stand or fall with the language."

All of the notices spoke well of Mrs. Browning's prose style, which they thought sincere, natural, human, and often lightened with humour. There was nothing in Kenyon's volumes which detracted from her reputation; her letters indeed added to her stature, so that to almost everyone she appeared to have the "most wonderful spirit," the "greatest soul," the "most truly passionate nature"—these and many similar expressions appear in the reviews—of anyone who wrote English verse in the nineteenth century.

The poet was being replaced by the personality, the woman, the wife, the friend. The New York Nation, which was typical of the other journals and newspapers in its approval of the letters, wrote, "We are enabled as never before to conceive of her character in its entirety; and there is nothing in the conception which does not enhance our sympathy with her aspirations as a poet and our admiration for her conduct of her life in every personal way."

The most respected newspaper in Boston, the Transcript, which was enthralled by this "pair of wonderful volumes," declared in the flowery language of the age that in the letters "there is a true life poem, an expression of a personality sound and sweet and wholesome, rounded and healthful, out-giving in loving kindness and in all the graces of beneficence, of unpretentious economy and of hospitality, with a firm unwavering hold of all the simplest, sweetest sources of happiness in life."

If similar passages from other reviews were cited, they would be in agreement that the letters showed Mrs. Browning to have been a woman with ardent impulses, wide and generous sympathies, independence of judgment, a rare faculty for seeing the best in people and institutions, a loving disposition, and a hatred of any kind of tyranny and injustice.

Early in 1899 and somewhat more than a year after the appearance of the Kenyon volumes, the love letters written by Elizabeth Barrett and Robert Browning were published at a time when there was a great public interest in the two poets. Pen Browning explained in a prefatory note that ever since his mother's death the letters had been kept by his father in an inlaid box, with each in its consecutive order and numbered by him.

The poet destroyed the rest of his correspondence and not long before his death handed the love letters to Pen, saying, "There they are, do with them as you please when I am dead and gone!" Many of the reviews expressed astonishment that the son would have published the letters, particularly in view of the pain his mother experienced whenever she felt that anyone had infringed upon her privacy. Although they questioned the propriety of Pen's decision, they agreed that his choice was lucrative for him and agreeable for the readers of the two volumes.

The Athenaeum, for example, said, "We should like to think that Browning never conceived the possibility of his son's publishing them; but, even if he had such an unexpressed idea, more honour would have been done to a great poet's memory by destroying them than by allowing it for a moment to be thought that he sanctioned their publication." Leslie Stephen felt that in reading the letters, which had been printed without omissions or alterations, he was overhearing confidences which neither of the correspondents had ever intended should one day be broadcast to the common ear.

It seemed to him, as it did to several other critics, that it might have been wiser to present a selection than the complete text. Everyone was agreed that there was nothing in the closely packed 1,100 pages which did not redound to the credit of both correspondents. To cite from a typical review, the Boston Literary World asserted, "Such a high-minded, delicate, unselfish pair of lovers as Robert Browning and Elizabeth Barrett it would be hard to parallel in fact or fiction."

The critics were charmed by the correspondence and thought that it was one of the most precious contributions to nineteenth-century literary history. As the Spectator expressed it, "We venture to think that no such remarkable and unbroken series of intimate letters between two remarkable people has ever been given to the world." On the whole the reviews were more interested in Elizabeth's than in Robert's letters.

It was through her eyes that the readers of the volumes saw for the first time the extent of Mr. Barrett's tyranny and the shock she received from the Pisa business in the fall of 1845. With two or three exceptions everyone believed that her letters justified the private marriage and the removal to Italy. The critics also maintained that Elizabeth, with her courage, her absence of pretension and self-pity, and her breadth of outlook was indeed worthy of the noble passion she had inspired. In the words of the Edinburgh Review, the woman seen in these letters was "a poet in every fibre of her, but adorably feminine, weak with more than a woman's weakness and strong with more than a woman's strength."

In comparing her prose style with Browning's, many of the journals commented upon the ease with which she expressed herself, in contrast to her fiancé's stiff, awkward manner and his long, contorted sentences in which he often failed to make his meaning clear. Furthermore, a number of critics observed that she had more humour in her letters than he.

As the Edinburgh Review wrote, "she could be relied upon never to see the droll side of a thing at the wrong moment, either for herself or for another." It may have been the publication of part of Mrs. Browning's correspondence and of the love letters which awakened a fresh interest in her poetry. In commenting on the various editions of her Poetical Works which were issued during the later Victorian years, critical journals repeatedly placed her far above Emily Brontë and Christina Rossetti and declared that she stood alone in the expression of the womanhood in her. Her poetry, they said, appealed chiefly to women because of her understanding of the depth, tenderness, and humility of the love which is given by women.

Her works were also being read and discussed in French periodicals, and it was a French woman, curiously enough, who produced the first full-length biography based on the recently published letters. Germaine-Marie Merlette issued in 1905 La Vie et l'Œuvre d'Elizabeth Barrett Browning, which was her thesis for the doctorate at the University of Paris. Although Mlle. Merlette did not have access to Mrs. Browning's manuscripts and presented no biographical information which had not appeared in print, she succeeded in compiling a sound, well-balanced study which was well received in England and long remained the standard work in its field.

The Year 1906 was marked by many publications in

observance of the centenary of Mrs. Browning's birth. The March issue of Book News, which was published in Philadelphia, was devoted to a series of articles on her life and writings. In one of these essays Thomas Wentworth Higginson recalled the day more than sixty years ago when a cousin brought him a manuscript copy of "The Lay of the Brown Rosary," which had not yet been published in America.

Along with many of his young friends in Boston, he had soon learned it by heart, and a few months later they also memorized "Lady Geraldine's Courtship," a copy of which they saw before its publication. Afterward he had shown great interest in her career and now and then heard James and Maria Lowell in Cambridge read from the letters they had received from her in Italy. In this commemorative issue of BookNews News another American critic Henry S. Pancoast wrote on her present reputation.

He maintained that although her vogue had passed, her place among the great English poets was secure because she "gave something to English poetry that with all its riches it had never before possessed. It is the woman that speaks in her descriptions of babies; in her love of children, in her heartbreak over pain." The editors of the New York Bookman announced that they were not planning to issue a special number to commemorate the anniversary. They added, however, that if they had done so, they would certainly have made "more of a to-do over Mrs. Browning than over her husband, for she was undoubtedly in pure poetry a greater genius than he."

That Browning had the greater intellect was in their opinion indisputable, but they thought that "for sheer beauty of diction and for perfect music" her best work was finer than anything he achieved. Few critics at this period were so generous in their judgments of her poetry. Percy Lubbock, who published in 1906 a volume of Mrs. Browning's selected letters interspersed with his own comments on her life and writings, expressed the prevailing opinion that much of her work which had been enthusiastically received two generations earlier was unfamiliar to many readers.

Now that poets were paying more attention to form, he believed that her careless craftsmanship could not be condoned. Yet he was convinced that she had possessed a great soul and was one of the most fiery geniuses of the nineteenth century and that however much her poetic reputation had declined, her point of view had become all the more interesting since the publication of her letters.

It was not many years after the centenary of his mother's birth that Pen Browning died at his home in Asolo, Italy, after an uneventful and fruitless life. Since he had no children, the books, manuscripts, art objects, furnishings, and other relics which he had inherited from his parents were bequeathed to a number of relatives, who had the collections sold at auction in May 1913.

The decision of the Moulton Barrett cousins to dispose thus of the property may have been justified economically, but Browning scholarship would have been better served if the materials had been kept together and made available for future students. After the Sotheby sale the holographs of Mrs. Browning's poems and letters went into the hands of dealers and collectors on both sides of the Atlantic and remained in hiding for more than a generation until they found their way into permanent collections. Thus no one during this long period attempted any serious study of her life or writings.

Many critics and poets during the late Victorian and the Edwardian eras had been discussing her poetry, but they did so only on the basis of her published letters and poems. In America E. C. Stedman, Richard Watson Gilder, Lewis Edwards Gates, and William James Dawson were drawn to her, and among British critics Edmund Gosse, Theodore Watts-Dunton, Edward Dowden, George Saintsbury, Henry Jones, and many others dealt sympathetically with her poetry. While all of these writers admitted her shortcomings, they were in agreement that in a few poems she rose to the highest levels and was unsurpassed by any other woman poet.

Furthermore they all realized that no one had taken her place since her death. Although her poetry was read and discussed during the first World War and the following decade, it was not until the late 1920's that the story of the Brownings seemed once again to captivate the public, even more so than it had a generation earlier at the time of the publication of the love letters.

In response to this great interest at least eight volumes were issued between 1928 and 1931 on Elizabeth or on the Brownings as a couple, with most of the books dwelling on the romance. One of the most important contributions to Browning studies during this period was the volume of Elizabeth's letters to her sister Henrietta, edited by Leonard Huxley and published by John Murray in 1929.

Huxley left out about one third of the text: medical details, repetitious comments on Pen, discussions of family matters, and remarks about obscure friends, all of which he thought would be of little general interest. In the passages he published, however, some of the names of the men and women to whom Mrs. Browning refers are indicated by blanks, even though in 1929 the persons whose names were thus erased had long been dead and, furthermore, had not been treated with disrespect in the letters.

The correspondence, which was written between 1846 and 1859, presented a new aspect of Mrs. Browning's life; as more than one reviewer noticed, the most important figure to emerge from the letters was Pen, with his burnished curls and velvet frocks.

As for the mother herself, the critical notices agreed that she seemed more attractive in her personality and richer in human sympathies than they had supposed her to be. In the opinion of the London Mercury, she portrayed herself as a woman who was "eager, warm-hearted, emotional, a little inclined to gush, full of the typical prejudices of her time, yet very human and likeable after all."

Likewise Bonamy Dobrée wrote in the National Review that in spite of the bric-a-brac of her surroundings, she was still an appealing figure not only because of the poetic quality in her but also because of the emotional richness of her life. Although the letters to Henrietta explained the mother, the wife, and the sister rather than the poet, several reviews, after describing the new material, considered her present position among English women poets.

In their judgment she was in her artistic achievement below Christina Rossetti, though they felt that without doubt Mrs. Browning's letters were by far the more interesting. But even more than the correspondence to Henrietta and the romantic biographies, it was Rudolf Besier play The Barretts of Wimpole Street which made the story familiar to hundreds of thousands in London and New York.

After the appearance of the Hollywood screen version of the play, the romance of the Brownings was known to millions, many of whom had never before even heard of the two poets. Although Besier took many of his lines from the published letters, he manipulated his material freely for dramatic purposes. The scene is Elizabeth's room, and the action is concentrated in the few months before her wedding, to which the Barretts refer at the end of the play after the heroine has fled to France. With the exception of Elizabeth and Henrietta, the family is dominated by the tyrannical and almost insane father, who is tormented by sexual repressions and has an affection for Elizabeth which she herself perceives is incestuous in its impulses.

At first Elizabeth appears to be sick, apathetic, and resigned to her prison, but in the course of the action she is drawn to Browning because of his high spirits, his courage, and his faith. The play is true to the spirit of the romance since it presents the noble qualities of both Browning and Elizabeth. There is, however, no historical basis for the final scene in which Mr. Barrett expresses his rage and frustration after he has heard of Elizabeth's marriage. In point of fact, no one knows precisely what he did or said on that occasion. Nor is there any evidence that Elizabeth's father had the abnormal desires with which Besier endowed the character. (Three of Mrs. Browning's nephews vigorously protested in a letter to The Times the "disgusting" charge which had been brought against their grandfather, whose memory, they asserted, had been sullied by this "gross violation of the canons of literary decency.")

Besier's play, which was first produced at the Malvern Festival in England in the summer of 1930 and enjoyed a long run in London during the following season, apparently stimulated Virginia Woolf to write about Mrs. Browning's poetry and life.

In an article which appeared simultaneously in the Yale Review and The Times Literary Supplement, Mrs. Woolf introduced her discussion of Aurora Leigh by suggesting that as a result of an irony which might have amused the Brownings themselves they were now better known in the flesh than they had ever been in the spirit: "Like so many other Victorian worthies they have been transformed in the past few years into figures of romance, passionate lovers with curls and side whiskers, peg-top trousers and sweeping skirts.

In this guise thousands of people must know and love the Brownings who have never read a line of their poetry." However much Aurora Leigh had been applauded during the decade or two after its publication, Mrs. Woolf believed that no one looked at it any more. Yet in spite of its many absurdities the poem held her enthralled with its speed, energy, and selfconfidence.

It seemed to Mrs. Woolf that Aurora Leigh gave the reader a feeling of life, that the characters were struggling bravely with the great problems of the Victorian age. She thought the poem still inspired respect and deserved a better fate than the oblivion into which it had fallen.

Two years later, in 1933, Mrs. Woolf added her contribution to the many popular treatments of the lives of the Brownings with her charming and original study entitled Flush, a Biography. In her essay on Aurora Leigh Mrs. Woolf wrote with humorous exaggeration that no one now read Mrs. Browning's poetry, which was considered by all primers of literature to be second-rate and hopelessly old-fashioned. To be sure, few cultivated people on either side of the Atlantic probably had a first-hand acquaintance with her novel in verse, her angel poems, or her romantic ballads.

The "Sonnets from the Portuguese," however, have not been forgotten. After Mrs. Browning's death late Victorian critics ranked them with Shakespeare's sonnets and without hesitation asserted that they were of their type among the greatest poems in the language.

E. C. Stedman thought it "no sacrilege to say that their music is showered from a higher and purer atmosphere than that of the Swan of Avon." Likewise Edmund Gosse believed that although Shakespeare's sonnets had a more admirable style, "those addressed by Elizabeth Barrett to her lover are hardly less exquisite to any of us, and to many of us are more wholesome and more intelligible." James Ashcroft Noble was "thrilled and melted" by the "Sonnets," and it seemed to him that it could "hardly be presumptuous to predict that for generations to come the Sonnets from the Portuguese will remain, what they undoubtedly now are, the noblest anthology for noble lovers which our language has to show." Quotations from almost all the other late-Victorian critics would show opinions no less enthusiastic.

Serious literary historians are now less impressed by the "Sonnets"—which nevertheless have continued to fascinate a portion of the general reading public. In 1886 Ticknor and Company issued in Boston the first separate edition of the "Sonnets," in the form of a large, heavy folio with elaborate border designs. Since that date scarcely a year has passed in which an edition has not been published in some country. The catalogue of the Harvard College Library records forty different editions (including translations), which have appeared in America, England, France, Germany, Italy, and Spain; and both the Library of Congress and the British Museum have copies of editions which are not in the Harvard collection.

Although many readers may have purchased the "Sonnets" with a firm belief in their high literary qualities, the arrangements of publication of the various separate editions are evidence of an attitude which has some of the characteristics of a cult. Most of the editions have been produced in a limited number of copies and by private, noncommercial presses rather than by large publishing houses. In some editions each copy is numbered and signed by the illustrator and was originally offered for sale in an attractive-appearing publisher's box.

Various editions were bound in white pigskin, calf, morocco, and gaycolored cloth. Some were printed on English handmade paper; others on Japanese vellum. Many have rubricated initials, decorated borders, and different kinds of ornamental designs.

One edition is a series of photographs of the poems, with each elaborately illuminated in the manner of a medieval manuscript. In one of the most striking editions, each poem was sketched on a separate plate, with different drawings above the poems. One hundred years after the first publication of the "Sonnets," the firm of Philip C. Duschnes of New York issued in 1950 the "Centennial Variorum Edition" in a printing limited to five hundred copies. The volume, which was daintily bound in flowered cloth, served a useful purpose by giving variant readings from the three original manuscripts, but it unfortunately failed to indicate the differences among the published texts of 1850, 1853, and 1856.

New editions have been published since 1950, and it seems likely that the "Sonnets" will be available at bookshops for many years to come because of their appeal to readers with romantic tastes. One of the most interesting of the recent editions is the Spanish verse translation by an Argentine poet which was published as a modestlooking paperbound pamphlet in Madrid in 1954.

It is scarcely surprising that the editors of a number of handsome, limited editions were more than generous in their estimates of the poems. For example, William Andrews Clark, Jr., in the introduction to his volume which he issued in San Francisco in 1927, for private distribution only, wrote that the "Sonnets" had secured Mrs. Browning's fame for all time and entitled her "to a high seat on Mount Parnassus beside Shelley, Keats, Byron, Browning, and other great gods of poesy." On the sound foundation of these sonnets "rests her renown as a poet—a foundation as eternal as the hills of Rome."

In addition to the "Sonnets," the story of her life, especially the romance is still of interest to the public. Within the last few years a full-length biography of her and two separate volumes on the Brownings have been published. As a literary craftsman she is now ranked by many critics below Emily Brontë and Christina Rossetti, both of whom in their day received much less acclaim. Yet most of Mrs. Browning's verse, in spite of its fire and energy, gives only a feeble representation of the exalted ideas which she was struggling to express. Except for a handful of her short poems, her ability to create failed to keep pace with her abundant thoughts and turbulent feelings.

And so it is not altogether as a poet (although she did have many poetical qualities) that she is attractive, but as one of the greatest personalities of an age which included among other English women of unusual abilities Charlotte and Emily Brontë, George Eliot, Mrs. Gaskell, Christina Rossetti, and Florence Nightingale.

With all of Mrs. Browning's foibles, her erratic poetical taste, her naïve acceptance of ready-made formulas to solve political problems, and her violent enthusiasms and antipathies, it is probable that she will be remembered as long as any woman of her time. It is the quality of her life even more than her artistic achievements which will live. Countless men and women will continue to find inspiration in the romance and the flight to Italy—where she found fulfillment as wife and mother —in her devotion to scholarship and letters, in her courageous and impassioned protests against injustice to individuals and subject peoples, and in her broad, generous, idealistic, Christian point of view.

Chapter 5

The Seraphim, And Other Poems

The reviewer in Blackwood's Edinburgh Magazine who asked, "What other pretty book is this?" discovered it to be The Seraphim, and Other Poems (1838) by Elizabeth Barrett Barrett. Barrett was thirty-two; she had already written an autobiography, Glimpses Into My Own Life and Literary Character (1820), and published three volumes of poetry, The Battle of Marathon (1820), An Essay on Mind, With Other Poems (1826), and Poems, 1833.

The Seraphim, however, was her first work both to receive a wide readership and extensive critical response, and also to represent "with all its feebleness and shortcomings and obscurities... the first utterance" of her "own individuality" (L, I:188). But the expression of that "individuality" was achieved through years of reading and imitating the male masters and of recognizing the relationship of gender to her determination to be a poet.

Her autobiography is a precocious, ebulliently self-confident document, in which the adolescent Barrett recorded her self-conscious training to be a poet. At age seven she "began to think of 'forming [her] taste'... to see what was best to write about and read about" (A, 8-9). As a consequence:

I read the History of England and Rome; at eight I perused the History of Greece and... first found real delight in po etry. "The Minstrel," Pope's "Illiad" [sic], some parts of the "Odyssey," passages from "Paradise Lost" selected by my dearest Mama and some of Shakespeare's plays among which were, "The Tempest," "Othello" and a few historical dramatic pieces....

At nine... Pope's "Illiad" [sic] some passages from Shakespeare and Novels which I enjoyed to their full extent.... At ten my poetry was entirely formed by the style of written authors and I read that I might write. Novels were still my most delightful study, combined with the sweet notes of poetic inspiration! At eleven I wished to be considered an authoress. Novels were thrown aside. Poetry and Essays were my studies and I felt the most ardent desire to understand the learned languages. To comprehend even the Greek alphabet was delight inexpressible. Under the tuition of Mr. McSwiney I attained that which I so fervently desired....

[At twelve] I read Milton for the first time thro' together with Shakespeare and Pope's Homer....

I perused all modern authors who have any claim to superior merit and poetic excellence. I was familiar with Shakespeare, Milton, Homer and Virgil, Locke, Hooker, Pope. I read Homer in the original with delight inexpressible, together with Virgil. [A, 9-15]

This astonishing record indicates that, even as a young girl, Barrett appreciated both the tradition she hoped to appropriate and also the crucial importance of the classics in the education of an English poet. That formal education she was denied by virtue of gender she sought to gain for herself. As an adolescent, she received permission to study with her brother's tutor, Mr. McSwiney. Then, as a young woman, she acted as an amanuensis to Hugh Boyd, a blind, rather pedantic, and second-rate Greek scholar, who lived near the Barrett house at Hope End, Malvem, and had written to the young poet in 1826 after the publication of An Essay on Mind. This educational history was not the equivalent of Eton and Oxbridge, but it demonstrates Barrett's understanding of the apprenticeship necessary for a poet.

Years later she reevaluated the time spent pondering the minutiae of Greek grammar and working on a study of the Greek. Christian poets with Boyd, recognizing it as wasted labour. In I845 she wrote to a Miss Thompson, who had requested some translations from the Greek for an anthology: "Perhaps I do not... partake quite your 'divine fury' for converting our sex into Greek scholarship.... You... know that the Greek language... swallows up year after year of studious life. Now I have a 'doxy',... that there is no exercise of the mind so little profitable to the mind as the study of languages. It is the nearest thing to a passive recipiency—is it not?—as a mental action, though it leaves one weary as ennui itself. Women want to be made to think actively" (L, I:260-61).

Barrett never analyzed why Greek scholarship induces a "passive recipiency" in woman, precluding her need to "think actively." It is tempting to infer her conviction that study of the classics forces woman to read herself always as the object of male narrative, while to "think actively" necessitates claiming herself as subject of experience and discourse. However valid this mature evaluation of classical study for women may be, Barrett was wise to immerse herself in such study as a young poet. It gave her the credentials to be taken seriously by the critics and enabled her as a poet to engage in the epic terms she would finally realise in Aurora Leigh, not merely in the lyrical verse of the affections associated with the popular "poetesses."

The young Barrett, to use de Beauvoir's terms, "play[ed] at being a man" by linguistically "dress[ing] up in men's clothes" (MRM, 2:7). At fourteen, in her Preface to The Battle of Marathon, she declared Homer as the model for her epic poem based on the Greek defence against Persian invaders on the plains of Marathon in 490 B. C.: "It would have been both absurd and presumptuous, young and inexperienced as I am, to have attempted to strike out a path for myself" (W, I:9). Yet even in this work, Barrett demonstrated strategies for appropriating the "path" that this literary father had walked. She assumed a male identity: "He who writes an epic poem must transport himself to the scene of action; he must imagine himself possessed of the same opinions, manners, prejudices, and belief; he must suppose himself to be the hero he delineates" (W, I:7-8). Yet earlier she had revealed the poem's true hero: "Who can be indifferent, who can preserve his tranquillity, when he hears of one little city rising undaunted, and daring her innumerable enemies, in defence of her freedom?" (W, I:6).

The epic poet she designated, according to convention, as "he," and yet the "little city rising" she designated, again according to convention, as female. Naming her poetic self as male while creating the epic hero with whom "he" must identify not as a brave male but as a courageous female both located Barrett within a tradition and also subverted it by elevating a rebellious woman who is acting "in defence of her freedom" as subject of the story to be told. Barrett studied Homer not only in the original but also in Pope's translation. This informed her imitation of Pope in An Essay on Mind (1826), a poem remarkable only for demonstrating Barrett's erudition in philosophy. Barrett then returned to classical sources, and in 1833 she published her first translation of Aeschylus's Prometheus Bound, a Romantic endeavor that assumes an added dimension for a woman whose disobedient act of writing resonated to Prometheus's theft of fire from the gods.

In her Preface to the translation, reworked and published with her Poems of 1850, she described a kinship with Aeschylus as one of the "ancient Greeks [who]... felt passionately, and thought daringly" (W, 6:83). Barrett did not attempt a Shelleyan revision of the Prometheus myth, but her translation exhibited her classical credentials and also linked her with a writer who represented her own ambitions as woman and poet to feel passionately and be daring in thought. She recognized that "sometimes [Aeschylus's] fancy rushes in, where his judgment fears to tread" (W, 6:84), as she would later determine that the poem which eventually became Aurora Leigh would "rush into drawing-rooms & the like 'where angels fear to tread'" I:31). Certainly Barrett's intentions from an early age were infused with entrepreneurial energy. Whereas Tennyson's early poems had languid heroines, Barrett boldly walked where women had for too long feared to tread; her early publications demonstrate how centrally she wished to locate herself in English poetic tradition.

She conformed to the apprenticeship of imitating the fathers, yet she was also aware very early that her gender necessitated comment:

My mind is naturally independant [sic] and spurns that subserviency of opinion which is generally considered necessary to feminine softness. But this is a subject on which I must always feel strongly, for I feel within me an almost proud consciousness of independance [sic] which prompts me to defend my opinions and to yield them only to conviction!!!!!!!

My friends may differ from me: the world may accuse me but this I am determined never to retract!!

Better, oh how much better, to be the ridicule of mankind, the scoff of society, than lose that self respect which tho' this heart were bursting would elevate me above misery— above wretchedness and above abasement!!! These principles are irrevocable! It is not—I feel it is not vanity that dictates them! it is not—I know it is not an encroachment on Masculine prerogative but it is a proud sentiment which will never, never allow me to be humbled in my own eyes!!! [A, 24]

Aware that "subserviency of opinion" is conventionally demanded of women, she determined to nurture her right to an independent mind. The style, with all its exclamation points and exaggerated language, is adolescent in expression, yet it reveals Barrett's understanding that the independent thinking demanded of a poet would render women the "ridicule of mankind, the scoff of society." Although many poets have suffered such scorn, the young Barrett was aware that she would be ridiculed, not as men are for the content of their thought, but as women are, for the act of thinking at all.

She evidences how hard it was to sustain her commitment to the intellectual life in her surviving diary. When Boyd wrote to her after reading An Essay on Mind, inviting her to visit him and his family in nearby Malvern, Barrett's father forbade the visit: "as a female, and a young female" such a visit would be overstepping the established observances of society. Even when the friendship was finally established and Barrett visited Boyd as often as possible to work at Greek, her aunt "Bummy" (who cared for the family of ten after their mother's death in

1828) and her sister Henrietta frowned on this transgression of woman's social norm:

This evening, Henrietta proposed inviting Mrs. Griffith to drink tea here tomorrow, —upon which, Bummy insisted on my returning from Malvern sooner than I shd otherwise do!! I was annoyed & said so—& even refused going at all, in the case of my being obliged to come back, by anything else than darkness. Henrietta need not have asked Mrs. G tomorrow, —nor, if she had asked her, need I have been forced to receive her company. But the point was yielded at last—of course by me!

Her family was distressed at the "impropriety" of her feeling "more friendship for Mr. Boyd than for the Martins!... They have, as most people have, clearer ideas of the aristocracy of rank & wealth, than of the aristocracy of mind". How different must intellectual life have been for Tennyson in the company of the Apostles at Cambridge, or for Robert Browning in the home that his parents provided when he determined to be a poet, where his friendship with Carlyle developed. Her relationship with Boyd was analogous to the one Eliot imagined between Dorothea Brooke and Mr. Casaubon: "My dear friend Mr. Boyd!— If he knew how much it gratifies me to assist him in any way (I wish I cd do so in everyway) all his 'drudgeries' wd devolve upon me".

Although Boyd encouraged Barrett's studies, he also trivialized her:

[Mr. Boyd] asked me to talk to Mr. Spowers at dinner: "on his account, he thought I ought to do it." I promised to do my best; and as I went out of the room, he said that I must remember what I had promised, & that he wd ask Mrs. Boyd if I had been "naughty or good." I in a panic of course.... Down to dinner. I impelled myself to talk, whether I had anything to say or not—to talk about the country, & the newspaper, & the raven, & Joanna Baillie & Lord Byron. So that when I had to answer Mr. Boyd's "naughty or good," I could say "good."

It is hard to imagine Tennyson, Browning, or Arnold accused of valuing intellect more than afternoon tea, of being called "naughty" at twenty-five. Yet these comparisons reveal the very different issues at the heart of creative composition for men and women bound by such cultural conventions. As surely as Dickens's childhood experiences—the blacking factory and his parents' imprisonment for debt—defined the nature of his fiction, so Barrett's experience of growing up female while determining to be a poet defined the form of her poetry. Only when the basic issue for a woman is understood to be "dare she write" (what Gilbert and Gubar refer to as the "anxiety of authorship") as much as "what to write" (the "anxiety of influence") can she be appreciated on her own terms. Whereas in her intellectual life Barrett was studying and imitating the classics, emotionally she recognized the discrepancy between the world expressed in male poetry and that inhabited by middle-class woman.

Many women and men exhorted middle-class woman to her role of wife and mother: the sentiments of Sarah Stickney Ellis (whose Women of England was published in the same year as The Seraphim, and Other Poems) were typical:

Women, considered in their distinct and abstract nature, as isolated beings, must lose more than half their worth. They are, in fact, from their own constitution, and from the station they occupy in the world, strictly speaking, relative creatures. If, therefore, they are endowed with only such faculties as render them striking and distinguished in themselves, without the faculty of instrumentality, they are only as dead letters in the volume of human life, filling what would otherwise be a blank space, but doing nothing more.

Barrett, in a letter to Kenyon about The Seraphim, and Other Poems, insisted that the expression of her own "individuality" represented "maturity" and belonging to the "living". Conversely, Ellis exhorted women to remember that because by nature they are "relative creatures" to their parents, husbands, and children, "individuality" renders them "dead letters." Ellis's rather than Barrett's convictions informed the work of the two most popular nineteenth-century "poetesses," Letitia Landon and Felicia Hemans.

Landon in her Preface to "The Venetian Bracelet" identifies love as her "source of song": "For a woman, whose influence and whose sphere must be in the affections, what subject can be more fitting than one which it is her peculiar province to refine, spiritualize, and exalt? I have always sought to paint it self-denying, devoted, and making an almost religion of its truth." In the "Immolation of a Hindoo Widow" Landon takes such self-denial to its extreme in her depiction of suttee:

The red pile blazes—let the bride ascend,
And lay her head upon her husband's heart,
Now in a perfect unison to blend—
No more to part.

Hemans equally defines woman as a relative creature. Unlike Barrett who admired de Stael's poet heroine, Corinne, Hemans (recalling a scene in the novel in which Corinne receives the poet's laurel) concludes "Corinne at the Capitol" as follows:

Happier, happier far than thou,
With the laurel on thy brow,
She that makes the humblest hearth
Lovely but to one on earth!

For the poetesses, woman's role was usually accompanied by suffering in the wake of betrayal, loss, and rejection. In "Madeline," from Records of Woman, Hemans describes woman's destiny as being to "suffer and be still." Sarah Stickney Ellis endorsed Hemans's attitude, taking those words as the epigraph for Women of England.

In the "Indian Woman's Death-Song" (Records of Woman), however, Hemans has a mother drown herself and her daughter after her husband deserted them:

"And thou, my babe! though bom, like me, for woman's weary lot,
Smile!—to that wasting of the heart, my own! I leave thee not;
Too bright a thing art thou to pine in aching love away—
Thy mother bears thee far, young fawn! from sorrow and decay."

Hemans's recognition that "woman's weary lot" is intolerable represents a rage against the very condition she attempts to support. This rage, rumbling under the sentimental, domestic surface of both her work and Landon's, is portrayed as violence that is inflicted on women by themselves or others, and ultimately expressed as death. The anger, which cannot be turned on the men who make them suffer, destroys the devoted "angels" themselves. If the frequent deaths of women in the poetesses' work are viewed not only as a morbid or sentimental strain but also as an expression of this anger inflicted by robust women writers on their long-suffering heroine victims, then such deaths can be seen as a strategy to exalt suffering woman while desiring to kill her off as an image of womanhood. It was a strategy Barrett inherited.

Although Barrett's record of her early reading focused on male writing, certainly by her late teens she was familiar with the work of the poetesses. The two poems she most liked in The Literary Souvenir; or, Cabinet of Poetry and Romance for 1826 were Landon's "The Forsaken" and Hemans's "The Wreck." She eulogized both poets after their deaths in "Felicia Hemans" (W, 2:83) and "L. E. L.'s Last Question" (W, 3:117), revealing thorough knowledge of their work. Yet, although their verse engaged her and often found echoes in the choice, if not the treatment, of her own subject matter, Barrett recognized the limitations of both Hemans and Landon as poets as she assessed them to her friend, Mary Russell Mitford:

> *If I had those two powers to choose from.. Mrs. Hemans's & Miss Landon's.. I mean the raw bare powers.. I wd choose Miss Landon's. I surmise that it was more elastic, more various, of a stronger web. I fancy it wd have worked out better—had it been worked out—with the right moral & intellectual influences in application. As it is, Mrs. Hemans has left the finer poems. Of that there can be no question. But perhaps.. & indeed I do say it very diffidently.. there is a sense of sameness which goes with the sense of excellence, —while we read her poems—a satiety with the satisfaction together with a feeling "this writer has written her best,"—or "It is very well—but it can never be better."* [MRM, I:235]

Barrett never placed Hemans and Landon in the same class as Homer, Aeschylus, Milton, Pope, or Wordsworth—the class to which she aspired. Nevertheless, they offered her a valuable model of women whose lives had been devoted to writing poetry. Even though they wrote of women analogous to Milton's Eve, they modeled woman actively describing herself rather than being passively described. It is qualitatively different to "suffer and be still" and to suffer and write about it. Yet at best, Hemans, Landon, and their like offered Barrett problematic models: patronized by the critics; committed to the notion that it was better for a woman to "make the humblest hearth" than to "wear the laurel on [her] brow"; and diligent in their portrayal of woman's acceptance of her "weary lot."

Lacking the stature of the revered and envied precursors by which male poets were nurtured, they did not challenge the privileged male voice of English poetry.

Women prose writers pioneered an alternative image of womanhood for the young Barrett: "I read Mary Wolstonecraft when I was thirteen: no twelve!.. and, through the whole course of my childhood, I had a steady indignation against Nature who made me a woman, & a determinate resolution to dress up in men's clothes as soon as ever I was free of the nursery, & go into the world 'to seek my fortune.' 'How,' was not decided; but I rather leant towards being poor Lord Byron's PAGE".

Her "steady indignation against Nature" was Barrett's protest against woman as long-suffering relative creature. Wollstonecraft emphasized learning and education for women, even while stressing the importance of her role as educated wife and mother. However, by the time she wrote The Seraphim, and Other Poems Barrett had read Madame de Stael's Corinne three times. Here for the first time was woman, in her own "clothes," represented as a poet. De Stael juxtaposed the freedom possible in Italy for woman's artistic endeavors and sexual passion with a passive servitude and repression she depicted as required of English women. The Italian landscape and sensibility provided Barrett with a metaphor for artistic freedom (even before she lived there), which she later exploited fully in Aurora Leigh. These literary mothers, while not being precursors held in general esteem, provided models for Barrett's task of creating an image of woman from her felt reality. She was aware that it was in The Seraphim, and Other Poems that such a "reality" began to take shape.

Barrett's awareness that this volume revealed an original po etic voice was shared by reviewers whose responses appeared in many journals, including the Examiner, the Athenaeum, Blackwood's Edinburgh Magazine, the Quarterly Review, the North American Review, and the English Review. They paid unusually serious attention to this unknown woman poet, placing her in a male tradition, yet treating her as a woman poet.

Echoing Barrett's sense of her "own individuality," the Athenaeum found The Seraphim "an extraordinary volume", while the Quarterly Review, in a discussion of nine women poets, was representative in recognizing that Barrett both stood out "as well for her extraordinary acquaintance with ancient classic literature, as for the boldness of her poetic attempts," and failed to achieve a "success... in proportion to her daring".

However, the North American Review, like her mentors, Boyd and Kenyon (but unlike Robert Browning), lamented that as Barrett progressed from her early male imitations into a more original voice, she violated poetic decorum. In The Seraphim, which "contains more of original poetry" than both her former volumes, the reviewer found that "her mind has gone through essential changes, which are not in all respects for the better.... Her great defect is a certain lawless extravagance".

In their discussion of the title poem, "The Seraphim," reviewers saw Barrett as heir to a poetic tradition epitomized in their minds by Milton. Barrett talked of Aeschylus as her inspiration for this poem, but its focus on the Crucifixion evoked Milton's earlier treatment of the Fall. The Examiner felt that "sacred subjects" were "not fit for poetry," that even "Milton degraded the Deity" and "the presumption of Dante is at least equal to his genius". The Quarterly Review judged that "The Seraphim" was "a subject from which Milton would have shrunk." However, the English Review allowed the poem almost unqualified approval and, without "quot[ing] Milton in defence of our author," judged Barrett fully "justified in approaching such a theme".

Dante, Milton. The reviewers sensed in Barrett a poet who deserved mention with pillars of the male tradition. Yet in Aurora Leigh Romney argues against Aurora's being a poet:

You never can be satisfied with praise
Which men give women when they judge a book
Not as mere work but as mere woman's work,
Expressing the comparative respect
Which means the absolute scorn.

This double standard was widespread, as confirmed by the reviewers' treatment of Barrett as a woman poet. In Blackwood's, "Christopher North" admired Barrett's work. Yet he typifies those reviewers who in a patronizing tone created a halo round the smiling face of "our fair author," the "fair Elizabeth." He questioned, "What other pretty book is this? 'The Seraphim, and other Poems,' by Elizabeth Barnett [sic], author of a Translation of 'Prometheus Bound.' High adventure for a Lady —implying a knowledge of Hebrew—or if not—of Greek. No common mind displays itself in this Preface pregnant with lofty thoughts. Yet is her heart humble withal." Placing Barrett in a tradition of women poets—of Mary Tighe, Felicia Hemans ("that other Sweetest Singer")—and Letitia Landon—North queried, "Surely Poetesses (is there such a word?) are very happy, in spite of all the 'natural sorrows, griefs, and pains,' to which their exquisitely sensitive being must be perpetually alive". He dismissed the tensions manifest in Barrett's work: "And our Elizabeth—she too is happy—though in her happiness she loveth to veil with a melancholy haze the brightness of her childhood— and of her maidenhood."

This sentimentality also informed the Quarterly Review's discussion of Barrett among nine women poets:

We feel that we never did a bolder thing than now we do, in summoning these nine Muses to our Quarter Sessions. The very ink turns blue with which we write their names.

It is easy to be critical on men; but when we venture to lift a pen against women, straightway apparent facies; the weapon drops pointless on the marked passage; and whilst the mind is bent on praise or censure of the poem, the eye swims too deep in tears and mist over the poetess herself in the frontispiece, to let it see its way to either.

The review is, in fact, quite rigorous and insightful, but the reviewer adopted rhetoric associated with the female poet, making her a quite different species from the male. Detracting from a focus on her poetry, the North American Review, placing Barrett as one of the "tuneful tribe", lamented, "In regard to this lady...

We are ignorant of her lineage, her education, her tastes, and (last not least, where a lady is concerned,) her personal attractions". Only the English Review addressed the issue of male prejudice against women writers: "her scholarship, solid and genuine, can defy the charge of female pedantry: that jealous cant of ignorant men is now, indeed, almost exploded; and women may not only cultivate high knowledge, but confess, and dare to show it, without disparagement to womanhood".

Overall the reviewers preferred to imagine Barrett as a poetess; if, by invoking Milton's name, they saw "The Seraphim" as the quintessentially male poem of the volume, they found "Isobel's Child" the quintessentially female one—such that it was mentioned and quoted in almost every journal. Clearly they felt comfortable with that most feminine icon—mother and child.

The poem is a dialogue between a mother who is willing her sick infant to live and the infant who is desiring to die, to escape earth's suffering. The Athenaeum devoted two sentimental columns to quoting from and summarizing the poem. "Christopher North" found that "the workings of a mother's love through all the phases of fear, and hope, and despair, and heavenly consolation, are given with extraordinary power". The Quarterly Review considered this "somewhat fantastic poem... a fair specimen of Miss Barrett's general manner and power".

The North American Review acknowledged that it was a "poem of singular originality of conception and impassioned depth of feeling... suggested by an infant sleeping upon its mother's arm". The English Review chose "Isobel's Child" as its "favourite... tender, thoughtful, and imaginative, the poem flows naturally on, developing with fine pathos the meaning of its text." The reviewers did not wholeheartedly endorse the poem. But neither coincidence nor aesthetics determined so many to discuss "Isobel's Child": it was surely the fact that only this poem depicted woman in her "natural role," as a mother with her baby. To the reviewers Barrett's gender was a crucial issue, provoking both patronizing condescension and startled admiration. Either way they recognized in this volume representing her "own individuality" an original poetic voice: it was neither familiarly male nor, alarmingly and refreshingly, did it speak as a woman should.

The reviewers' recognition of Barrett both as heir to a male tradition and also as poetess dramatically presents the dialectic that operated throughout her career until she achieved her synthesis of these two roles in Aurora Leigh. In particular, two pairs of poems in The Seraphim, and Other Poems reveal this dialectic as Barrett simultaneously presents and challenges traditional literary images of woman: Barrett's revisionary reading of Aeschylus in "The Seraphim" and her "tender" "Isobel's Child"; her revisionary reading of Wordsworth in "The Poet's Vow" and her heroine of the affections in "The Romaunt of Margret."

In the Preface to the title poem, "The Seraphim," Barrett evoked a male precursor; she revealed her "thought, that had Aeschylus lived after the incarnation and crucifixion of our Lord Jesus Christ, he might have turned... from the solitude of Caucasus to the deeper desertness of that crowded Jerusalem where none had any pity". "The Seraphim," not one of Barrett's enduring achievements, is ostensibly an orthodox Christian celebration of divine love made manifest through the Crucifixion.

However, her "vision of the supreme spectacle" from "a less usual aspect", namely that of two angels, covertly, if not self-consciously, allowed Barrett to create a narrative strategy both for presenting woman's relationship to public events and also for analyzing her subjective experience of that relationship.

In Aeschylus, Prometheus and those who visit him speak; Milton's narrative allowed for extensive dialogue between the principals of the action. Barrett, although following epic tradition in designating her angels male, chose an "aspect" for them suggestive of women's relation to public events; her protagonists are spectators of, not actors in, the public drama. How consciously Barrett at this stage linked woman and angel it is impossible to know, but it was certainly an established connection after Coventry Patmore published "The Angel in the House".

Using the "less usual aspect" of the angels, Barrett decentered the male narrative; however, she did not allow woman's subjective experience to replace it:

A woman kneels
The mid cross under,
With white lips asunder.
And motion on each.
They throb, as she feels,
With a spasm, not a speech.

The Crucifixion could not be viewed from Mary's point of view —an equally "less usual aspect"—because as woman she had to "suffer and be still," to feel with "a spasm, not a speech." In "The Seraphim," however, Jesus, recognized by Zerah and Ador, the two angels, as both "man's victim" and "his deity", suggests the paradox of Victorian middle-class woman's being viewed both as powerless "relative creature" in a society venerating masculine industrial power and also as "angel" worshipped for her moral integrity. Jesus thereby dramatizes woman's position, creating an analogy between the divine Jesus's assuming the human condition and woman's entering male public life. The poem's fascination with dangerous public events of earth rather than with the safe security of the angels' Heaven serves as a metaphor for female desire to be included in such events, whatever the cost.

The angels assess this public life on earth, comparing it with their protected home, Heaven. Zerah, convinced that "Heaven is dull,/ Mine Ador, to man's earth", describes the former:

The light that burns
In fluent, refluent motion
Along the crystal ocean;
The springing of the golden harps between
The bowery wings, in fountains of sweet sound,
The winding, wandering music that returns
Upon itself, exultingly self-bound
In the great spheric round
Of everlasting praises.

In spite of these sensuous qualities, Zerah yearns for involvement in earthly "dust and death": the "fluent, refluent" Heaven with its "winding, wandering music" cloys beside earth's harsher realities. Far from having "bowery wings," nature is destructive: "The yew-tree bows its melancholy head / And all the undergrasses kills and seres"; and, as Ador recognizes, humans are greedy: "having won the profit which they seek, / Men lie beside the sceptre and the gold / With fleshless hands that cannot wield or hold". Zerah contrasts Heaven, where "seraphic faces" continually grow more "beautiful with worship and delight" with earth, where the three who are crucified hang "'Ghast and silent to the sun. / Round them blacken and welter and press / Staring multitudes". Barrett conveys the horror of the Crucifixion by the crowd's reaction to it as they push and shove to watch rather than by Jesus's suffering.

Whereas in Heaven "light... burns... Along the crystal ocean" and the air is filled with "the springing of the golden harps," on earth light and sound reveal suffering and cruelty:

Can these love? With the living's pride
They stare at those who die, who hang
In their sight and die. They bear the streak
Of the crosses' shadow, black not wide,
To fall on their heads, as it swerves aside

When the victims' pang
Makes the dry wood creak.

Like the Lady of Shalott, the angels desire to be on earth, with all its suffering. Barrett fuses these male angels with female spectators desirous of some involvement in public events. In the male world of patriarchal struggle enacted at the Crucifixion women have no part. With "a spasm, not a speech" the woman is a powerless and silent observer to the public world of male decision making (God, Herod, Pilate, Judas, Jesus, Peter, the soldiers). Barrett as a woman and a poet partially circumvents this: she assumes the persona of the powerless observer, but gives the angels (closer to androgyny than to traditional masculinity) the right to speech rather than spasm. Zerah identifies himself as "tearless" because he is nonhuman, in contrast to Mary who weeps. This links the Miltonic angel as poet interpreter between God and man, and the notion of woman as angel so prevalent in nineteenth-century rhetoric.

Fusing here her two traditions—male and female—Barrett, however consciously, dramatizes her desire to engage in activities hitherto reserved for men. It is not an easy task: the angels are fearful of leaving their sheltered domain. They experience "the fear of earth" and understand postlapsarian corruption. Nevertheless, whatever their hesitations while still in Heaven, they find earth preferable to their earlier protected existence. Their reasoning is not persuasive. There is nothing in the language that convinces us earth is a better place. The preference results merely from a belief that Christ/God, taking on human form, makes heaven dull in comparison with "man's earth" for all its corruption, suffering, and death. Such fear, yet determination, suggests the nineteenth-century "angels'" fear of leaving the male-sheltered house for creative combat in a world that denied them place.

Barrett fuses here a woman's desire to engage in the public concerns of humanity with her conviction that such an engagement is the poet's task. She embraces a poetic creed that provides an aesthetic cover for legitimizing her woman's desire for involvement in public concerns, not just domestic issues.

In the epilogue, when the speaker touches on the blasphemy of her enterprise in writing of a sacred subject, Barrett implies the parallel blasphemy of "counterfeiting" male texts by transforming the angels into female speakers whose "language [has] never [been] used or hearkened":

And I—ah! what am I
To counterfeit, with faculty earth-darkened,
Seraphic brows of light
And seraph language never used nor hearkened?
Ah me! what word that seraphs say, could come
From mouth so used to sighs, so soon to lie
Sighless, because then breathless, in the tomb?
Forgive me, that mine earthly heart should dare
Shape images of unincamate spirits
And lay upon their burning lips a thought
Cold with the weeping which mine earth inherits.

The female mouth is "so used to sighs," rather than to the transcendental male privilege of speech, that, having accomplished her task of "shap[ing] images" and "lay[ing]... a thought," the speaker asks forgiveness for her daring. In contrast to the external, male-dominated setting of "The Seraphim," "Isobel's Child" is set indoors and the protagonists are a mother, her infant son, and his nurse. There is one brief mention of the child's father. A three-month-old dying child is brought by the nighttime ministrations of his nurse and his mother, the Lady Isobel, back to health. Smiling over his recovery, his mother is oblivious to the ominously raging storm outside.

The tempestuous "external nature" that "broke / Into such abandonment" mysteriously (and repressively) transforms its energies into "A sense of silence and of steady / Natural calm" when it enters the "human creature's room". Here the mother, praying for her child's life, compares herself to "Mary mild" who was not denied "mother-joy" but was "blessèd in the blessèd child". The boy lives, but after the storm mysteriously dies down, the infant loses his "baby-looks" for the "earnest gazing deep" of an old man and precociously tells his mother of his desire for death. This "dark... dull / Low earth, by only weepers trod" cannot compare to his knowledge of the "happy heavenly air" seen in a Wordsworthian "vision and a gleam":

"I saw celestial places even.
Oh, the vistas of high palms
Making finites of delight
Through the heavenly infinite,
Lifting up their green still tops
To the heaven of heaven!"

He challenges the efficacy of poetry to provide him with a comparable vision:

"Can your poet make an Eden
No winter will undo,
And light a starry fire while heeding
His hearth's is burning too?
Drown in music the earth's din,
And keep his own wild soul within
The law of his own harmony?"

He longs for the "little harp... whose strings are golden" that waits for him in heaven. The mother, in her happy acceptance of her child's wish, seems unnatural. As Sandra Donaldson points out, the "theme of Christian consolation... seems almost formulaic" as the childless Barrett demonstrates how mothers "should be grateful their child is now in heaven.... By asking the mother why she would want him to live, the child pushes the theme of Christian consolation to its logical but deadly conclusion." Obviously, "The Seraphim" and "Isobel's Child" can be seen as exercises in orthodox religious thought—God's great love manifest in the Incarnation and Crucifixion, and the consolation of heaven. But what concerns me is the opposing visions these two poems represent in the context of their settings.

The public male drama, played out at the Crucifixion at which Mary is speechless and powerless, makes heaven seem dull and earth, if not exciting or attractive, at least appealing in its dynamic energy. On the other hand the private female drama, enacted in the domestic interior of the Lady Isobel's castle, around which a turbulent external world whirls, exhibits only "dreary earthly love" in a world of "weepers." In comparison, the open spaces of heaven, offering "vistas of high palms" and the "sweet life-tree that drops / Shade like light across the river", promise a more enticing vision to the infant, one of a future not spent with women in the castle but outside in highways of heaven bustling with a "thousand, thousand faces," where he can play his harp "tuned to music spherical, / Hanging on the green life-tree / Where no willows ever be". Whereas the woman in "The Seraphim" is silent and powerless, the male infant of "Isobel's Child" convinces his mother his words should be privileged.

"The Seraphim" stresses the desire for involvement in the turmoil and joy of humanity, thereby privileging the public world, which is associated with men. "Isobel's Child" sees in the domestic world of the female only suffering on earth and finds death and heaven to be preferable states. While Christian consolation may be the overt message of both poems, covertly they repudiate the claustrophobia perceived in female-dominated internal space and endorse the attraction of "man's earth," male dominated external space.

"The Romaunt of Margret" and "The Poet's Vow" should also be viewed as companion poems. Barrett's acknowledged intention was to show in "The Romaunt of Margret" that the "creature cannot be sustained by the creature," and in "The Poet's Vow" to "enforce a truth—that the creature cannot be isolated from the creature". However, at the same time she also challenges cultural assumptions about woman and the male poet. In "The Romaunt of Margret" woman, identified purely as a relative creature, dies. The male poet in "The Poet's Vow" is deluded when he imagines he can retreat from human interaction and substitute maternal nature for woman.

"The Romaunt of Margret" is a ballad. The poetesses had already appropriated the revived form by introducing issues of domesticity. Landon's "Song of the Hunter's Bride" (from The Troubadour) is a conventional tale of a woman anxiously awaiting her husband's return from hunting. As it grows late she fears he has been hurt, then complains,

Why stays he thus?—he would be here
If his love equall'd mine;—

Methinks had I one fond cage dove,
I would not let it pine.

This complaint is undercut by her joy at her husband's eventual return, "My Ulric, welcome home." But the image of woman as analogous to a "fond cage dove" lingers. In Hemans's "Troubadour Song" a warrior fights valiantly in a grisly battle. His life of external masculine activity is juxtaposed with the feminine passivity of the woman left behind in her "smiling home." The warrior survives the "thousand arrows" to return, but the woman meanwhile had "died as roses die, / That perish with a breeze."

Although the poem stereotypes the knight and lady, its final question, "There was death within the smiling home— / How had death found her there?" suggests a murderous idle domesticity. Barrett takes this fatal domesticity to its extreme in "The Romaunt of Margret." A fairly conventional ballad narrative, in which Margret dies because she has lost her love, reveals a domestic subtext dramatizing the killing of the Angel in the House. In Professions for Women Virginia Woolf records how, as a writer, she had to do battle with a phantom, suggestive of Ellis's "woman of England":

She was intensely sympathetic. She was immensely charming. She was utterly unselfish. She excelled in the difficult arts of family life. She sacrificed herself daily. If there was chicken, she took the leg; if there was a draught she sat in it—in short she was so constituted that she never had a mind or a wish of her own, but preferred to sympathize always with the minds and wishes of others. Above all—I need not say it—she was pure.... Had I not killed her she would have killed me. She would have plucked the heart out of my writing.

Woolf knew that to write demands "having a mind of your own,... expressing what you think to be the truth about human relations, morality, sex. And all these questions, according to the Angel in the House, cannot be dealt with freely and openly by women; they must charm, they must conciliate, they must—to put it bluntly—tell lies if they are to succeed." Woolf battled this image of woman, consuming time better spent on "roaming the world in search of adventures." She recognized that "killing the Angel in the House was part of the occupation of a woman writer."

Barrett's 1838 and 1844 ballads evoke a figure like Woolf's An gel. Alethea Hayter describes "Mrs. Browning's Ideal Woman, noble, constant, self-sacrificing, and all blushes, tears and hair down to the ground" as a "tiresome creature." While Hayter's sense that she is "a perfectly nineteenth-century figure" may be accurate, I would argue that it is the age's rather than Barrett's "Ideal Woman."

However unconsciously, "The Romaunt of Margret" reveals a narrative desire to "kill off" this "tiresome creature," not endorse her; Margret dies because she fulfilled her female duty to tend to others and it proved insufficiently lifesustaining. Certainly Margret is a "relative creature": she embroiders her brother's "knightly scarf," attends his animals, waits at home for his return, sings "hunter's songs" to him, and pours him his "red wine"; she combs her sister's hair, gives her her own special bird, shares flowers with her, and rears her in Godliness. She is also her father's special handmaiden (more favored than the "hundred friends" in his court); denying herself the delight of watching the knights at tournament, she reads him a "weary book" and cherishes "his blessing when [she's] done."

When not caring for her family, she sits by the river thinking of her "more than a friend / Across the mountains dim." She wears his "last look in [her] soul, / Which said, I love but thee!" Margret is indeed an ideal daughter of England, a veritable Angel in the House. Why does she die? Ellis would say that such unrequited love as Margret gives to her family and the suffering engendered by the separation from her lover merely require her to "suffer and be still." Margret dies because her daemon, the shadow that rises from the water and sits beside her, engages Margret in dialogue, confronting her with a subversive message. The narrator's response is to lament that earthly love will not last: "O failing human love!... O false, the while thou treadest earth!" But the daemon suggests that an existence predicated entirely on Ellis's notion of the "faculty of instrumentality," of being identified as always in a serving relationship to others, kills women. The daemon challenges the idea that the self-identified woman, with "faculties [that] render her striking and distinguished" in herself, is merely a "dead letter in the volume of human life"; she implies that the "relative creature" cannot sustain her own life.

Margret's main fantasies focus on her absent lover, but it is not, as Gardner Taplin asserts, merely his death that kills her: it is the gradual recognition of the murderous instrumentality of her existence. As the daemon asserts that her brother, her sister, and her father love their material possessions more than they love Margret, the physical environment around her withers, representing the withering of her own life:

The sounding river which rolled, for ever
Stood dumb and stagnant after.
You could see each bird as it woke and stared
Through the shrivelled foliage after.
And moon and stars though bright and far
Did shrink and darken after.

Margret exists solely in her serving relation to others and on the fantasy of a lover: when that role proves to be futile, she dies. The daemon asphyxiates the angel. The narrator, a troubadour, begins her singing of the "wild romaunt" in the present tense as though describing a scene unfolding before her.

This continues until the daemon ("the lady's shadow") leaves the water: "It standeth upright in the cleft moonlight, / It sitteth at her side." The narrator now addresses Margret, forcing her to look at the daemon, her own death: "Look in its face, ladye." At this the narrator seems frightened by her own tale for she removes herself from the action, changes to the past tense, and the rest of the tale is a record of, rather than an involvement with, Margret's story.

Whereas in the first stanza the narrator knows her tale is of death—"The yew-tree leaf will suit"—by the last stanza she feels inadequate to telling her tale: "I have no voice for song. / Not song but wail, and mourners pale, / Not bards, to love belong." Her exclamatory ending shifts from narration to rhetorical chant and her lament certainly lends credence to the notion of the poem as one of transitory love:

O failing human love!
O light, by darkness known!
O false, the while thou treadest earth!
O deaf beneath the stone!

But she feels that "mourners" not "bards" belong to love (echoing Mary's feeling with "a spasm, not a speech" in "The Seraphim"). Does this imply that the poet's function is not to tell the story of "failing human love," but to indict a society that suggests that its middle-class women can and must survive only on love?

The confused relationship of the narrator to her tale suggests an anxiety about the implications of her subject matter, determined to an extent by the autobiographical impulse informing this poem. Dwelling on Barrett's invalidism, Porter and Clarke focus on such an impulse: "Elizabeth must have been the painter's manikin, serving as first model for Margret.... The hold on life through the love of others in life, —for the sake of a peculiarly loved brother's love, a cherished little sister's, a fondly proud father's, —these are all longing snatches at the life about to elude Margret which must have quivered through the outstretched fingers of her own actual experience". What Porter and Clarke fail to recognize is that life is only about to elude Margret because she realizes that her love is not returned and that she is a drudge.

Much of the autobiographical significance lies not in Barrett's precarious health (as Porter and Clarke imagine), but in the relationship between Barrett and her mother. The narrator offers no explanation for the missing mother, but the implication is that she died in the same way as Margret dies, through unrequited self-sacrificing love. It is also ominously suggested that Margret's younger sister, who "wears / The look our mother wore" will die this inevitable female death. Margret, successfully educated to be womanly, has taken on her mother's role: she is sister/lover to her brother, sister/mother to her sister, and daughter/wife to her father. The poem, therefore, repeats Barrett's own family situation with her brothers, younger sisters, and her father.

Through study and invalidism, Barrett had sought to avoid the female occupations, thereby incurring the wrath of her sister, Henrietta. She was subject to the departures and returns of her favourite brother, Edward, whose masculine freedom she envied in her youth. And, although he encouraged her writing, her father was peremptory, authoritarian, and emotionally contained. In I828, when Barrett was twenty-two, her mother died, having given birth to twelve children (one died). Barrett wrote about her to Browning: "Scarcely was I woman when I lost my mother— dearest as she was & very tender,... but of a nature harrowed up into some furrows by the pressure of circumstances.... A sweet, gentle nature, which the thunder a little turned from its sweetness—as when it turns milk—One of those women who never can resist, —but, in submitting & bowing on themselves, make a mark, a plait, within,.. a sign of suffering. Too womanly was she—it was her only fault").

Barrett describes her mother in language analogous to Woolf's angel, "A sweet, gentle nature.... One of those women who can never resist... submitting and bowing." To Barrett being such a woman was a "fault." The angel cannot sustain her sweet submissive nature because the "thunder" (Mr. Barrett?) "a little turned [her] from its sweetness—as when it turns milk." Barrett is ambivalent in both admiring and condemning her mother for being such a woman; yet she attributes her mother's death to embracing that role. It was not a role her eldest daughter intended to assume. And, as though dramatizing these responses to her mother's life, in "The Romaunt of Margret" she examines the fate of a woman who was "too womanly... it was her only fault." However, the narrator never spells out the implications of her tale, that a woman who refuses to see herself as the relative creature Margret is, and who realizes herself through "such faculties, as render [her] striking and distinguished" in herself, will survive. Such a woman could be a poet.

Barrett's early resistance to marriage and her suspicion

of romantic love are dramatized by Margret's death when the lover across the "mountains dim" (was he ever real?) dies. Romantic love is unreliable. Margret's death then is not merely a melancholy repetition of ballad conventions, but a questioning of their assumptions. The poem annihilates woman's self-annihilative role. The heroine's death, which we expect to mourn, becomes in fact a liberating act, freeing Barrett from the "Ideal Woman's" fate. The protagonist's death is an equally sorrowful yet liberating act in "The Poet's Vow," Barrett's revisionary reading of Wordsworth and of Romantic ideology about Nature. Barrett's overt admiration of and covert entrapment by Wordsworth as a precursor are revealed in "The Book of the Poets," her critical essay on the history of English poetry published in the Athenaeum.

She laments how the followers of Dryden and Pope reduced poetry to "the trick of accoustical mechanics," how in their writings "thought had perished... and we had the beaten rhythm without the living footstep." In their work Nature had been "expelled". But Cowper, Bums, and Coleridge heralded a change consummated by Wordsworth, "the chief of the movement." These poets allowed "Nature, the long banished, [to redawn] like the morning." To accomplish this they abandoned, after a hard struggle, the "conventional dialects" of poets, conventional words, attitudes, and manners, consecrated by "wits." Wordsworth "in a bravery bravest of all... to the actual scandal of the world which stared at the filial familiarity,... threw himself not at the feet of Nature, but straightway and right tenderly upon her bosom... trustfully as child before mother". Barrett cites Wordsworth as the primary poet of Nature, suggesting that he and his rhetoric of Nature had a much stronger influence on her than other Romantic poets. Indeed, she outgrew her adolescent fervor for Byron, admired Keats, but found Shelley too cold and distant as a poet.

Wordsworth was spokesman for a literary tradition that posited Nature as a maternal figure. A psychoanalytic scenario of this would, thereby, have the male precursor poet as the father, and the female presence in Romantic poetry as Mother

Nature, the silent other, the woman. The son, the young poet, engages in a struggle of desire for and separation from her, and is both subject to and yet controls her power. In "The Poet's Vow" Barrett dramatizes the dilemma Wordsworth's representation of nature posed for her as a daughter poet.

The poem tells of an unnamed male poet who rejects his fellow human beings in order to live with the "touching, patient Earth" to "feel [her] unseen looks / Innumerous, constant, deep":

"And ever, when I lift my brow
At evening to the sun,
No voice of woman or of child
Recording 'Day is done.'
Your silences shall a love express,
More deep than such an one."

Barrett portrays a clichéd Romantic poet for whom nature, assuming female qualities, is preferable to a wife welcoming him home. But a new aspect of man's relationship to and exploitation of "Earth" is presented by this poet. He believes that, while God created a "very good" earth, man made it "very mournful," a violently crazed place instead of a calm and silent haven:

"Poor crystal sky with stars astray!
Mad winds that howling go
From east to west! perplexèd seas
That stagger from their blow!
O motion wild! O wave defiled!
Our curse hath made you so."

To restore the paradisal bond between man and nature (son and mother's breast), the poet breaks his bonds with other people. Forsaking adult concerns, he hopes again (as a child fantasizes) to control this mother turned madwoman, this woman who is neglecting his needs.

The narrator, however, establishes the error of his vision:

This poet daringly,
—The nature at his heart,
And that quick tune along his veins
He could not change by art, —

Had vowed his blood of brotherhood
To a stagnant place apart.
He did not vow in fear, or wrath,
Or grief's fantastic whim,
But, weights and shows of sensual things
Too closely crossing him,
On his soul's eyelid the pressure slid
And made its vision dim.

What he sees as a "touching, patient Earth," the narrator views as a "stagnant place apart." What he feels to be the "dessicating sin" of human involvement, she describes as the "weights and shows of sensual things / Too closely crossing him." Nature is not a maternal figure to the narrator, but a mere stagnant place unless populated by human intercourse. In Part 2 ("Showing to Whom the Vow was Declared"), the poet assigns all his silver and gold to his "crowding friends." The narrator tellingly describes how the friends are "solaced" by "clasping bland his gift, —his hand / In a somewhat slacker hold".

Only his friend, Sir Roland, and his fiancée, Rosalind (his childhood companion), remain, and he dismisses them to marry each other, with his lands as Rosalind's dowry. Rosalind refuses to be so assigned, and, although she describes herself as "half a child" and the poet as "very sage", it is she who will eventually demonstrate how fallacious his romance with nature is. She learns from his face the "cruel homily" of "the teachings of the heaven and earth". Preferring to remain "untouched, unsoftened" by their beauty, she dissociates her female identity from "the senseless, loveless earth and heaven".

Sir Roland also tries to persuade the poet that his understanding of the relationship between people and the earth is destructive.

The poet's response reveals a masochistic vision of his desired natural environment:

"I go to live
In Courland Hall, alone:
The bats along the ceilings cling,

The lizards in the floors do run,
And storms and years have worn and reft
The stain by human builders left
In working at the stone."

His "touching, patient Earth" is destructive. His retreat, a cobwebby squalor, undercuts his notion of nature's "unseen looks / Innumerous, constant, deep," and her "silences" that "love express". In his male hands domestic space resembles an unfeminized gothic interior. In Part 3 ("Showing How the Vow was Kept") Barrett wrote an uncanny counterpoint to Tennyson's "The Lady of Shalott." Although critics commented on certain similarities of style between Barrett and Tennyson, neither had read the other's work at this stage. A comparison between the two is, however, illuminating.

In Tennyson's poem the woman inside the tower knows only that a curse of unknown origin is on her. This confines her inside, prohibiting her from looking through her window. She longs to go outside—"I am half sick of shadows"—but remains the artist, weaving representations of the images from outside reflected in her mirror. Love finally compels her to look at the handsome Sir Lancelot, but such engagement in the world causes her death. Tennyson, the male poet who is free, whatever his psychopathology, to move in the world beyond his house and engage in its activities, projects a fantasy of escape from the public world onto a female artist whom he condemns to stay removed from the world and its destructive energies.

Barrett, a woman writer confined to a domestic sphere, transforms such domestic enclosure into the gothic habitat of a male poet who deliberately turns from love and the world, and chooses to stay within his tower. To the narrator this is a curse: "a lonely creature of sinful nature / It is an awful thing". Unlike the Lady of Shalott, who only saw shadowy reflections in her mirror yet longed to look out, this "poet at his lattice sate, / And downward looked he". Free to look down and walk about, he only peered through his window at the churchgoers, the bridal party, and the child who "Stood near the wall to see at play / The lizards green and rare". The poet neither joined them nor blessed them, but purposely withdrew.

This brought him not solace but fear:
He dwelt alone, and sun and moon
Were witness that he made
Rejection of his humanness
Until they seemed to fade;
His face did so, for he did grow
Of his own soul afraid.
The self-poised God may dwell alone
With inward glorying,
But God's chief angel waiteth for
A brother's voice, to sing;
And a lonely creature of sinful nature
It is an awful thing.
An awful thing that feared itself;
While many years did roll,
A lonely man, a feeble man,
A part beneath the whole,
He bore by day, he bore by night
That pressure of God's infinite
Upon his finite soul.

The psychic disturbance caused by denial of "his humanness," defined as involvement in the world outside the home, turns the poet into an "awful thing that feared itself." Part 4 ("Showing How Rosalind Fared by the Keeping of the Vow") evokes Keats's "La Belle Dame Sans Merci." If the knight's encounter with "La Belle Dame" leaves him wasted and aimless, so Rosalind's rejection by the poet leaves her wasted: "In death sheets lieth Rosalind / As white and still as they".

His devotion to nature makes Rosalind turn from her "rival" and, in an exaggerated reaction to the poet's own behaviour, she insists that the windows in her room be closed so she hears nothing from outside and sees none of God's "blessed works".

When she is dead, she wants her corpse carried to Courland Hall via the natural landscape of her childhood—the long church grass, the river bank, the brook, the hill, the "piny forest still" and the "open moorland". Nature, instead of fulfilling its promise ("the brook with its sunny look / Akin to living glee"), has been used against her; only as a corpse will she traverse it again. In Part 5 ("Showing How the Vow was Broken") the poet (on the day Rosalind dies) revels alone in the beauty of the stars at midnight:

They shine upon the steadfast hills,
Upon the swinging tide,
Upon the narrow track of beach
And the murmuring pebbles pied:
They shine on every lovely place,
They shine upon the corpse's face.

The poet learns that Rosalind is dead; his "touching, patient Earth" cannot preserve him from human interaction. The sterility of his aesthetic is now challenged by a woman poet: attached to Rosalind's corpse is a scroll. Written before her death, the poem is in the Hemans-Landon tradition of love-laments: "'I have prayed for thee with bursting sob / When passion's course was free.'" She suffered silently and tearfully the years without him. Her poem, however, effects change. Rosalind insists that nature is not a substitute for woman: "'I tell thee that my poor scorned heart / Is of thine earth.'" Dead, she can no longer pray for him:

"The corpse's tongue is still,
Its folded fingers point to heaven,
But point there stiff and chill."

Like the ancient mariner, the poet's only salvation lies with himself:

"I charge thee, by the living's prayer,
And the dead's silentness,
To wring out from thy soul a cry
Which God shall hear and bless!"

"Triumphant Rosalind" awakens his "long-subjected humanness," manifest as a "lion-cry", and he weeps. Their roles reversed now, Rosalind, the "half-a-child," is a wise poet, and the male poet reveals "That weeping wild of a reckless child / From a proud man's broken heart". The man "who so worshipped earth and sky" is "found too weak / To bear his human pain", and he too dies.

Sir Roland, years later, brings his little son to the grave. When the boy, like the poet before him, turns "upward his blithe eyes to see / The wood-doves nodding from the tree," his father, echoing Rosalind, tells him:

"Nay, boy look downward,...
Upon this human dust asleep.
And hold it in thy constant ken
That God's own unity compresses
(One into one) the human many,
If not in love, on sorrow then, —
Though smiling not like other men,
Still, like them we must weep."

The religious overtones of Barrett's aesthetic creed matured as her poetry became boldly feminized through her understanding that her responsibility was to speak for those women who "suffer wrong... everywhere". She was convinced that the real work of poets is the work women have always been rooted in—human suffering and joy—but without its attendant self abnegation. Barrett's conviction that the poet must engage with social and political issues had its terrors and burdens for her, a woman imagining herself as a descendent of the great male poetic tradition, as the "fear of earth" had for the angels in "The Seraphim." She suggests such anxiety in her dramatization of other prominent women in "The Virgin Mary to the Child Jesus," "Victoria's Tears," and "The Young Queen." In the first of these, Mary's meditation over her sleeping son, Mary knows that future generations will say of her, "Thou art / The blessedest of women!", but Barrett examines the practical implications of this status.

Mary feels that her pure son was "created from my nature all defiled" and recognizes that:

No small babe-smiles my watching heart has seen
To float like speech the speechless lips between,
No dovelike cooing in the golden air,
No quick short joys of leaping babyhood.

Barrett imagines that Mary, knowing her son's destiny, will have painfully ambivalent feelings about the "majestic angel whose command / Was softly as a man's beseeching said" naming her as the chosen mother of Jesus. When she thinks of "the drear sharp tongue of prophecy, / With the dread sense of things which shall be done," of how her son will be called "despised" and "rejected," she feels: "I must not die, with mother's work to do, / And could not live—and see".

In "Victoria's Tears" Barrett imagines how this eighteen-year old girl, "Maiden! Heir of kings," must feel as a woman leading a country (in which women were disenfranchised) when she can "no longer lean" on her "mother's breast." The contrast between the adult woman with a public function—whether queen or poet —deprived of such maternal nurturance, and Barrett's sense of Wordsworth as one who "threw himself right tenderly upon [Nature's] bosom" is a poignant one. Barrett stresses the great pomp of the coronation, but

She saw no purples shine,
For tears had dimmed her eyes;
She only knew her childhood's flowers
Were happier pageantries!
And while her heralds played the part,
For million shouts to drown—
"God save the Queen" from hill to mart, —
She heard through all her beating heart,
And turned and wept—
She wept, to wear a crown!

Barrett suggests that token women who attain public prominence feel ambivalent about their status. As she reveals her own anxiety as a woman measuring her feet inside the shoes of her dead literary fathers, so she imagines Victoria to be similarly unnerved at her sudden power. In "The Young Queen," she delineates how "Her palace walls enring / The dust that was a king—/ And very cold beneath her feet, she feels her father's grave."

At fourteen Barrett had felt some comfort in walking in Homer's footsteps and not striking out a path for herself; now she imagines in chilling terms a severance from the father as woman appropriates power traditionally reserved for him. Instead of guiding her feet the precursor now numbs them with cold. It is a statement of loss; but it also determines the daughter to walk her own path.

The first tentative steps along such a path resulted from the "individuality" represented in The Seraphim, and Other Poems, in Barrett's conviction that in this "age of steam" the poet had to embrace the world "of dust and death" and "human pain." By taking Jesus, "man's victim" and "his deity"—with his engagement in human concerns—rather than God, the divine creator, as her model for the poet, Barrett legitimized her desire that woman engage in art and politics. In The Seraphim, and Other Poems Barrett initiated her departure both from the "frustration" of the male poetic tradition, which privileged the male voice as subject of poetic discourse with woman as object and other, and from the "delusion" of following the poetesses who overtly advocated resignation to woman's "weary lot" even while covertly transgressing their own dictum. She began in these poems to place woman as the subject of her own discourse.

When Kenyon expressed fond nostalgia for her early poems, Barrett dismissed The Battle of Marathon and An Essay on Mind as a "girl's exercise," convinced that "the difference between them and my present poems is not merely the difference between... immaturity and maturity; but that it is the difference between the dead and the living, between a copy and an individuality, between what is myself and what is not myself". Far from lamenting the past, she eagerly anticipated fashioning the "new manners" of the discourse expressing that subjectivity; her Poems of 1844 represented a decisive challenge to the "old manners" she was outgrowing.

Chapter 6

Poems of 1844: Eve's Alloted Grief

In her Preface to Poems of 1844 and her two sonnets to George Sand, "A Desire" and "A Recognition," Barrett explores an emerging poetics with greater consciousness of her position in relation both to the established male poetic tradition and also to a distinctly female literary one than she had in her previous volume. Those six years between the publication of The Seraphim, and Other Poems and Poems of 1844 were dominated by Barrett's invalidism and confinement. This confinement can symbolize woman's literary imprisonment in a male poetic tradition.

Conversely, to recognize Barrett's literary imprisonment necessitates understanding the nature and function of her invalidism. Barrett had always suffered ill health, but her doctors were so worried in the winter of 1838 that they advised her to leave London, where her family had lived since 1835, for a more favorable climate in Torquay on the south coast. Not until 1841 did she persuade her doctors and father to allow her return to London. Occasional carriage rides in the summers of 1845 and 1846 were the only relief from her invalid's room in the Wimpole Street house, until her secret marriage to Browning in September 1846.

Barrett's legendary invalidism is complex. Its origins may reach back to the young teenager's recognition of the divergence of sex roles once her favourite brother, Edward, was sent to public school:

Together have we past our infant hours,

Together sported Childhood's spring away,
Together cull'd young Hope's fast budding flowers,
To wreathe the forehead of each coming day!
Yes! for the present's sun makes e'en the future gay.
And when the laughing mood was nearly o'er,
Together, many a minute did we wile
On Horace' page, or Maro's sweeter lore;
While one young critic, on the classic style,
Would sagely try to frown, and make the other smile.
But now alone thou con'st the ancient tome—
And sometimes thy dear studies, it may be,
Are cross'd by dearer dreams of me and home!
Alone I muse on Homer—thoughts are free—
And if mine often stray, they go in search of thee!
["Verses to My Brother"]

Betty Miller astutely explores the effect on the young Barrett of this separation between boy and girl. She suggests that the passionate, energetic child felt that her place as firstborn was usurped by the first son, Edward. He was her closest companion during their childhood, yet his increasingly privileged masculinity aroused in her, "inconsolable for not being bom a man," a stormy "spirit of emulation." She was a lively "tomboy" who climbed walls, ladders, trees; roamed the countryside around Hope End; and loved the pouring rain and rolling in long grass.

Scorning both the governess and the sewing assigned to the Barrett girls, she so resented that "subserviency of opinion which is generally considered necessary to feminine softness" that she insisted on studying Greek and Latin with Edward's tutor, Mr. McSwiney. But when Edward was sent to public school, Mr. McSwiney dismissed, and Barrett left behind, she recognized, "The Dream has faded—it is o'er." She could not go with Edward through the gates of Hope End to school, out into the world of men; confined within the domestic sphere of women she languished, Miller concludes, recognizing the "inescapable realities of her own femininity."

After Edward's departure and the tutor's dismissal, doctors' reports reveal that Barrett experienced "pain in the head... very considerable debility and consequent nervous irritation, producing smallness and feebleness of the pulse—pain, and weakness in the back, which [would] not allow her sitting up, without support by pillows, and she [was] always rendered worse by exercise—The feet [were] generally cold." They found her illness mysterious and resistant to diagnosis. Subsequently it has been thought possible that it was associated with early symptoms of tuberculosis.

This sudden debility in such an energetic child, however, is puzzling. Maybe she enacted that branch of Victorian medical thought that determined middle-class femaleness to be an inherently sickly condition, in which "many a young life is battered and forever crippled in the breakers of puberty." Hampered by petticoats, confined at Hope End, witnessing her mother's yearly pregnancies and attendant weakness, Barrett's energies were transformed into exhaustion.

Aurora Leigh sank into a similar lethargy under her aunt's educational practices, suggesting Barrett Browning's own diagnosis of her invalidism. Whatever its etiology, Barrett employed her sickness as a strategy to resist activities deemed appropriate for a woman, and to gain time for study and writing.

Philip Kelley and Ronald Hudson, editors of Barrett's Diary, I83I-32, imagine that her "enforced idleness at this time, and her always indifferent health subsequently, turned her more and more to books and study, writing and introspection.... Her love of seclusion grew, and no doubt engendered the marked reluctance she later displayed whenever obliged to put aside her books and take part in the social round of visits.".

This is consistent with criticism that sees women's writing as compensation for a lack in their lives: viz., Dickinson wrote because she never married, Barrett Browning wrote because she was an invalid. However, Kelley and Hudson confuse cause and effect. In a culture which demanded that middle-class women be wives and mothers, women writers devised strategies for engaging and protecting their creative energies, such as refusing to marry, refusing to receive visitors, even invalidism. Barrett knew she needed time and room for her art; invalidism allowed her both.

Barrett Browning's contemporary, Florence Nightingale, understood, and for many years enacted, this ideology of invalidism. In "Cassandra", she denounced the frittering away of women's energy, intellect, and time:

Mrs. A has the imagination, the poetry of a Murillo, and has sufficient power of execution to show that she might have had a great deal more. Why is she not a Murillo? From a material difficulty, not a mental one. If she has a knife and fork in her hands during three hours of the day, she cannot have a pencil and a brush. Dinner is the great sacred ceremony of this day, the great sacrament. To be absent from dinner is equivalent to being ill. Nothing else will excuse us from it. Bodily incapacity is the only apology valid.

How do we explain then the many cases of women who have distinguished themselves..? Widowhood, ill-health, or want of bread, these three explanations or excuses are supposed to justify a woman in taking up an occupation. Women have no means given them, whereby they can resist the "claims of social life." They are taught from their infancy upwards that it is wrong, ill-tempered and a misunderstanding of "a woman's mission" (with a great M.) if they do not allow themselves willingly to be interrupted at all hours. Sickness provided time and "room of one's own" for a middle class woman's engagement in intellectual pursuit. When at twenty-five Barrett was forbidden by her father to stay a few days to help her friend, Mr. Boyd, with his work, she wrote, "You know I cannot do everything I like, or everything when I like. I only rule in my own room—where there are no subjects to be ill-governed—except the literary inanimate".

Barrett needed a valid "excuse" to spend time in that room. She recorded in her Diary how, after a day in which her aunt made her join "Mrs. Cliffe's pic nic," she returned "unwell with overfatigue. These kind [sic] of things do not agree with me". On the next day her aunt wanted her to visit Mrs. Martin, but again she became ill:

I felt so unwell, that I negatived the proposal, – & this

set B's combustible particles on fire. She spoke crossly to me, —& I who was on the very verge of hysterics, & required only a finger touch to impel me forwards, burst into tears, & had that horrible dead precursive feeling all thro' my hands & feet.... I lay down on my bed after my breakfast, because I cd scarcely sit up—and yet when time drew near for us to meet Mrs. Martin, I sent Henrietta in to Bummy to carry my palinodia. I wd go, if she wished it so. No!—it wd not do.

Once Henrietta and Bummy had departed, however, she "read Mr. Beverly's pamphlets..; the letter to the Archbishop of York, & the Tombs of the prophets... a good deal of Lamartines, —second volume of Meditations poetiques et religieuses". I do not mean to suggest that Barrett consciously feigned illness to write. Rather, the illness, whether formed from or intensified by a complex reaction to the consciousness of her femaleness in adolescence, enabled Barrett to adopt invalidism as a strategy for finding freedom at least in her own room. However, after years of such invalidism Barrett recognized her dilemma: such a self-protective life resembled imprisonment. She gave a stark account of her situation to a friend (October 1843):

I live in London, to be sure, and except for the glory of it I might live in a desert, so profound is my solitude and so complete my isolation from things and persons without. I lie all day, and day after day, on the sofa, and my windows do not even look into the street. To abuse myself with a vain deceit of rural life I have had ivy planted in a box, and it has flourished and spread over one window, and strikes against the glass with a little stroke from the thicker leaves when the wind blows at all briskly.

Barrett revealed how hard it was to inhabit such "a desert" in a later letter to Mrs. Martin (December 1845) about the closing of the "prison doors":

Do you think I was bom to live the life of an oyster, such as I do live here? And so, the moaning and gnashing of teeth are best done alone and without taking anyone into confidence.... For me, I am not yet undone by the winter. I still sit in my chair and walk about the room. But the prison doors are shut close, and I could dash myself against them sometimes with a passionate impatience of the needless captivity. I feel so intimately and from evidence, how, with air and warmth together in any fair proportion, I should be as well and happy as the rest of the world, that it is intolerable. The "moaning and gnashing of teeth," that restless captive energy, were eased in Barrett by opium. When Browning expressed concern about its use, she explained that sleep "will not easily come near me except in a red hood of poppies" and acknowledged.

It might strike you as strange that I who have had no pain no acute suffering to keep down from its angles should need opium in any shape. But I have had restlessness till it made me almost mad—at one time I lost the power of sleeping quite and even in the day, the continual aching sense of weakness has been intolerable besides palpitation as if one's life, instead of giving movement to the body, were imprisoned undiminished within it, & beating & fluttering impotently to get out, at all the doors & windows. So the medical people gave me opium... [and] the tranquillizing power has been wonderful.

The image of Barrett as pale invalid yields to that of monster, housing restlessness enough to make her mad: in her third-floor room Barrett moaned and gnashed her teeth. As isolated as Bertha Mason, she was confined to one room where her father visited her daily to say prayers, and where the male doctors tranquilized her "restlessness" with opium; among them was a doctor who believed that for a woman to be a poet "was a mortal malady & incompatible with any common show of health under any circumstances". She was the madwoman in the straightjacket. The invalidism she exploited when younger to gain time for her studies became an instrument of the patriarchy to subdue her. She must always have been subliminally aware that her father desired her imprisonment; it was clarified for her the year after the publication of the Poems of 1844 when doctors warned that for Barrett to live she had to winter in Italy. Mr. Barrett refused to allow this, forcing Barrett to realise that the father she adored would "rather see me dead at his foot than yield the point".

There is so much legend surrounding Elizabeth Barrett, Robert Browning, and Mr. Barrett that I do not wish to add to it. I am not interested here in the psychological complexities surrounding this daughter-father relationship. It is, however, necessary to outline how Barrett described the relationship and transmuted it into her art, in order to illuminate the latter. Concerning Mr. Barrett, she explained to Browning, "[His] principle of passive filial obedience is held drawn (& quartered) from Scripture. He sees the law & the gospel on his side". Barrett felt that her father both cared for his ten children and took seriously "all those patriarchal ideas of governing grownup children 'in the way they must go!'" She appreciated that there could never be a "truer affection in a father's heart" but condemned the "evil [that] is in the system" to which her father subscribed: "to make happy according to his own views of the propriety of happiness—he takes it to be his duty to rule like the Kings of Christendom, by divine right".

While many Victorian fathers may have behaved similarly toward their sons and daughters, the Barrett children were subject to a peculiarity in their father, namely his attitude toward their sexuality and possible marriage: "he never does tolerate in his family (sons or daughters) the development of one class of feelings". Elizabeth Barrett was not the only child disowned by Mr. Barrett because of her marriage; her sister, Henrietta, and her brother, Alfred, was also cut from Mr. Barrett's life and will. The other surviving children remained single. Barrett described her father as an exaggeratedly authoritarian upholder of the patriarchy; yet, she imagined the isolation that resulted for him with an empathy that reveals as much about her situation as her understanding of his: "We can alter nothing by ever so many words. After all, he is the victim. He isolates himself—& now and then he feels it the cold dead silence all round, which is the effect of an incredible system.

If he were not stronger than most men, he could not bear it as he does". However, her compassion did not blind her to his contribution to her isolation. When he declared she would incur his grave displeasure if she wintered away from home, she submitted to his will, "taking up [her] chain again" and remaining in her "cage". As her desire to live, encouraged by Browning, grew, she understood how her isolation had been "imprisonment" and her father the "gaoler."

Barrett recognized how different her life as a young female poet had been from Browning's as a young male one:

What you say of society draws me on to many comparative thoughts of your life & mine. You seem to have drunken of the cup of life full, with the sun shining on it. I have lived only inwardly, —or with sorrow, for a strong emotion. Before this seclusion of my illness, I was secluded still—& there are few of the youngest women in the world who have not seen more, heard more, known more, of society, than I, who am scarcely to be called young now. I grew up in the country had no social opportunities, had my heart in books & poetry, & my experience, in reveries. My sympathies drooped towards the ground like an untrained honeysuckle.... It was a lonely life—growing green like the grass around it. Books and dreams were what I lived in—& domestic life only seemed to buzz gently around, like the bees about the grass. And so time passed, and passed—and afterwards, when my illness came & I seemed to stand at the edge of the world with all done, & no prospect (as appeared at one time) of ever passing the threshold of one room again, —why then, I turned to thinking with some bitterness... that I had stood blind in this temple I was about to leave that I had seen no Human nature, that my brothers & sisters of the earth were names to me,.. that I had beheld no great mountain or river—nothing in fact. I was as a man dying who had not read Shakespeare & it was too late!— do you understand?

And do you also know what a disadvantage this ignorance is to my art—Why, if I live on & yet do not escape from this seclusion, do you not perceive that I labour under signal disadvantages.. that I am, in a manner, as a blind poet? Cer tainly, there is compensation to a degree. I have had much of the inner life—& from the habit of selfconsciousness of self analysis, I make great guesses at Human Nature in the main. But how willingly I would as a poet exchange some of this lumbering, ponderous, helpless knowledge of books, for some experience of life & man. Barrett offered no feminist analysis of her adolescence, of her "seclusion," of her invalidism, beyond her complaint that she "had no social opportunities." There was social intercourse at Hope End for "ladies," but none for a poet. Barrett imagined her art as limited by her social restrictions; Woolf offered a similar analysis: "It cannot be doubted that the long years of seclusion had done her irreparable damage as an artist. She had lived shut off, guessing at what was outside, and inevitably magnifying what was within."

A restricted environment does not automatically limit a writer, secure in the subjectivity of that experience; when, however, the experience belongs to the realm of the female "other," it has traditionally been trivialized. Barrett and Woolf both internalized this masculine notion when they found "disadvantage' or "irreparable damage" to Barrett's art as resulting from her seclusion. In that early letter to Browning, Barrett reflected on how her years of confinement affected her art and how "as a blind poet" she would "exchange some of this lumbering, ponderous, helpless knowledge of books, for some experience of life & man"; her feelings echoed or resulted from the reviewers' response to Poems of 1844.

They continued to admire her work, but lamented that Barrett's poems originated in books, not life. Sarah Flower Adams in the Westminster Review summed up this critical reservation: Barrett's being "an exile... secluded from society" resulted in a "style, not unfrequently, wanting the ease of colloquial expression. Books her only companions, she [was] led to adopt their language," which "weakened instead of assisting the development of real power." Barrett herself grew "to despise book-knowledge & its effect on the mind... when people live by it" because they cloister "their souls under these roofs made with hands, when they might be under the sky.

Such people grow dark & narrow & low, with all their pains. Barrett imagined she "stood blind in this temple [she] was about to leave.. that [she] had seen no Human nature," but her art is not diminished because she represented those experiences of being woman and artist that shaped her aesthetic. Her solitude can be seen not as detrimental to her art but rather as a fortuitous and essential stage in her progress toward a mature poetic voice.

Certainly Browning did not share Barrett's feelings about her work: he recognized there an integrity of voice that he felt eluded his own work: "Your poetry must be, cannot but be, infinitely more to me than mine to you—for you do what I always wanted, hoped to do, and only seem now likely to do for the first time.

You speak out, you, —I only make men & women speak—give you truth broken into prismatic hues, and fear the pure white light, even if it is in me: but I am going to try. We value Browning precisely because he made "men & women speak," prefiguring modernism in his recognition that truth is not absolute but "broken into prismatic hues." However, this appreciation of Barrett's work, even allowing for the enthusiasm of a new lover, was genuine and enduring.

Alice Meynell cast light on the apparent contradiction between Barrett's fear that poetic limitation would result from her seclusion and Browning's recognition that her work was sincere. Meynell preferred the "Mrs. Browning" who "rose from her sofa, stood at a husband's side, received his friends," to the Barrett "lurking in that delusive bower which secluded writers—those who are women—are apt to build for themselves out of their fancies as to what they probably seem to be in the mind and thought of the world of their readers." Nevertheless, she understood that "nothing but the secrecy of a dark sick-room and a sofa could give a sensitive woman the strange courage of Elizabeth Barrett's poems.

Out of sight she had no fear of the vociferous though sweet part she took in the world." Barrett may have felt limited by solitude and encumbered by book knowledge, but she also appreciated how her "strange courage" was fostered by her isolation: she refused an invitation to visit Mrs. Martin in 1846, saying, "I can lose nothing here, shut up in my prison, and the nightingales come to my windows and sing through the sooty panes. If I were at Hastings I should risk the chance of recovering liberty, and the consolations of slavery would not reach me as they do here".

Although the rhetoric of "shut up," "prison," and "sooty panes" belies the notion of contentment in that room, Barrett recognized that her poems ("the nightingales singing at her window") were the "consolations of slavery":

Have I not felt twenty times the desolate advantage of being insulated here & of not minding anybody when I made my poems?—of living a little like a disembodied spirit, & caring less for supposititious [sic] criticism than for the black fly buzzing in the pane?—That made me what dear Mr. Kenyon calls "insolent,"—untimid, & unconventional in my degree; and not so much by strength, you see, as by separation—You touch your greater ends by mere strength; breaking with your own hands the hampering threads which, in your position wd have hampered me.

Barrett knew that to reach the "greater ends" of poetry each poet must break "the hampering threads" that bind her or him. To Bloom this would mean the threads of the precursor's poems that bind the imagination of the son. In Barrett's case it meant that, and also the "hampering threads" of woman's role.

It is an ironic image, reflecting as it does the sewing that occupied middle-class women's fingers instead of the pen. Browning had the advantage of strength, a male power; Barrett the advantage of seclusion, a female condition. If she had moved as freely as Browning in literary society, she would have been "hampered" from touching her "greater ends." She explained: "I never learnt to talk as you do in London.... If my poetry is worth anything to any eye, —it is the flower of me". The "desolate advantage" of her isolation freed her from woman's role; protected her from exposure to criticism of her writing and herself; and cut her off from the way "to talk... in London," from the "threads which... wd have hampered me," so she could hear her own voice, see her own vision, be "'insolent,'—untimid, & unconventional," be unladylike.

Barrett paid for freedom of imagination with imprisonment of body: her confinement produced a rhetoric of imprisonment, which in turn impelled her—who knows how consciously—both to expose woman's textual imprisonment and to revise the assumptions of poetic tradition. Her Preface to Poems of 1844 reveals her awareness of the former, whereas her sonnets to George Sand, "A Desire" and "A Recognition," illustrate that her identification with Sand encouraged her to attempt the latter. The Preface to Poems of 1844 demonstrates Barrett's "anxiety" about Miltonic "influence" and about her own "authorship."

Her self-consciousness about his influence suggests a possible strategy for solving the dilemma of the daughter's struggle with the strong precursor father poet. A clue to this strategy lies in Barrett's dedication to the 1844 volume, "To My Father." Protest against the authority of the father—that "alien tyranny / With its dynastic reasons of larger bones / And stronger sinews"—rumbles under and sometimes explodes through the surface obedience of many poems in the volume.

Yet the energy and even violence manifested are absent in the sweetness of the dedication in which she recalls "the time far off when I was a child and wrote verses, and when I dedicated them to you who were my public and my critic." She expresses gratitude for an "existence which has been sustained and comforted by you as well as given," culminating in her feeling—as a thirty-eight-year-old woman—that though "somewhat more faint-hearted than I used to be, it is my fancy thus to seem to return to a visible personal dependence on you, as if indeed I were a child again; to conjure your beloved image between myself and the public, so as to be sure of one smile, —and to satisfy my heart while I sanctify my ambition, by associating with the great pursuit of my life its tenderest and holiest affection".

Barrett set her "ambition" at the age of ten: "No woman was ever before such a poet as she would be. As Homer was among men, so would she be among women, —many persons would be obliged to say that she was a little taller than Homer if anything."

She also understood the cultural imperative that to be a good (middle-class) woman was not to be a poet "taller than

Homer" but to have the qualities of a child. Her emphasis in the dedication on imagining herself "a child again" and in the Preface on her "lowness" and "weakness" suggests acceptance of, while in fact rebelling against, the "alien tyranny" that defined her as woman-child in both literature and life. Barrett's comments in the Preface on the composition of "A Drama of Exile," a lyric drama about Adam and Eve just after their expulsion from the Garden of Eden, enact this strategy. The long passage merits careful study.

The subject of the Drama rather fastened on me than was chosen; and the form, approaching the model of the Greek tragedy, shaped itself under my hand, rather by force of pleasure than of design. But when the excitement of composition had subsided, I felt afraid of my position. My subject was the new and strange experience of the fallen humanity, as it went forth from Paradise into the wilderness; with a peculiar reference to Eve's alloted grief, which, considering that self-sacrifice belonged to her womanhood, and the consciousness of originating the Fall to her offence, —appeared to me imperfectly apprehended hitherto, and more expressible by a woman than a man.

There was room, at least, for lyrical emotion in those first steps into the wildemess, —in that first sense of desolation after wrath, —in that first audible gathering of the recriminating "groan of the whole creation,"—in that first darkening of the hills from the recoiling feet of angels, —and in that first silence of the voice of God. And I took pleasure in driving in, like a pile, stroke upon stroke, the Idea of EXILE, —admitting Lucifer as an extreme Adam, to represent the ultimate tendencies of sin and loss, —that it might be strong to bear up the contrary idea of Heavenly love and purity.

But when all was done, I felt afraid, as I said before, of my position. I had promised my own prudence to shut close the gates of Eden between Milton and myself, so that none might say I dared to walk in his footsteps. He should be within, I thought, with his Adam and Eve unfallen or falling, —and I, without, with my EXILES, —I also an exile! It would not do.

The subject, and his glory covering it, swept through the

gates, and I stood full in it, against my will, and contrary to my vow, —till I shrank back fearing, almost desponding; hesitating to venture even a passing association with our great poet before the face of the public.

Whether at last I took courage for the venture, by a sudden revival of that love of manuscript which should be classed by moral philosophers among the natural affections, or by the encouraging voice of a dear friend, it is not interesting to the reader to inquire. Neither could the fact affect the question; since I bear, of course, my own responsibilities. For the rest, Milton is too high, and I am too low, to render it necessary for me to disavow any rash emulation of his divine faculty on his own ground; while enough individuality will be granted, I hope, to my poem, to rescue me from that imputation of plagiarism which should be too servile a thing for every sincere thinker. After all, and at the worst, I have only attempted, in respect to Milton, what the Greek dramatists achieved lawfully in respect to Homer.

They constructed dramas on Trojan ground; they raised on the buskin and even clasped with the sock, the feet of Homeric heroes; yet they neither imitated their Homer nor emasculated him.... To this analogy—the more favourable to me from the obvious exception in it, that Homer's subject was his own possibly by creation, —whereas Milton's was his own by illustration only, —I appeal.

To this analogy—not to this comparison, be it understood—I appeal. For the analogy of the stronger may apply to the weaker; and the reader may have patience with the weakest while she suggests the application. Barrett initially denies responsibility for the subject matter of "A Drama of Exile": "it rather fastened on me than was chosen." She places herself in a male tradition when she claims that her poem was "approaching the model of Greek tragedy," but immediately undercuts such assertiveness, "I felt afraid of my position." Yet the ensuing description of the poem reveals not fear, but a confident exposition of her subject matter as "the new and strange experience of the fallen humanity."

She elaborates on the aspect of the Fall that most interests her, "Eve's alloted grief," then quietly challenges Milton: this aspect has been "imperfectly apprehended hitherto, and [is] more expressible by a woman than a man." Her assertion is tempered, however, by an apologetic justification, as though she already felt her own posi tion challenged: "There was room, at least, for lyrical emotion in those first steps into the wilderness."

She imagines "that first silence of the voice of God," as both a "desolation after wrath" and also a silence that allows her "pleasure... in the Idea of EXILE." Her concern for "Eve's alloted grief" shifts to the male actors in this drama: "I took pleasure in driving in like a pile, stroke upon stroke, the Idea of EXILE, —admitting Lucifer as an extreme Adam, to represent the ultimate tendencies of sin and loss." Yet Barrett ends the burst of verbal "masculine" energy on the anticlimactic "feminine" notes of "Heavenly love and purity."

Like Milton's, Barrett's rhetoric indicates a greater delight in the energies of the exiled than the obedience of the pure. Having embraced her commitment to "Eve's alloted grief" and the vigour of the "Idea of EXILE," she follows her tame commitment to "love and purity" by reiterating "I felt afraid." Her fear is that of a daughter who has "dared to walk in [the father's] footsteps."

As though confessing an "anxiety of influence," Barrett states that she had tried to "shut close the gates of Eden between Milton and myself." This is the first mention of Milton's name, though his presence haunts the Preface. In a reversal of conventional gender roles, Barrett tries to confine Milton inside a place of domestic innocence: "He should be within... with his Adam and Eve unfallen or falling." Barrett places herself outside in the male world of experience: "and I, without, with my EXILES, —I also an exile!"

This crucial claim has a felt urgency inexplicable from the context. Its meaning can only be surmised as speaking to her sense of exile as a writer from the Miltonic tradition. This is not, however, a totally negative position: her rhetoric reveals delight in her usurpation of the masculine sexual rhythms implicit in her "pleasure in driving in like a pile, stroke upon stroke, the Idea of EXILE." Yet "exile" also dramatizes her felt duty to abandon such energy for the submissively asexual female world of "love and purity."

The Preface states what "A Drama of Exile" demonstrates, Barrett's failure to achieve a truly visionary rereading of Milton's poem. She could not keep Milton confined in his text, in his garden of innocence; she could not rewrite his poem from her exiled female perspective. The Preface speaks more clearly to this issue than does the poem itself: "The subject, and his glory covering it, swept through the gates, and I stood full in it, against my will, and contrary to my vow, —till I shrank back fearing, almost desponding" (emphasis mine). The "alien tyranny" of Milton's text overpowered her, not because she believed in man's supremacy, but because she was subject to it "against [her] will."

Although she rallied, "took courage for the venture" and wrote her poem, the result is dominated by Milton's male ideology. Barrett's closing remarks on the "Drama" rationalize her attempt to speak to "Eve's alloted grief" and the "Idea of EXILE." Sensitive to criticisms of and expectations about women's work, she clears herself from charges of imitation and emasculation by claiming that her work in relation to Milton's is analogous to what "the Greek dramatists achieved lawfully in respect to Homer." Homer's "subject was his own possibly by creation" whereas Milton's was his "by illustration only."

Milton interpreted the gender economy according to his ideology; Barrett claims implicitly the right to redefine that economy her way. She rationalizes her right through legal language, reflecting on what the Greek dramatists "achieved lawfully" and reiterating that hers is a case she can rightfully "appeal." But the woman who dedicated herself as a child to her biological father ends the dialectic between assertion and submission with the latter, referring to herself, Milton's literary daughter, as the "weakest" writer.

The Preface is the key to Barrett's poetics: "Eve's alloted grief... imperfectly apprehended hitherto, and more expressible by a woman than a man." Yet its very rhetoric dramatizes the difficulties she had in realizing her aesthetic. The traditionally male rhetoric in which Barrett expresses her determination to explore the hitherto male territory of "the wilderness... in that first silence of the voice of God," gives way to the rhetoric of the "poetesses," rife with "fear," "love," "purity," and weakness. She juxtaposes the assertive woman's usurpation of patriarchal power with the woman-as-child-as-poetess's appeasement of the "alien tyranny" of the Father—be it God, Milton, or Mr. Barrett.

If Milton's voice was the paternal influence inhibiting Barrett's portrayal of Eve in "A Drama of Exile," George Sand's was the maternal voice confirming Barrett's attempts to liberate herself from the "alien tyranny" of Milton's vision. Barrett first men tioned Aurore Dupin, Baronne Dudevant, George Sand, in a letter to Mary Russell Mitford, dated November 21, 1842, in which she confessed her "secret" of "reading... the new French literature."

She questions, rather coyly, whether Mitford thinks "it is very naughty of [her] to read naughty books." "Curious beyond the patience of [her] Eve-ship," she justifies such reading because she lives "out of the world altogether" and is "lonely enough & old enough & sad enough & experienced enough in every sort of good & bad reading, not to be hurt personally by a French superfluity of bad." Among those writers she mentions is the "shameless" George Sand. It is unclear whether Barrett's reference to her "Eve-ship" refers to her writing of "A Drama of Exile" or to her impatience with the role of innocence, silence, and submission culturally assigned to the suffering Eve/woman. However, George Sand's novels of female passion and assertion, of questioning the inequality in marital relationships, modeled an alternative that soothed some of her earlier "steady indignation against Nature who made [her] a woman".

Her reading of French novels, and especially of the "shameless" George Sand, invited charges of shamelessness against herself. Barrett reveals in her letters on the subject curious contradictions. She writes Mitford that Sand is "a true woman of genius" and allows to Browning that she is one woman who does not demonstrate an intellectual inferiority to men, who has "all that breadth & scope of faculty which women want"; her Consuelo is "a sort of rambling Odyssey, a female Odyssey". Yet she also refers to Sand as "this brilliant monstrous woman", as one who is "eloquent as a fallen angel", as a woman who "has something monstrous in combination with her genius". Barrett's sense of Sand as "monstrous" is, she explains to Mitford, "a bare expression of the sort of feeling with which one regards a woman whenever she leans to the aggrandizement of the physical aspect of passion".

Sand's frank portrayal of female sensuality may have caused Barrett less embarrassment than a feeling of duty to express such sentiments to the proper Miss Mitford, who felt "righteous indignation on the subject of Madame Dudevant". Barrett allows that Lelia is a "serpent book" of "soul-slime", the reading of which made her blush "in my solitude to the ends of my fingers".

Such "vileness" notwithstanding, French literature, and Sand's work in particular, made Barrett's "whole being" ache so that her quotidian existence at home seemed "all so neutral tinted and dull and cold by comparison." She respected this literature's refusal to be bound by convention: "It is as if the soul of the thinker were given to the four winds & the multitudinous waters, without hold or compass, —& as if in this great tornado of being she lost sight of the localities & relations both of Heaven & Earth".

Sand offered Barrett womanhood beyond the "love and purity" of her "Eve-ship": "she who is man & woman together", "this brilliant monstrous woman." Barrett claimed Sand's passionate intellect while apparently repudiating it by calling her "monstrous." Sand united Jane Eyre with Bertha Mason, harmonizing the "angel" and "monster" of female experience documented by Gilbert and Gubar in The Madwoman in the Attic. In her admiration of Sand as a writer who is "eloquent as a fallen angel," Barrett embraced the satanic implications of Sand's work for women. Whatever ambivalences Barrett felt or was obliged to feel about Sand, she acknowledged her "naughty secret" publicly by publishing her two sonnets addressed to Sand in the Poems of 1844. She told Mitford: "Mr. Kenyon told me I was 'a daring person' for the introduction of those sonnets. He had heard an able man say at his table a day or two before, that no modest woman would or ought to confess to an acquaintance with the works of George Sand".

Maybe part of the daring was embodied in the form of the poems. Although Milton, Wordsworth, and Keats had adapted the sonnet, its origins lay in love. Certainly Barrett was aware of the original "very strictest Italian form", and Patricia Thomson underscores this resonance: "The love affair of Elizabeth Barrett with George Sand is much less celebrated than her romance with Browning, but, in its own way, it was as intense, as liberating and as clearly, if not as fully, documented." Barrett's two sonnets, "To George Sand, A Desire" and "To George Sand, A Recognition," overtly documented this literary affair. In the opening of "To George Sand, A Desire," Barrett ad dresses George Sand by her "self-called" male name, evoking the God-like creativity and male power over words that Sand has usurped. Sand violates the accepted gender economy by valorizing her woman's intellect with man's emotions.

The "lions" of her "tumultuous senses," with which her soul answers "roar for roar," represent her "monstrous" aspect. Barrett recognizes, however, that Sand's readers misperceive her passionate soul and senses when they respond to her as to an "applauded circus"; her sexuality has become a popular act. In the second quatrain she wishes Sand to transcend, therefore, her lionlike physicality and represents her soul as a demiangel with powerful swan wings beating from her "strong shoulders."

The masculine force of the lion is still implied in the power necessary for this ascent. Rescuing Sand's "nobler nature" from the "tumultuous senses" that her readers vulgarize, Barrett imagines how Sand's true genius, her "strength and science," could be freed from the contamination of her sexuality to flood the world with "holier light." The sestet desexes Sand totally: the swan's wings become angel's wings, the setting is neither earth nor sky, but Heaven. Barrett separates Sand's soul from physicality, purifying the woman whose life is imaged as an "applauded circus."

She represents her as one whom an innocent "child and maiden" can "embrace" and "kiss upon [her] lips a stainless fame." Sexual passion is transformed into a kiss of innocence, the woman artist into the domestic angel. The poem works with exaggeration, both of the gross way in which readers turn Sand into an "applauded circus" and of the purity which is the alternative.

It demonstrates the monster-angel dichotomy of woman and is unable to offer any integration of the two. The sonnet's language and rhythm emphasize its anticlimactic nature: the assertive stresses of the opening line, "Thou large-brained woman and large-hearted man," are dramatically contrasted with the almost tripping rhythm of the last, "To kiss upon thy lips a stainless fame."

It is hard to tell whether this transformation of Sand represents Barrett's true feelings, or whether, as Thomson hypothesizes, it is "revealing, both of Elizabeth Barrett's own deep involvement and her consciousness of a censorious public, whom she attempts to propitiate with such terms as 'angel,' 'pure,' 'holier,' 'stainless,' 'maiden,' 'no bler.'" It does allow Barrett both to acknowledge her admiration for Sand publicly and also to defend herself from the criticism that "no modest woman would or ought to confess an acquaintance with the works of George Sand."

"To George Sand, A Recognition" is quite another kind of sonnet. Again it uses the Petrarchan form, but carries none of the Petrarchan idealizing of the beloved that "A Desire" exploits. Having appeased her public with the first sonnet, in the second Barrett states the nature of Sand's importance for her. This sonnet speaks to the dialectic between Milton's influence and Sand's own. If the recitative is Barrett's statement in the Preface that she intends to speak with "peculiar reference to Eve's alloted grief," then the aria in "A Recognition" elaborates on that "grief," and on Sand's articulation of it. The opening quatrain is a question. Drawing from her notion that

George Sand is "she who is man & woman together", Barrett emphasizes that masculine qualities can never disguise Sand, who is a "true woman" possessed of a "woman's nature" that connects her to "the gauds and armlets worn / By weaker women in captivity." Recognizing women as a class, Barrett questions whether Sand for all her apparent "manly scorn" can ever deny belonging to that class. "Ah, vain denial" dismisses such severance as impossible. This connects her with Sand: the 1844 poems demonstrate both Barrett's own separation from the traditional role of woman and also her very real sense of "captivity."

This sonnet seeks to define woman ("true woman," "woman's nature," "weaker women," "woman's voice," "woman's hair," and "woman-heart"); it is a bleak definition. The Biblical notion of "Eve's alloted grief" triumphs: woman is in "captivity," she sobs and speaks with "voice forlorn," and knows "dishevelled strength in agony." She is, however, beyond "Eve-ship" in her capability of speaking about her lot with a "revolted cry." Barrett recognizes Sand's accomplishment as resonating to her own purposes: to be a spokeswoman for those who are not privileged and who feel with "spasm, not a speech," a Promethean usurper of the God-granted male power of language.

The second quatrain (which extends into the ninth line) answers the question the speaker poses in the first. No costume can mask woman's essential nature, and woman, traditionally assigned to a life of suffering, must express her condition. She will, thereby, find her strength, symbolized by the wild hair that is freed or tamed in so much of Victorian literature as either expression or suppression of woman's passion and imagination. If the second quatrain answers the first, the sestet explains the answer, with a curious dichotomy between the "world" and "we." "The world" sees Sand as a poet burning in a "poet-fire," but "we" see "thy woman-heart beat evermore / Through the large flame." The "world" implies men (or all readers who— wittingly or not—read within patriarchal blinkers) who know her as a writer; whereas "we," the women, recognize how Sand's "woman-heart" informs her work.

Women's literature was conventionally patronized and trivialized. However, women writers who, defying their cultural roles, wrote "through the large flame" of the hitherto male "poet-fire"—as did Sand, and as Barrett aspired to do—challenged the identification of male with universal. Sand wrote of the "revolted cry" of woman, Barrett of "Eve's alloted grief": women, if not the "world," recognize the shift in gender and poetic assumptions when the "poet-fire" is informed by a "woman-heart."

"A Recognition" is essentially an aesthetic manifesto, rooted (if a little spasmodically) in the actual world. But the last two and a half lines are curious: with a quick switch, echoing "A Desire," Barrett imagines Sand again unsexed on the "heavenly shore," a spirit. Although there is a linguistic/imagistic transition from "the woman-heart" beating to "beat purer, heart," the rhetorical and emotional transition feels forced. The final image is of death, the "heavenly shore." Only there will God "unsex" Sand, liberate her from the demands her "poet-fire" puts on her "woman-heart." The switch from earth to heaven is analogous to the switch in Barrett's Preface from the assertive energy of imagining the "pleasure in driving in, like a pile, stroke upon stroke, the Idea of EXILE" to the passive stasis of "heavenly love and purity." It may repudiate the "dishevelled strength in agony" of woman's lot, but it also detracts from the passion of the "body" of the sonnet, by "purifying" it into spirit. The religious language of the last lines, "purer," "unsex," "heavenly," "unincarnate," "purely," deflect from Sand's and Barrett's earthly purpose as women writers.

The influence of Milton and Sand, demonstrated so dramatically in the Preface and the George Sand sonnets, dominates the Poems of 1844. Milton evokes the male tradition that locates woman as his object: Sand confirms Barrett's subversion of that text. When woman speaks back, hers will be a different and equally important story. The Poems of 1844 reveal some progress toward this latter ideal over The Seraphim, and Other Poems, but they demonstrate most noticeably a dialectic between, not a synthesis of, the two influences. Barrett's seclusion led her, in Poems of 1844, both to recognize and rebel against her literary confinement: whereas the Preface and the George Sand sonnets speak to those issues, her ballads are the most interesting dramatization of them. Poe, for all his reservations about Barrett's idiosyncratic work, recognized and admired its "happy audacity of thought and expression never before known in one of her sex." If the conscious awareness of Milton inhibited Barrett when she attempted to imagine the Fall from woman's perspective, the revisionary programme she identified in her Preface is obliquely manifest in the rebellion against the patriarchy dramatized by the courtly ladies of her ballads. They foreshadowed Barrett's own rejection of what she painfully came to understand as imprisonment in her father's room.

Chapter 7

Woman and Artist: Both Complete

In Casa Guidi Windows Barrett Browning demonstrated confidence in her mature voice: her decision to free herself from the yoke of her father's "alien tyranny" informed her commitment to Italian liberation; and the unification she desired for Italy resonated to the unification of "woman" and "poet" that Casa Guidi Windows enacts. Secure in her position vis-à-vis the poetic past that had both nurtured and imprisoned her, Barrett Browning made public her "highest convictions upon Life and Art" and dramatized in Aurora Leigh the process whereby she achieved that integration of woman and poet.

Bloom has asserted that all poets are both nurtured and imprisoned by their poetic past and must free themselves from their precursors' influence. As feminist criticism on Barrett Browning and other female poets has shown, however, the process of liberation is quite different for a female than for a male poet. The male poet bears the same relationship to the world as his precursor; both imagine themselves as the subject of experience. Aurora Leigh suggests that as long as poetry is imagined as a predominantly male endeavor, a female poet enacts her liberation by transforming herself from being the object of male narrative to being the subject of her own story.

In The Battle of Marathon, her translation of Prometheus Bound, "The Seraphim," and "A Drama of Exile," Barrett Browning attempted themes and forms associated with the male poetic tradition. Encouraged by these attempts to take herself seriously as a poet, she was nevertheless inhibited by her precursors, and those poems are interesting revelations more of the costs of "anxiety of influence" and of "authorship" than of accomplishment. Aurora Leigh is her mature appropriation of the tradition. In the blank verse of Milton's epic, Barrett Browning writes of a heroine who refuses to be merely a helpmate. In spite of being taught by her aunt and lectured by her cousin Romney in the Miltonic ways of womanhood, Aurora insists on claiming for herself the Adamic privilege of naming the world.

Although Aurora Leigh was published in 1856, Barrett Browning had been planning such a poem for many years. In one of her earliest letters to Browning she wrote:

My chief intention just now is the writing of a sort of novel-poem—a poem as completely modern as "Geraldine's Courtship," running into the midst of our conventions, & rushing into drawing-rooms & the like "where angels fear to tread"; & so, meeting face to face & without mask the Humanity of the age, & speaking the truth as I conceive of it, out plainly.

That is my intention. It is not mature enough yet to be called a plan. I am waiting for a story, & I won't take one, because I want to make one, & I like to make my own stories, because then I can take liberties with them in the treatment. Barrett Browning's original intention of "making" rather than "taking" a story seems thwarted in Aurora Leigh's echoes of Corinne, George Sand, Ruth, Jane Eyre, and "The Princess," such that the whole poem appears "an overlapping sequence of dialogues with other texts."

Nevertheless, her epic poem uniting woman and poet tells a story essentially her own, and this early letter identifies the crucial qualities of what came to be Aurora Leigh: its insistence on modernity, on "this live, throbbing age"; its defiance of conventions—the female poet questions the sex/gender economy and writes of rape, prostitution, illegitimacy, and the working class; and its location of heroic action in "drawing-rooms" rather than on the battle-fields with medieval "Roland [and] his knights at Roncesvalles". Barrett's refer ence to "rushing into drawing-rooms & the like 'where angels fear to tread'" now has an ironic cast.

Identifying herself with the "fools [who] rush in" rather than with the timid angels, Barrett asserts an earthiness over a spirituality. But her statement carries for us now the paradox that the Victorian middle-class woman, who ideologically belonged in the drawing-room with her sewing, flower arranging, morning visitors, and piano, was spiritualized into Angel in the House. Barrett, however, imagines the "angels" as being afraid of drawing-rooms, implying that "angels [will] fear to tread" in the drawing-room of her design. Even at such an early stage of her "intention," Barrett Browning named the form Aurora Leigh was to take, the "novel poem."

Her adoption of a persona suggests she needed "fictional characters to carry the charge of her experience as a woman artist" so that she could speak "the truth... out plainly," and belies her intention to meet "face to face & without Mask the Humanity of the age." But her writing of a "novel-poem" is also the synthesis of the male and female traditions between which she shifted uneasily throughout her career. Aurora's assertive "I write" is the culmination of the progression in Barrett Browning's work from "I thought" (Sonnets from the Portuguese), to "I stand" ("The Runaway Slave at Pilgrim's Point"), and "I heard" (Casa Guidi Windows); it combines a female speaker with a hitherto male-defined activity. The male epic tradition and the female novel form her voice.

The female tradition, to which Aurora Leigh was heir, included the influences of both women novelists and poetesses. First, the heroine of Madame de Stael's Corinne provided, as Ellen Moers demonstrates, a generation of women writers with the typology of England as a land of repression and Italy as a place of creative and sexual possibility for women. Corinne, however, although a renowned poet, ultimately dies from lack of love. George Sand's "revolted cry," her "woman's voice," her "dishevelled strength in agony," had long influenced Barrett Browning. Sand's life-long reevaluation of gender relations is also one of Aurora's concerns and Sand's life in Paris resonates in Aurora's life as a writer in London. The initial freedom these French influences offered was reinforced by Barrett Browning's English contemporaries. She wrote to Mrs. Martin in 1853: "Tell me if you have read Mrs. Gaskell's 'Ruth.' That's a novel which I much admire. It is strong and healthy at once, teaching a moral frightfully wanted in English society.... 'Villette,' too... is very powerful".

Ruth must have suggested or confirmed Barrett Browning's conviction that a story such as Marian Erle's should be the subject not only of novels but of poetry, and Villette shares with Aurora Leigh an unreliable narrator who ultimately finds professional and sexual fulfillment outside of England. The second female influence was that of the poetesses. When Aurora finally acknowledges her love for Romney, she claims, "Art is much, but Love is more". Whereas Barrett eschewed the "affections" of the poetesses to model her poetry after the male tradition, Barrett Browning's mature voice incorporated their concerns into art. Aurora initially imagines such affections as associated with Romney's types of "doating mothers, and perfect wives, / Sublime Madonnas, and enduring saints", but she comes to understand through her engagement with Marian Erle in Paris that art is enriched by the love of a "common woman." Her statement, far from a renunciation of her art, claims a denigrated female tradition as an integral aspect of poetry, yet redefines that tradition to include the subjectivity of woman's sexual passion.

Although Ruskin wrote to Browning that Aurora Leigh was the greatest poem in the English language and "the first poetical expression of the Age," and Swinburne recorded, "no English contemporary poet by profession has left us work so full of living fire," the reviewers' responses were more complex, providing a remarkable counterpoint to the poem; they betrayed in their discussion the very ideologies that Aurora Leigh addressed. Response was mixed over what Barrett Browning was attempting in her epic infused with female concerns. The Athenaeum represented those disturbed by "a mingling of what is precious with what is mean—of the voice of clarion and the lyric cadence of harp with the cracked school-room spinet—of tears and small talk—of eloquent apostrophe and adust speculation—of the grandeur of passion and the pettiness of modes and manners." Although admiring the "glorious chords and melodies" of some passages, the reviewer was distressed that "Milton's organ is put by Mrs. Browning to play polkas in May-Fair drawing-rooms."

The Dublin University Magazine, however, saw the contrast between Aurora's meditation on art in Book 5 and the subsequent episode of the party at Lord Howe's as part of a tradition epitomized by Shakespeare in his depiction of "the coarse or foolish, or the low in thought and expression, following quickly upon the elevated and poetic." This representation was felt to be true to "real life": "The common-place and prosaic ever touching upon but not blending with the sublime and poetic, like colours which set off each other when in juxta-position, but do not lose their distinctive characters by fusion. Such a fusion the author might easily have effected by clothing the sentiments of the ball-room men and women in poetic language; but she would then have been neither true to their nature nor to her own art."

Even this sensitive critic did not fully appreciate Barrett Browning's achievement: Shakespeare separated the "low in thought and expression" from "the elevated" by the use of prose rather than poetry. Barrett Browning, however, incorporated both the "common-place and prosaic" and the "sublime and poetic" into what the Westminster Review identified as the "high fever" of Aurora's narration. C. Castan described more precisely "the particular tonal quality" as one in which the "narrating suffering Aurora, moves along the mountain range of her passion."

The crucial point here is that, while the vocabulary may represent high and low life, the same voice narrates both the sublime and the commonplace in the epic form: an intelligent woman's life perforce included in easy or uneasy juxtaposition both the life of the intellect and of the drawing-room in a way that a man's culturally did not. The Athenaeum accurately predicted readers' responses to this portrayal of woman in saying: "To some [Aurora Leigh] will be so much rank foolishness, —to others almost a spiritual revelation". Barrett

Browning had "expected to be put in the stocks and pelted with the eggs of the last twenty years' 'singing birds' as a disorderly woman and freethinking poet! ", so she was surprised to hear of "quite decent women taking the part of the book in a sort of effervescence" which led her to "modify [her] opinions somewhat upon [people's] conventionality, to see the progress made in freedom of thought". She also heard the response she feared, "the 'mamas of England' in a body refuse to let their daughters read it".

Such "mamas"' fears inform the responses of even sympathetic reviewers to the issues Aurora Leigh addresses. The Dublin University Magazine is paradigmatic: "We are disposed to think that no better test can be found of the civilization and enlightenment of any people than the position which woman attains to amongst them, both in a social and intellectual point of view". It lauded Barrett Browning's protest against the "social wrongs of woman" in her "greatest poem", and yet, belying its earlier liberalism, the review ended with a reactionary conclusion:

Indeed in the effort to stand, not on a pedestal beside man, but actually to occupy his place, we see Mrs. Browning commit grave errors. She assumes as it were the gait and the garb of man, but the stride and the strut betray her. She is occasionally coarse in expression and unfeminine in thought; and utters what, if they be even truths, are so conveyed that we would hesitate to present them to the eye of the readers of her own sex. There is nothing that detracts so much from the pleasure which the perusal of this poem has given us, as this conviction, that the authoress has written a book which is almost a closed volume for her own sex. The days when such women as Aphra Behn can hope to be palatable to the female sex are, we believe, gone for ever. Woman must be ever true to her womanly instincts if she would be the meet helper as well as companion of man. We grieve to find such a woman as Elizabeth Barrett Browning, even in a phrase or sentiment, forgetful of that nature.

Unlike George Eliot, who celebrated Barrett Browning as "the first woman who has produced a work which exhibits all the peculiar powers without the negations of her sex," the Dublin University Magazine saw Barrett Browning as usurping man's place. The passage is rife with irony. First: the fact that she "utters... truths" of women's lives—work, rape, prostitution, illegitimacy, maternity, and the sex/gender economy—designates the work "a closed volume" to the women whose experience it depicts. Second: depicting women's lives in verse "coarse in ex pression and unfeminine in thought" violates Barrett Browning's "womanly instincts" making her "forgetful of [her] nature." Marian Erle speaks to this:

We wretches cannot tell out all our wrong
Without offcncc to dcccnt happy folk.
I know that we must scrupulously hint
With half-words, delicate reserves, the thing
Which no one scrupled we should feel in full.

The review maintains that woman's "social and intellectual" position is of concern only insofar as it conforms to patriarchal definitions of "womanly instincts" and "nature." When a woman tells her own nature she "assumes... the gait and the garb of man." The reviewer privileges male fantasy over female experience of women. The ultimate irony is that when Barrett Browning finally wrote as "I" she was condemned as being too much like a man, whereas earlier when her femaleness wore a male disguise she was lauded as the best poetess. The reviews manifest two misreadings of Aurorà Leigh. The Dublin University Magazine epitomizes the first by arguing that the poem intended to exemplify woman in her role as "meet helper as well as companion to man." To praise the poem as Barrett Browning's "greatest" while reinterpreting it is double speak.

The reviewer praises the revelation of woman's "social suffering" and her "highest intellectual development," yet declares the poem a failure in its refusal of Biblical and Miltonic precepts: "In the failure both of Romney and Aurora to work out to a prosperous issue their own theories, is finally exhibited to an extent, perhaps beyond what the author intended, the ulter dependence of each sex upon the other, the truth that if a primaeval decree gave man the dominion, it was as much for woman's happiness as his own—a dominion which the holy principle of love turns into a blessing to both, by making obedience an anticipating assent". Although Aurora Leigh may conceivably demonstrate the "dependence of each sex on the other," it emphatically does not illustrate "the truth that if a primaeval decree gave man the dominion, it was as much for woman's happiness as his own." It is puzzling to see how the blinded Romney exhorting Aurora to her work and, in effect, becoming her muse could be expressing his dominion over her.

The reviewer's need for such a resolution is echoed by the Athenaeum's finding the "argument unnatural", by Blackwood's wishing "Mrs. Browning had selected a more natural and intelligible theme," and by Coventry Patmore's dismissal of the poem in the North British Review because the "development of [Aurora's] powers as a poetess is elaborately depicted; but as Mrs. Browning is herself almost the only modem example of such development, the story is uninteresting from its very singularity." Patmore's reasoning is especially disturbing; if being a poet is problematic for a woman because the tradition has been male-defined, then that system is perpetuated if a poem about the growth of a woman poet's mind is ignored for its "singularity."

The second misreading is represented by those who dismiss Aurora, discovering the poem's excellence in the depiction of Marian Erle. They endorse a conservative ideology restricting woman to her maternal role. Thus Blackwood's regretted that "the extreme independence of Aurora detracts from the feminine charm, and mars the interest which we otherwise might have felt for so intellectual a heroine," whereas Marian "does undoubtedly attract our sympathies more than the polished and high-minded Aurora,... as the mother of a hapless child. There indeed, Mrs. Browning has achieved a triumph".

Likewise the Westminster Review appreciated the "picture of innocence and maternal fondness such as perhaps has never before been realized in verse," whereas the poet-narrator's "self-consciousness repels—her speculations do not much interest us". In sum, the reviewers reveal the very patriarchal ideologies that Barrett Browning was addressing: they admire the poem, but dislike Aurora's independence and exalt Marian as mother with child; they sympathize with Barrett Browning's indictment of women's "social wrongs," yet accuse her thereby of "prov[ing] her manhood"; they admire Barrett Browning's poem, yet want to see Aurora under man's dominion as Romney's helpmate; they are touched by Marian's story but dislike the coarseness with which it is expressed.

In short, they reflect the age's turmoil over the representation of woman.

Aurora Leigh's story dramatizes how she reconciled these con tradictions. First, as a poet she identifies with the male tradition until she realizes, to use de Beauvoir's terms with which I began this study, that "to play at being a man [is] a source of frustration." Second, through Marian Erle she owns her "woman's passion", then experiences how "to play at being a woman is also a delusion" when she offers herself to Romney as object of his love and need. Finally, she engages sexually and intellectually as Romney's equal, and on a symbolic level she renders him (who in his blindness evokes the blind precursors, Homer, Aeschylus, Milton, and even Mr. Boyd) into her muse. Her development parallels Barrett Browning's "frustration" in her work through the Poems of 1844, her "delusion" in the Sonnets from the Portuguese until she objectifies the poet-beloved as her Muse, and her assertive subjectivity in "The Runaway Slave at Pilgrim's Point," Casa Guidi Windows, and Aurora Leigh.

The structure of Aurora Leigh is significant as a representation of Aurora's transformation. Castan established the narrative time scheme of the poem: through Book 5 Aurora is twenty seven years old, narrating her life story on the evening she decides to leave England and return to Florence; by the end of Book 5 the "youthful confident" Aurora has caught up with the "sadder" narrator who, unlike those in Jane Eyre and Great Expectations, does not know the outcome of her story, and therefore is not fully reliable; in Books 6-9 the "story has caught up with the narrator and till the end of the poem they stay together." I want to extend these observations: the later books resemble journal entries in that Aurora records events as they occur. Her readers, thereby, experience the denouement as Aurora does, rather than mediated by her mature knowledge. The tightly structured plot is as important as the narrative time sequence: the events recorded in Books I-4 are repeated in reverse order in Books 6-9, dividing the poem into two parts:Written in England:

- Aurora's parents' marriage, her childhood in Italy, adolescence in England, birth as a poet.
- Romney's proposal on Aurora's twentieth birthday.
- Aurora as a writer in London, introduction of Lady Waldemar, Marian Erle's story.
- Marian's story continued, the abortive wedding.
- A pivotal book: Aurora's meditation on Art, Lord Howe's party, Aurora's decision to leave England for Italy.

Written in Paris and Italy:

- Aurora's discovery of Marian in Paris, Marian's explanation of the abortive wedding, Marian's second story.
- Marian's story continued, the journey to Italy, letters to Lord Howe and Lady Waldemar.
- Romney's arrival in Florence, his and Aurora's reassessment of the discussion that took place on her twentieth birthday.
- Marian's refusal to marry Romney, Aurora's union with Romney, her rebirth as a poet.

Aurora repeats, in the last four books, the experiences of the first four, but engages in them very differently. Whereas Book I records the union of Aurora's parents, Book 9 celebrates the union between Romney and Aurora. Book 2 records Romney's proposal and Aurora's rejection of it, whereas Book 8 contains the cousins' reinterpretation of that day. Books 3 and 7 tell of the attempted and actual rape of Marian, whereas Book 4 records the abortive wedding and Book 6 gives

Marian's explanation for her failure to appear at it. The poem describes a narrative return that can be schematized:

England		Abroad
I	Union	9
2	Romney and Aurora,	8
	her twentieth birthday	
3	Marian's story	7
4	Marian's story,	6
	the wedding	
	5	
	Art	

Whereas the first books offer a mediated though unfinished autobiography, the last four demonstrate in episodic fashion the stages in Aurora's integration of woman and poet, her transfor mation from being the object of Romney's gaze to being the subject of her own vision. The *National Review* had an inkling of this in its assessment of the poem's controversial ending:

She learns the error of her life, —that she had striven to be an artist instead of a woman, rather than been content to be a simple woman, and let her art spring from that true basis; and the truth, which is the deepest moral of the work, overwhelms her with its sudden conviction, that great as is art, greater is the human life of the artist; and greatest, love, which is the centre of that life and of all life—... As the theme deepens, and the faulty artist forgets herself in the true poet, the verse runs smooth and clear.

The transformation of the "faulty artist" into the "true poet" is effected by Aurora's refusal to identify "artist" as "man." Whereas the relationship of Aurora to her father and his books informs the first half of the narrative, Marian Erle's experience controls the second half; Aurora's story resolves the conflicts between the male literary and female cultural economies to which Barrett Browning was heir.

Beginning her autobiography on the evening she decides

to leave England, her father's country, for Italy, her mother's land, is Aurora's first step from "faulty artist" to "true poet"; her assumed male identity no longer tolerable, she initiates the journey to womanhood:

Of writing many books there is no end;
And I who have written much in prose and verse
For others' uses, will write now for mine, —
Will write my story for my better self.

Aurora will write "for [her] better self" in order to create that self.

The twenty-seven-year-old Aurora narrates two events exemplifying the sex/gender economy that circumscribes her: her reaction as a child to her dead mother's portrait and her response to Romney's sudden appearance as she crowned herself poet with an ivy wreath on her twentieth birthday. Aurora narrates how her mother's death when she was four left her with a "mother-want about the world". The young child lacked a mother's love, but also a role model; she grew to define being female for herself. Aurora recalls her mother's portrait, a macabre picture painted from the corpse, which was dressed not in the customary funeral shroud, but in her red evening gown. As a young child Aurora found this picture "very strange"; "half in terror, half / In adoration" she would gaze at the "swan-like supernatural white life / Just sailing upward from the red stiff silk". Her gaze transformed the picture on the canvas into different representations of woman that later haunt her narrative. The adult Aurora realizes that as a child she created these images "mixed, confused unconsciously" from "whatever [she] last read or heard or dreamed":

Ghost, fiend, and angel, fairy, witch, and sprite,
A dauntless Muse who eyes a dreadful Fate,
A loving Psyche who loses sight of Love,
A still Medusa with mild milky brows
All curdled and all clothed upon with snakes
Whose slime falls fast as sweat will; or anon
Our Lady of the Passion, stabbed with swords
Where the Babe sucked; or Lamia in her first

Moonlighted pallor, ere she shrunk and blinked
And shuddering wriggled down to the unclean;
Or my own mother.

She recognizes that woman's identity is created by the cultural economy: as a child she read and heard not about woman as artist, but as Muse, Psyche, Medusa, Lamia, and the suffering Madonna. Imprisoned by such literary representations of woman as object of narratives formed from men's terror or adoration of her, part of Aurora's task as a poet is to test these representations against her own experience. Only the Westminster Review commented on this crucial passage, denigrating it as "a perfect shoal of mangled and pompous similes". The criticism is unwittingly ironic: the very muddle that the critic identifies replicates the muddled images of woman available to Aurora.

Aurora does not assume all the roles she identifies in her mother's portrait, but casts Lady Waldemar and Marian into its mythic types. If Lady Waldemar dramatizes Medusa and Lamia, then Marian is cast as Psyche, "who loses sight of love," and "Our Lady of the Passion, stabbed with [metaphoric] swords / Where the Babe sucked." At Lord Howe's party, Aurora "the printing woman" feels alienated from the seductive self-presentation of Lady Waldemar with her "alabaster shoulders and bare breasts, / On which the pearls, drowned out of sight in milk, / Were lost, excepting for the ruby clasp!".

The white of Lady Waldemar's shoulders and breasts and the red of her ruby clasp are reminiscent of the uncanny portrait of Aurora's mother. And, whereas her "heavy ringlets" and "that coil / Of tresses" suggest Medusa, the "twenty stinging snakes" of Lady Waldemar's hatred toward Aurora confirms her as the "Lamia-woman". Aurora writes of these women through patriarchal eyes: Lady Waldemar is neither as monstrous nor Marian as angelic as Aurora fictionalizes them.

The second event representing the sex/gender economy, which in retrospect Aurora recognizes as revealing how she had internalized woman as object of the male gaze, is her reaction to Romney's surprising her when she crowned herself poet. She narrates how on her twentieth birthday, feeling "so young, so strong, so sure of God", she imagined wearing the poet's laurel (as Corinne had been crowned) "In sport, not pride, to learn the feel of it". Aurora recalls choosing ivy, not laurel: "I drew a wreath / Drenched, blinding me with dew, across my brow". However, Romney's appearance transformed her from a woman actively crowning herself a poet to an art object for his gaze, a transformation to which she acquiesced:

I stood there fixed, —
My arms up, like the caryatid, sole
Of some abolished temple, helplessly
Persistent in a gesture which derides
A former purpose.

At twenty-seven, though still not fully formed as an artist, Aurora understands the anachronistic nature of such a gesture. She repressed the energy with which she had earlier "bounded forth" into stasis: "I stood there fixed." Although acknowledging the sacredness of the tradition in which she was represented as a sculpture, a "caryatid," the older Aurora knows that the "temple" or tradition that she then upheld in that role must be "abandoned." Aurora characterizes her situation: "Woman and artist, —either incomplete, / Both credulous of completion". At twenty she had been "helplessly persistent" in her conformity, and yet her gesture of standing "there fixed" under the male gaze only mocked a tradition enriched in its "former purpose" by such a gesture.

Aurora's response to these two events was to assume the identity of subject and [male] poet, rather than of object and woman, an identity suggested by her early association with poetry through her dead father's books. Reading them she felt as though her father "wrapt his little daughter in his large / Man's doublet, careless did it fit or no". As overwhelmed as her creator, who was inhibited by "Milton's glory" when writing "A Drama of Exile," Aurora felt "Among the giant fossils of [her] past, / Like some small nimble mouse between the ribs / Of a mastadon".

Yet her turbulent response to poetry— "my soul, / At poetry's divine first finger-touch, / Let go conventions and sprang up surprised"—presented an alternative to the female occupations privileged by her aunt. The latter included an education in a smattering of religion, languages, mathematics, geography, history; a "general insight into useful facts"; embroidery; and the reading of books that proved woman's "right of comprehending husband's talk," "their angelic reach / Of virtue," and their "potential faculty in everything / Of abdicating power in it". Until she read poetry Aurora recalls,

I only thought
Of lying quiet there where I was thrown
Like sea-weed on the rocks, and suffering her
To prick me to a pattern with her pin,
Fibre from fibre, delicate leaf from leaf,
And dry out from my drowned anatomy
The last sea-salt left in me.

Under her aunt's tutelage, Aurora almost sank into female invalidism, until reading and writing of poetry averted it. Her "quickening inner life" so distressed her aunt that Aurora, projecting her rage onto "teas[ing] / The patient needle till it split the thread," learned deception as a strategy for survival while her "soul was singing at a work apart / Behind the wall of sense". Because her aunt had inculcated in her female duties, Aurora associated poetry with male activity.

Her early poems, like her creator's, were imitations:
And so, like most young poets, in a flush
Of individual life I poured myself
Along the veins of others, and achieved
Mere lifeless imitations of live verse.

At twenty-seven Aurora reflects as a male poet on her early work, on the facile ease with which she wrote it, laughing at the young self who easily summoned the muse "As if we had seen her purple-braided head, / With the eyes in it, start between the boughs / As often as a stag's." She humorously recalls her "effete results / From virile efforts," her "cold wire-drawn odes," the "bucolics," and "didactics, driven / Against the heels of what the master said". Whereas Aurora will come to admire most a poetry that is "unscrupulously epic", she remembers the "counterfeiting epics" of her youth, in much the same way as her creator recalled her "Battle of Marathon." As Barrett Browning wrote to Kenyon that her 1838 poems in comparison with her earlier work revealed the "difference... between a copy and an individuality", so Aurora knows:

I wrote
False poems, like the rest, and thought them true
Because myself was true in writing them.
I peradventure have writ true ones since
With less complacence.

Romney's marriage proposal was the first assault on Aurora's youthful poetic "complacency" on her twentieth birthday. Ironically, his patronizing and dismissive attitude toward Aurora and her work functioned positively for her. Romney, spokesman of a culture, represented also by Robert Southey in his famous letter to Charlotte Brontë, insisted that Aurora accept the incompatibility between being woman and poet. In fact, he confirmed Aurora in her determination to write, yet forced her to recognize she was a female poet, not a male one. She could not easily discard the "frustration" of the latter any more than her creator could, but the scene signifies her first awareness of her dilemma.

Aurora recreates the dialogue between the cousins, unmediated by her older self. Romney's refusal to read her poetry—as he explains, "I saw at once the thing had witchcraft in't, / Whereof the reading calls up dangerous spirits: / I rather bring it to the witch"—presents woman and artist as irreconcilable opposites. His reassurance only emphasizes her deviance: "I have seen you not too much / Witch, scholar, poet, dreamer, and the rest, / To be a woman also".

To his urging her not to defile her "clean white morning dresses", Aurora, however, asserts, "I choose to walk at all risks". Barrett Browning, who once had not "dared to walk in [Milton's] footsteps", has her heroine striking out her own path and fearlessly walking in it. Romney insists that she realise she is female and therefore not a serious poet; as a poetess, she will receive the "comparative respect / Which means the absolute scorn" of male critics, who will dismiss her work "not as mere work but as mere woman's work" and praise her because "Among our female authors we make room / For this fair writer.../... competent to... spell".

The tone of Romney's comments echoes the critical timbre Barrett, "the fair Elizabeth," received, especially about The Seraphim, and Other Poems. Romney (the voice, as Gelpi interprets him, of Aurora's internalized critic) forces Aurora into verbalizing the cultural conflict between being a woman and an artist:

"You have read
My soul, if not my book, and argue well
I would not condescend... we will not say
To such a kind of praise (a worthless end
Is praise of all kinds), but to such a use
Of holy art and golden life.
... I would rather dance
At fairs on tight-rope, till the babies dropped
Their gingerbread for joy, —than shift the types
For tolerable verse, intolerable
To men who act and suffer. Better far
Pursue a frivolous trade by serious means,
Than a sublime art frivolously."

Aurora measures herself by the standards of Art; Romney judges her a woman fit only to be one of the "doating mothers, and perfect wives, / Sublime Madonnas, and enduring saints". If earlier, referring to Aurora as a "witch," he conjured up the monstrous image of woman represented in Aurora's mother's portrait, he now condemns her to the portrait's angelic aspects. These, Romney imagines, qualify her as wife, as co-worker in his utopian visions of social reform for the poor. Aurora acknowledges his work as worthy but rejects it for herself as his help meet. In refusing Romney, she refuses the Biblical dictum, reinforced in Paradise Lost, that "He [was] for God only, she for God in him." Aurora's declaration is analogous to Jane Eyre's rejection of St. John Rivers:

"What you love
Is not a woman, Romney, but a cause:

You want a helpmate, not a mistress, sir,
A wife to help your ends, —in her no end."

Aurora recognizes Romney's desire for her as object of his life, not subject of her own. Romney, mistaking totally the thrust of her argument, taunts her with being so preoccupied with literature that she desires a literary lover, a sonneteer, who would address her elaborately:

"Lady, thou art wondrous fair,
And, where the Graces walk before, the Muse
Will follow at the lightning of their eyes."

He misses the irony that he is the one condemning Aurora to literary and cultural myths of woman. Aurora's answer to Romney speaks not just to him, but also to Tennyson's Prince, who at the end of "The Princess" insists on the complementarity of man and woman, and, indeed, to Mrs. Ellis, who condemns woman to be a "relative creature":

"You misconceive the question like a man,
Who sees a woman as the complement
Of his sex merely. You forget too much
That every creature, female as the male,
Stands single in responsible act and thought
As also in birth and death. Whoever says
To a loyal woman, 'Love and work with me,'
Will get fair answers if the work and love,
Being good themselves, are good for her—the best
She was born for."
"... But me your work
Is not the best for, nor your love the best."
"I too have my vocation, —work to do."

That women should have work of prime importance is as incomprehensible to Romney as to Aurora's aunt. Aurora echoes Carlyle's insistence on work, but applies it to women as well as men; and whereas Romney echoes Macaulay's and the utilitarians' concern with material needs, Aurora reflects the Victorian emphasis of Carlyle and Arnold, who insisted on feeding the spirit also. Once people are fed, Aurora asks, "What then, / Unless the artist keep up open roads / Betwixt the seen and unseen?"

At twenty Aurora confidently rejected Romney to pursue her commitment as poet. However, when she was questioned by her aunt on Romney's sudden departure Aurora's submissiveness demonstrates how fragile that confidence was: "The lion in me felt the keeper's voice / Through all its quivering dewlaps; I was quelled / Before her, —meekened to the child she knew". Culturally Aurora was seen as "child," or potential wife, as she struggled to be poet, "lion." Reflecting on that day she faces Romney's objections and is ambivalent about her decision. As poet she cannot, she feels with some longing, be a "common woman." By refusing to be "child," or wife, she has rejected being;

happier, less known and less left alone,
Perhaps a better woman after all,
With chubby children hanging on my neck
To keep me low and wise.

In Lady Waldemar's words, Aurora records the cultural economy that creates this separation:

"You stand outside,
You artist women, of the common sex;
You share not with us, and exceed us so
Perhaps by what you're mulcted in, your hearts
Being starved to make your heads: so run the old
Traditions of you."

Such a statement of her own psychic dilemma, voiced by one she loathes, reinforces Aurora's conflict; it is not, however, the monstrous woman who effects the reconciliation of "artist woman" and the "common sex" but the one whom Aurora imagines as angelic. Much of her autobiography records Marian Erle's life; to tell that life, however, Aurora uses different narrative techniques before and after leaving England. In England she emphasizes that the story is in her own language, not Marian's. Practically, this solves a narrative problem for Barrett Browning, allowing her to employ a diction close to her own rather than attempting—as Eliot, Dickens, and Gaskell did—a working-class speech alien to her protected middle-class experience; it also functions structurally in the book. Aurora records:

We talked. She told me all her story out,
Which I'll retell with fuller utterance,
As coloured and confirmed in after times
By others and herself too.
I tell her story and grow passionate.
She, Marian, did not tell it so, but used
Meek words that made no wonder of herself
For being so sad a creature.
She told the tale with simple, rustic turns, —
Strong leaps of meaning in her sudden eyes
That took the gaps of any imperfect phrase
Of the unschooled speaker: I have rather writ
The thing I understood so, than the thing
I heard so. And I cannot render right
Her quick gesticulation, wild yet soft.

Aurora acknowledges her embellishments of Marian's story: she gives it "fuller utterance," with a passion missing in Marian's version.

She is sympathetic to the suffering in Marian's world: to how Marian's father "cursed his wife because, the pence being out, / She could not buy more drink. At which she turned /... and beat her baby in revenge / For her own broken heart"; to how Marian's mother wanted to prostitute her daughter to the squire: "'He means to set you up, and comfort us'"; to how Marian's friends turn to prostitution: "'Poor Rose,... / I heard her laugh last night in Oxford Street'"; and to how the sempstresses must live:

"we've used out many nights,
And worn the yellow daylight into shreds
Which flapped and shivered down our aching eyes
Till night appeared more tolerable, just
That pretty ladies might look beautiful,
Who said at last... 'You're lazy in that house!
'You're slow in sending home the work, —I count
'I've waited nearly an hour for't.'"

But whereas Marian speaks "simple, rustic turns" with "imperfect phrase," Aurora writes not what Marian said but her interpretation of it. The alienation from Marian this implies is reflected in Aurora's subsequent self-reproach "I have been wrong", and her acknowledgement:

I had done a duty, in the visit paid
To Marian, and was ready otherwise
To give the witness of my presence and name
Whenever she should marry...
... I felt
Tired, overworked.

The result is a fiction, apparently empathic with the plight of the poor, yet one that appropriates Marian to Aurora's own likeness:

She told me she was fortunate and calm
On such and such a season, sat and sewed,
With no one to break up her crystal thoughts,
While rhymes from lovely poems span around
Their ringing circles of ecstatic tune,
Beneath the moistened finger of the Hour.

This echoes Aurora's own solace during her adolescent hours of sewing with her aunt. Aurora's middle-class fiction allows her, like Romney, to feel charity toward a poor sufferer while scoming her class. Such scorn informs her attitude to the poor who came to Marian's wedding:

They clogged the streets, they oozed into the church
In a dark slow stream, like blood.
Those, faces? 'twas as if you had stirred up hell
To heave its lowest dreg-fiends uppermost
In fiery swirls of slime.

Aurora finds a kinship with Marian as a woman, even though they are divided so crudely along class lines. When Romney preaches of his "common love" for the "loveless many," Aurora records:

I turned
And kissed poor Marian, out of discontent.
The man had baffled, chafed me, till I flung
For refuge to the woman
She, at least,
Was not built up as walls are, brick by brick,
Each fancy squared, each feeling ranged by line.

Aurora's frustration with the system of man allows her to identify with a woman of a different class for a brief "refuge," which is prophetic of her later meeting with Marian in Paris. What is radical about this fiction, however, even at this stage of Aurora's development, is the inclusion of Marian as a major character in her epic autobiography. Although Aurora objectifies Marian, as Romney does (and as Dante Gabriel Rosetti objectifies the prostitute in "Jenny"), her record of her is a powerfully ironic juxtaposition to Romney's patronizing praise,

"You, at least,
Have ruined no one through your dreams. Instead,
You've helped the facile youth to live youth's day
With innocent distraction."

Although Romney no longer labels her "witch," he condemns her as a poetess in his summary of her work as an "innocent distraction" and with his injunction, "Dear, be happy. Sing your songs, / If that's your way". Writing her "better self," Aurora's task is to make clear the difference between her "song" and that expected of the poetesses, and to refuse to be hampered by "this vile woman's way" of caring more for one man's (Romney's) approval, than for "Art's pure temple". This task informs Aurora's review both of her career as poet and of poetics in the pivotal fifth book. Like her creator, Aurora has written successful ballads, but found them too confining. She has written pastorals that failed because they were not "humanised".

And certainly Barrett Browning must have been referring to her own medieval ballads when Aurora rejects the poet who "trundles back his soul five hundred years". She rejects all the forms that the poetesses were allowed, thus privileging the masculine epic. The epic contains the age; it does not restrict the writer to a brief lyric "song." Aurora Leigh's blank verse ties it to Paradise Lost; and like The Prelude it treats the growth of a poet's mind. And yet, as if naming her own autobiographical poem, Aurora declares that a poet should be "unscrupulously epic" and appropriate the form to her own uses:

Trust the spirit,
As sovran nature does, to make the form;
For otherwise we only imprison spirit
And not embody.

She insists on the heroic in the ordinary, as did the Victorian novelists, which was at variance with much of Victorian poetic practice, which preferred classical or medieval heroes—or even the bishops, dukes, and intellectuals of Browning's work. And yet, though her book was wrung from her "life-blood", Aurora is dissatisfied with her art. She feels its passion, yet: "There's more than passion goes to make a man / Or book, which is a man too".

Aurora's use of "man" to describe herself as poet is both conventional and literal. Although she is a professional, something eludes her as a poet. She does not name this lack, but in essence describes it as she muses on herself as an artist:

I am sad.
I wonder if Pygmalion had these doubts
And, feeling the hard marble first relent,
Grow supple to the straining of his arms,
And tingle through its cold to his burning lip,
Supposed his senses mocked, supposed the toil
Of stretching past the known and seen to reach
The archetypal Beauty out of sight,
Had made his heart beat fast enough for two,
And with his own life dazed and blinded him!
Not so; Pygmalion loved, —and whoso loves
Believes the impossible.

But I am sad: I cannot thoroughly love a work of mine, Since none seems worthy of my thought and hope More highly mated. He has shot them down, My Phoebus Apollo, soul within my soul, Who judges, by the attempted, what's attained, And with the silver arrow from his height Has struck down all my works before my face While I said nothing. Is there aught to say? I called the artist but a greatened man. He may be childless also, like a man.

Aurora identifies herself—as she must as creator—with Pygmalion, not Galatea. It is a significant choice of model;

Pygmalion typifies the artist who creates woman according to his gaze, not her reality. Aurora, oblivious to this irony, claims that the difference between herself and Pygmalion as artists is due, not to gender, but to the fact that "Pygmalion loved," which allowed him to "believe the impossible." She, however, "cannot love a work of mine." Galatea proved a fertile muse for Pygmalion; whereas Aurora's muse, Phoebus Apollo, "soul within my soul, /... Has struck down all [her] works before [her] face." Her adoption of a male muse should indicate that she imagines herself a female poet.

Yet her effort is fruitless, confirming the psychic contortions Aurora must undergo to imagine herself as a poet at all: "I called the artist but a greatened man. / He may be childless also, like a man." Pygmalion was a "greatened man"; she is "childless, like a man." Her identification as a poet has much to do with gender; while the analogy between labour and the creation of Art is a convention, Aurora imagines the poet here as specifically male, deprived of the reproductive capacities that differentiate him from the female. Her feeling "I am sad," if connected with her childlessness, indicates her alienation from the procreative potential that defines her sex. It suggests both Aurora's desire to identify herself as a woman and the barrenness of not doing so. Through her close contact with the procreative role of woman enacted by Marian Erle in the second half of her story, Aurora finally claims her female identity.

Although she cannot yet realise herself as a woman, Aurora understands that love and passion are the price she has paid for being an artist:

How dreary 'tis for women to sit still,
On winter nights by solitary fires,
And hear the nations praising them far off,
Too far! ay, praising our quick sense of love,
Our very heart of passionate womanhood,
Which could not beat so in the verse without
Being present also in the unkissed lips
And eyes undried because there's none to ask
The reason they grew moist.

Aurora writes here almost as a poetess, yet the epic context elevates the "affections" described. Aurora recognizes the irony in men's praising women for the "very heart of passionate womanhood" that imbues their "verse" while paradoxically condemning women artists not to feel it in their lives. That lovers respond to the passion in her work while she sits alone leads her to admit she's "hungry". Her "mother-want" is transformed into hunger for the "love of one" rather than for the generalized love of all. Although she cannot name Romney, she both muses on Pygmalion's love and envies her male contemporaries, not for "native gifts or popular applause" but for "a girl... with brown eyes"—a mother or a wife who supports them in their work. Aurora associates her doubts about her work with her inability to give and take as the male poets, with whom she aesthetically identifies, can from their mistresses or wives. Prefiguring her union with Romney, Aurora here glimpses the fact that love is essential for art.

Yet publicly she can, on the very evening she begins writing her "better self," say to Lord Howe at his party:

"you shall not speak
To a printing woman who has lost her place
(The sweet safe comer of the household fire
Behind the heads of children), compliments,
As if she were a woman. We who have clipt
The curls before our eyes may see at least
As plain as men do. Speak out, man to man."

But in private afterwards she finds the separation of poet from woman intolerable. Whereas metaphorically she described herself as one who "clipt the curls before [her] eyes" like a man, she records:

And I breathe large at home. I drop my cloak,
Unclasp my girdle, loose the band that ties
My hair... now could I but unloose my soul!
We are sepulchred alive in this close world,
And want more room.

Aurora can release the symbol of her womanhood, her hair, and reveal the female body within the clasping "girdle," but cannot fully inhabit her femaleness, her soul. Such denial feels like death, as surely as it did for the nun in "The Lay of the Brown Rosary"; Aurora feels "sepulchred alive," imprisoned. However, the hair she has loosened, even when she keeps her soul imprisoned, assumes the strength of Aurora's own repressed passions as she dwells on the prospective marriage of Romney and Lady Waldemar, "a woman still":

My loose long hair began to burn and creep,
Alive to the very ends, about my knees:
I swept it backward as the wind sweeps flame,
With the passion of my hands
... made a knot as hard as life
Of those loose, soft, impracticable curls.

The dramatic image of Aurora's "loose long hair... alive to the very ends," which Aurora must with "passion" repress into a "knot as hard as life," represents Aurora's passionate female life and its sublimation into masculinity. The force of the repression threatens to overwhelm her; imprisonment becomes unbearable. Aurora finally acts on her need for "more room" to loose her soul from being "sepulchred alive." Her decision to leave England is as significant as Barrett Browning's own. Her raising money for her literal journey by selling both the "residue of [her] father's books" and also the manuscript (the writing of which liberated her from their influence), parallels Barrett Browning's transcendence of Milton's hold on her art and her rejection of her father's authority. Aurora is ready for her psychic journey, uniting poet and woman.

Whereas the first five books of Aurora Leigh were written at one time, the last four, written in Paris and Florence and spanning a three-year period, were written in several sittings. The second part is divided into Aurora's first sight of Marian in Paris; her discovery of Marian and their conversation; and their journey to Italy and Aurora's final reunion with Romney. Aurora comments on the journal style of this second half, "I have written day by day".

In Paris, Aurora reveals she is initially in the sway of

conventional patriarchal ideology. When she first glimpses Marian, she cannot acknowledge that Marian is holding a child: "The arms of that same Marian clasped a thing /... I cannot name it now for what it was". She enacts both female silence about the reality of women's lives and also patriarchal horror at the "fallen woman," translating "stolen" sexual pleasure into the language of actual thievery:

A child. Small business has a castaway
Like Marian with that crown of prosperous wives
At which the gentlest she grows arrogant
And says "My child." Who finds an emerald ring
On a beggar's middle finger and requires
More testimony to convict a thief?
A child's too costly for so mere a wretch;
She filched it somewhere.

Aurora dismisses Marian as "damned", then catches herself : "Stop there: I go too fast; / I'm cruel like the rest". Instead of stereotyping Marian, she imagines another explanation for the child—it is a neighbour's. Although Aurora is still incapable of accepting the child as Marian's, such questioning of her own responses determines her to find Marian, "And save her, if she will or will not—child / Or no child, —if a child, then one to save!"

The transformation from imagining the child as a "thing" to determining to help both mother and child is Aurora's first altruistic move. Until this point, survival for her in a society that demanded woman's self-abnegation necessitated Aurora's absorption in her own affairs. But, as for many other Victorian characters, human maturity depends on what Maggie in The Mill on the Floss names the "abandonment of egoism"; indeed, even Pip in Great Expectations learns the importance of such abandonment if he is to render others intelligible to his own mind. Aurora's growth into a harmonious selfhood is achieved through love as well as art, and through a compassionate sympathy for Marian's situation on Marian's terms, not according to convention. Marian is the instrument of this transformation.

When Marian told her story to Aurora in London, it was

unthreatening; indeed it reinforced middle-class ideology about the working-class and evoked middle-class charity. But Marian's story in Paris, unlike her earlier London tale, directly assaults Aurora's values: she refuses to be defined by Aurora's middle class ideology and language.

Instead of a narrative "coloured... in after times" and told more according to the "thing [she] understood so, than the thing [she] heard so", Aurora records a story in which Marian insists on her version, refusing to "scrupulously hint / With half-words, delicate reserves, the thing / Which no one scrupled [she] should feel in full".

The narrative technique is quite different from Aurora's earlier fiction objectifying Marian; in Paris Aurora records the dialogue whereby she first learns to articulate the subjectivity of female experience. Such dialogue is still suspiciously middle-class, underlining the fact that Marian's function is still to be absorbed into and exploited by Aurora's middle-class story, not dramatized as exemplifying the dilemmas of the poor.

When Aurora finds Marian in Paris, she is initially shocked at the ease with which Marian refers to her past and to Romney, and she asserts with patriarchal reticence: "'Therefore come,' / I answered with authority. —'I think / We dare to speak such things and name such names / In the open squares of Paris!'".

The ambiguity here, as to whether "We dare to speak" represents a new freedom or a reprimand against Marian's assumption of such freedom, is resolved by Marian's silently accompanying Aurora in response. The affairs of women's lives are for the domestic interior, not for the "open squares," suggesting that Aurora endorses a prohibition against such naming in the "open squares" of poetry.

Silent at first, Marian "followed closely" where Aurora "went, / As if [she] led her by a narrow plank / Across devouring waters, step by step", until she had to return to her child, necessitating that Aurora give up her authority and follow. She submitted to Marian's lead, and, whereas earlier Marian crossed the treacherous "devouring waters" into her domain, Aurora now experienced an equal threat to her own psychic structures:

Then she led The way, and I, as by a narrow plank Across devouring waters, followed her, Stepping by her footsteps, breathing by her breath, And holding her with eyes that would not slip.

Aurora's "breathing by [Marian's] breath" moves her from the circumscribed world of the "printing woman," who dared not speak of woman's experience except as "coloured" by the teller, into the subjectivity of Marian's world, that of the "common woman." A gulf initially separates the two women. Crossing that gulf has already proved treacherous for Marian, exploited by the middle-class world as an experiment, and it threatens Aurora now with loss of autonomy. She has hitherto resisted following anyone's lead: outwardly she acquiesced in her aunt's upbringing, while inwardly resisting; and, sensing the danger Romney posed to her autonomy, she refused his proffered authority.

Aurora's emotions stir, watching the "extremity of love" (6.600) between Marian and her son. Yet she still evokes patriarchal morality about the "fallen woman" when, "trying to be cold", she suppresses her enjoyment of the mutual smiles between mother and child. Unless a mother be pure, she insists:

"I would rather lay my hand,
Were I she, on God's brazen altar-bars
Red-hot with burning sacrificial lambs,
Than touch the sacred curls of such a child."

Marian, "plung[ing] her fingers in his clustering lock" and speaking with "indrawn steady utterance," reproaches Aurora for her piety, which cannot "find grace enough for pity and gentle words". Aurora insists in a "grave and sad" voice on Marian's impiety in stealing the child; Marian is "no mother, but a kidnapper," who will deprive her child of a "pure home," "pure heart," "pure good mother's name and memory". Whereas Aurora summons the pious platitudes of middle class religion to judge Marian, the latter responds with quite a different social analysis.

Comparing herself to "any glad proud mother" with her

"church-ring" who might evoke the law to judge her, Marian declares:

"I talk of law! I claim my mother-dues
By law, —the law which now is paramount, —
The common law, by which the poor and weak
Are trodden underfoot by vicious men,
And loathed for ever after by the good."

When Aurora insists she "filched" her child, Marian rejects being blamed as victim:

"What, what,... being beaten down
By hoofs of maddened oxen into a ditch,
Half-dead, whole mangled, when a girl at last
Breathes, sees... and finds there, bedded in her flesh
Because of the extremity of the shock,
Some coin of price!... and when a good man comes
(That's God! the best men are not quite as good)
And says 'I dropped the coin there: take it you,
And keep it, —it shall pay you for loss,'—
You all put up your finger—'See the thief!
'Observe what precious thing she has come to filch.
'How bad those girls are!'"

The very God whom Aurora imagines as judge Marian sees as compensating her with the child for the brutality she has suffered. "Angry with the world," she turns Aurora's argument upside down to reveal its empty rhetoric:

"Ah, ah! he laughs! he likes me. Ah, Miss Leigh,
You're great and pure; but were you purer still, —
As if you had walked, we'll say, no otherwhere
Than up and down the New Jerusalem,
... the child would keep to me,
Would choose his poor lost Marian, like me best."

Aurora adamantly persists in her disapproval; yet her anger is directed not at Marian, but at her own empathy with the young victimized mother. Believing "a child was given to sanctify / A woman", she reproaches Marian for turning her "faults" into "easy virtues." Marian, "with most despairing wonder," questions:

"What have you in your souls against me then,

All of you? am I wicked, do you think?
God knows me, trusts me with the child; but you,
You think me really wicked?"

When Aurora accuses her of being "complaisant," of committing a "wrong" for "certain profits" from a seducer, Marian seems to share her middle-class rhetoric and ideology when she claims she had "chaste pulses" because she was not sexually willing, not "fouled in will / And paltered with in soul by devil's lust", but was rather a victim of "man's violence". However, she rejects such a sexual economy:

"What, 'seduced's your word!
Do wolves seduce a wandering fawn in France?
Do eagles, who have pinched a lamb with claws,
Seduce it into carrion? So with me.
I was not ever, as you say, seduced,
But simply, murdered."

Although she shares Aurora's horror at unlawful sexual complicity, she educates Aurora to the fact that often the "fallen woman" was not complicitous in her "fall" but a brutalized victim. She places the blame where it belongs, on men, rather than on its traditional recipients, women. Marian speaks of female experience in a way quite new to Aurora. Her narrative disrupts Aurora's patriarchal discourse and transforms woman from scorned object to angry subject. Aurora is thereby empowered to identify herself as female:

But I, convicted, broken utterly,
With woman's passion clung about her waist
And kissed her hair and eyes, —"I have been wrong,
Sweet Marian."

Her old attitudes "broken utterly," Aurora experiences her "woman's passion." She allows herself the physical expression of feelings suppressed since she first met her aunt and "clung about her neck," only to receive in return a kiss from "cold lips" before "with some strange spasm / Of pain and passion, she wrung loose my hands / Imperiously, and held me at arm's length". She acts both as child again as she clings about Marian's waist and also as adult as she kisses her hair and eyes. Romney's criticisms and corrections had only served to harden Aurora's resolve to "walk at all risks," whereas Marian's serve to reunite Aurora with her repressed womanhood. However, her language and images are inappropriate for these new values: she switches from calling Marian harlot to identifying her as "Sweet holy Marian".

Earlier Marian refused to allow Aurora's patriarchal rhetoric to describe her experience as "fallen woman"; now she resists its cult of true womanhood. Aurora proclaims Marian "innocent"; Marian vehemently insists Aurora face the truth:

that world of yours has dealt with me
As when the hard sea bites and chews a stone
And changes the first form of it. I've marked
A shore of pebbles bitten to one shape
From all the various life of madrapores;
And so, that little stone, called Marian Erle,
Picked up and dropped by you and another friend,
Was ground and tortured by the incessant sea

And bruised from what she was, —changed! death's a change,

And she, I said, was murdered; Marian's dead.

Aurora, complicitous in Romney's experiment, denied her affinity with the "common woman," and betrayed her. Although Aurora still cannot unite her heart and speech, she does offer Marian practical help, a home for her and the child in Italy:

"I am lonely in the world,
And thou art lonely, and the child is half
An orphan. Come, —and henceforth thou and I
Being still together will not miss a friend,
Nor he a father, since two mothers shall
Make that up to him."

Aurora provides for the mother and child; although no longer an artist "childless like a man," she does not imagine herself as "father" but assumes a mother's role. She thereby confirms her new role as a poet: to include the joyful and painful subjectivity of women's lives in her work. Although she can juxtapose Marian's language with her own platitudes,

Aurora is still dependent on the fictions of the latter: "in my Tuscan home I'll find a niche / And set thee there, my saint, the child and thee". Aurora imagines Marian as a Madonna figure, but by including Marian's version of her experience in her autobiography, Aurora demonstrates the fallacy of such fictions, even while not fully able to reject them. Most important, she demonstrates that the reality of women's lives should be the subject matter of poetry.

Barrett Browning effects the transformation of woman as object into woman as subject via the stories of women who, like the runaway slave and Marian Erle, are outside the linguistic, social, and political systems typified by middle-class white men. Whereas Aurora, a middle-class woman, could assume a male identity as a poet, the slave and Marian are bound by their biological destiny. Through the stories of such marginal women Barrett Browning and her creation, Aurora Leigh, identify with the female voice essential to their true maturation. Although Barrett Browning is unusual among high Victorian poets in her concern for slavery and the working-class woman, there are ideological ramifications in such a gesture. In "using" under-class women— as the runaway slave and Marian Erle—to effect her own transformation into subjectivity, Barrett Browning exploits as well as dramatizes such women, who then disappear from the poems.

She was not, however, purely exploitative, as she reveals to Thackeray:

> *I am not a "fast woman." I don't like coarse subjects, or the coarse treatment of any subject. But I am deeply convinced that the corruption of our society requires not shut doors and windows, but light and air: and that it is exactly because pure and prosperous women choose to ignore vice, that miserable women suffer wrong by it everywhere. Has paterfamilias, with his Oriental traditions and veiled female faces, very successfully dealt with a certain class of evil? What if materfamilias, with her quick sure instincts and honest innocent eyes, do [sic] more towards their expulsion by simply looking at them and calling them by their names?* [L, 2:445]

It is analogous to, but with a quite different moral emphasis from, Wordsworth's focus on ordinary people. Aurora records how she was powerfully moved by her "wom an's passion" when Marian named the wrong she suffered; yet identifying herself as a woman is difficult and troubling for her:

My head aches,
I cannot see my road along this dark;
Nor can I creep and grope, as fits the dark,
For these foot-catching robes of womanhood.

The "robes of womanhood" had been a potent image for Aurora since Romney first warned her that writing poetry "defiles / The clean white morning dresses" (2.95-96), and she herself acknowledged:

A woman's always younger than a man
At equal years, because she is disallowed
Maturing by the outdoor sun and air,
And kept in long-clothes past the age to walk.

Only after hearing Marian's story, however, does Aurora understand she cannot escape her sex, try as she will to clip the "curls before [her] eyes". This realization releases her suppressed feelings as she thinks on Romney, "the man I love—I mean / The friend I love". She allows herself for the first time the feelings of a "common woman," yet in terror quickly subverts them:

Poor mixed rags
Forsooth we're made of, like those other dolls
That lean with pretty faces into fairs.
It seems as if I had a man in me,
Despising such a woman.

While Aurora has, through Marian, felt her woman's passion, it still discomforts her. Hearing that Kate Ward wears a cloak modeled on her own—representing, as her friend Vincent Carrington, the artist, says, "How women can love women of your sort"—Aurora muses, "Kate loves a worn-out cloak for being like mine, / While I live self-despised for being myself". Yet she also acknowledges, "I've a heart / That's capable of worship, love, and loss; /... I'll be meek / And learn to reverence, even this poor myself". She admits, "I'm a woman, it is true;/ Alas, and woe to us, when we feel it most!" Feeling "it most" means experiencing love and passion, yet Aurora imagines that her rejection of Romney has forfeited such a possibility.

Leaving England, her father's land, allowed Aurora, through Marian, to realise her subjectivity. Her fame as a poet and her return to Italy, her mother's country, enables her to inhabit that subjectivity. As if to confirm this she visits the house where she had lived with her father: "I rode once to the little mountain house / As fast as if to find my father there". But the house is changed, and Aurora leaves: "That was trial enough of graves". She cannot assume her old role of wearing her father's masculine "doublet." While such separation makes her feel like a "restless ghost", she also finds in it a new freedom. Through extolling the virtues of being out of England, she expresses also a confidence in the "better self," a female one, she is creating:

I'm happy. It's sublime,
This perfect solitude of foreign lands!
To be, as if you had not been till then,
And were then, simply that you choose to be.
possess, yourself,
A new world all alive with creatures new,
New sun, new moon, new flowers, new people—ah,
And be possessed by none of them!

But she has no model for how to possess this "new world" and succumbs, as de Beauvoir describes the state, to the "delusion" of "play[ing] at being a woman." Obsessed with what she imagines to be the loss of Romney—"Romney, Romney! Well, / This grows absurd!—too like a tune that runs / I' the head"—she watches women at church, praying in their sorrow. Identifying with them, she "drop[s her] head upon the pavement too, / And pray[s]" that God will not hear her words but "only listen to the run and beat / Of this poor, passionate, helpless blood".

Being a "common woman" threatens to silence Aurora, enabling her only to feel, as Barrett Browning had once imagined Mary's feeling at the foot of the cross, "with a spasm, not a speech." And indeed, she sinks into passivity when "ended seemed [her] trade of verse":

I did not write, nor read, nor even think,
But sat absorbed amid the quickening glooms,
Most like some passive broken lump of salt
Dropped in by chance to a bowl of oenomel,
To spoil the drink a little and lose itself,
Dissolving slowly, slowly, until lost.

In terms reminiscent of her description of suffering her aunt to "dry out from [her] drowned anatomy / The last sea-salt left in [her]", she now imagines herself passive, broken, bitter, and "lost." Her only models for being female are the women she has read about, her mother's picture, her aunt, her view of the monstrous Lady Waldemar and the saintly Marian, those of her readers like Kate Ward who look to her as their model, and the suffering women she sees in Italian churches.

If the end of Book 7 dissolves the "faulty artist," then the last two books create the "true poet." Aurora wavered earlier between imagining herself as male or female. Now she falters between her cultural engendering and her subjectivity. In her creation of a "better self" who can "exhibit all the peculiar powers without the negations of her sex," she redefines woman by uniting the expression of her intellectual powers with the realization of "the very heart of passionate womanhood".

The first sign that Aurora will rescue herself from the "delusion" of "play[ing] at being a woman" is her filling the "quickening glooms" with the fantasy of a mythic sea-king:

Gradually
The purple and transparent shadows slow
Had filled up the whole valley to the brim,
And flooded all the city, which you saw
As some drowned city in some enchanted sea,
Cut off from nature, —drawing you who gaze,
With passionate desire, to leap and plunge
And find a sea-king with a voice of waves,
And treacherous soft eyes, and slippery locks

You cannot kiss but you shall bring away
Their salt upon your lips.

Appropriately, Aurora finally activates her imagination both by hearing Marian laugh as she plays with her son (passionate womanhood) and also by reading (intellectual endeavor). Aurora has a "book upon [her] knees to counterfeit / The reading that [she] never read at all". Marian's laugh startles her out of the "drowsy silence" so that she finally reads her book, "Boccacio's tale, / The Falcon's, of the lover who for love / Destroyed the best that loved him". Identifying with the protagonist, Frederigo, who killed his favourite falcon to feed his mistress, Aurora implies—by saying, "Some of us / Do it still"—that she has destroyed the best part of herself, "my trade of verse," in her love for Romney. Aurora's response to Marian's laugh and Boccaccio's tale is to transform herself from a "passive broken lump of salt" into a poet: the "salt" on her lips expresses the subjectivity of her desire in imagining the male, the "sea-king," as object of her passion.

When Romney appears—almost as a physical manifestation of her imagined sea-king—Aurora (ignorant of his blindness) believes he is married to Lady Waldemar. She recognizes her love for Romney yet simultaneously accepts that she has lost him. In a lengthy discussion the cousins address the issues they first raised ten years previously on Aurora's twentieth birthday. Romney, impressed by Aurora's mature poetry, accepts now the status of object that men must necessarily have in woman's vision. Endowing her with the God-like power of the creator, he feels Aurora rightly "turned [him] from the garden" because of his arrogance:

"I should push
Aside, with male ferocious impudence,
The world's Aurora who had conned her part
On the other side the leaf! ignore her so,
Because she was a woman and a queen,
And had no beard to bristle through her song,
My teacher, who has taught me with a book."

The power of Aurora's poetry has convinced him that there is "the other side the leaf" from his. Previously, when Aurora crowned herself a poet, his gaze transfixed her to stone:

now he understands how egocentric his vision was: "certainly / I stood myself there worthier of contempt, / Self-rated, in disastrous arrogance". His arrogance toward Aurora was matched by his arrogance toward the world's poor, "one great famishing carnivorous mouth, — / A huge, deserted, callow, blind bird Thing" whom only he could save. When the poor reject his methods, he understands the fallacy of his beliefs. He tells Aurora, "I yield, you have conquered". In light of Aurora's later humbling of herself before Romney in a show of love and self-abnegation, Romney's self-derogation is crucial. As Romney will later say to her, so Aurora replies, "I am not so high indeed, / That I can bear to have you at my foot".

Aurora's apparent self-debasement before Romney in her final declaration of love concerns critics, who refer to it as the poem's "conventional happy ending," "the self-abnegating servitude with which Aurora Leigh concludes," and the "perfection of self-sacrifice" that Aurora enacts to cope with the "guilt of self-centered ambition." And indeed Aurora's declaration is disturbing as she begs Romney, "stoop so low to take my love / And use it roughly, without stint or spare". It is, however, a logical stage in her maturation, and it parallels a similar one in Barrett Browning's life, recorded in the Sonnets from the Portuguese when the speaker queries, "How, dearest, wilt thou have me for most use?"

Indeed the very "competition" between Aurora and Romney as to who should sit at whose feet evokes the early correspondence between Barrett and Browning, each vying for position of humblest lover and weakest poet. It is also a persuasive stage within the terms set by the poem, Aurora Leigh. Aurora can confidently assert, "I'm an artist, sir, / And woman", and outline her poetics by saying, "I'm plain at speech, direct in purpose" and "I use the woman's figures naturally".

Yet her only model for a woman's experience of love is the self abnegating one dictated by her culture. (Such an objectification Aurora saw at its extreme in Marian's experience, for all the subjectivity with which Marian insisted on in narrating it.) Romney's refusal to allow Aurora to objectify herself enables her to reject the "delusion" of this "play at being a woman." To be fully a woman does not necessitate rejecting the role of artist, but redefining it. On her twentieth birthday Aurora felt herself incomplete as both "Woman and artist"; her determination was to "complete" herself. By thirty she recognizes that she can only complete herself as artist by realizing herself as woman:

Passioned to exalt The artist's instinct in me at the cost Of putting down the woman's, I forgot No perfect artist is developed here From any imperfect woman.

What her long story, from her description of her mother's portrait to her declaration of love for Romney, has taught her is that in her very attempt to define herself as an artist, following the "high necessities of Art", she violated her fundamental nature. To be fully a "common woman" is to own fully her passionate nature. As an artist she must fully own that nature to be a "true poet."

Aurora's final freedom is initiated when she hears that her ancestral home, inherited and lived in by Romney, burned to "a great charred circle, where / The patient earth was singed an acre round". Blinded subsequently by the shock, Romney is "turned out of nature," "a man, upon the outside of the earth". Whereas Barrett in the Preface to Poems of 1844 describes herself as an "exile," Aurora, with her father's and lover's house razed, records how the male is now exiled, on the "outside of the earth." He has become object. The final stage of Aurora's autobiography parallels her creator's. Romney's blindness means Aurora is no longer the object of his gaze, echoing Barrett's realization of her subjectivity in the Sonnets when her beloved's "di vinest Art's / Own instrument didst drop down at [his] foot / To hearken what [she] said".

In "The Poet's Vow," "A Vision of Poets," and "Lady Geraldine's Courtship" Barrett dramatized the convention of the female muse guiding the male poet. The enquiry into other possibilities for the figuration of poet and muse, begun at the end of "A Vision of Poets" and continued through Casa Guidi Windows, is consummated in Aurora Leigh. Aurora's union with Romney, on a literal level a man with whom she can live as a sexual and intellectual equal, provides the book with its conventional happy ending. However, he functions symbolically as Aurora's muse, which transforms the conventional ending into a radical one. A male poet competes with the precursor father for the muse's favour; Aurora competed with the cultural definitions of woman, dramatized in the monstrous Lady Waldemar and the angelic Marian, for the favors of this male muse.

Romney appears, therefore, to be the "composite precursor" exemplifying the dilemma Joanne Feit Diehl identifies as fundamental to the nineteenth-century woman poet: "For Rossetti and Browning as well as for Dickinson, the precursor becomes a composite male figure; finding themselves heirs to a long succession of fathers, these women share the vision of a father/lover that surpasses individuals. And so for them the composite father is the main adversary." A male poet separates his precursor father from "the image of the fecund if idealized or distant muse" whom he may win from the father for himself. The nineteenth-century woman poet's dilemma is that her composite precursor and her muse are the same (male) figure. He always, therefore, retains the inhibiting power Milton's glory held over Barrett in "A Drama of Exile." Diehl identifies this problem for Barrett Browning in her reading of "A Musical Instrument". Yet she acknowledges that Dickinson, Rossetti, and Barrett Browning do not "reveal identical pressures." Barrett Browning's work exemplifies an alternative to that engagement with the composite precursor which Diehl identifies as dominating Dickinson's work.

Unlike Dickinson, Barrett Browning approaches the dilemma by initially imagining a muse who is not such a precursor or father/lover. She identifies as muse one in the gender/power economy who bears a position analogous to the one the female muse holds in relation to the male poet. She imagines not a silent lover but an infant boy. Whereas the son was privileged over the mother in "Isobel's Child," after Barrett Browning's move from her father and England, she recasts that muse into one without such inhibiting power. Although the slave's son wants "the master-right" to become that inhibiting figure, his mother, burying him in the "dark earth," denies him that status, retaining the idealized relationship with him that male poets have with the muse, liberating her song. In Casa Guidi Windows the muse is initially an anonymous boy singing "bella libertà." However, Barrett Browning concludes the poem by evoking one to whom she has literally given birth—her son.

Diehl claims that "for the male poet, the birth of a poem fulfills his maieutic impulse; he becomes both midwife and mother of his art"; Barrett Browning becomes midwife and mother to both her art and muse. The mother poet invites the muse infant, "Let me see thee more," and commands his total attention: "Now look straight before, / And fix thy brave blue English eyes on mine". She thus summons the silent object of her desire to inspire her vision of the "new springs of life".

In Aurora Leigh the figure of the muse changes. As demonstrated, Marian Erle is the agent of Aurora's transformation into subjectivity, thus evoking the earlier figure of George Sand's liberating the potential for her "woman's voice." However, Marian only gains that powerful function by virtue of her infant son. Her need to return to care for him necessitates Aurora's following Marian, "as by a narrow plank / Across devouring waters". He is the silent object around whom the competing ideologies and discourses of Aurora and Marian whirl, until finally Aurora embraces her woman's passion. Aurora assumes the poet/mother role toward him; he "will not miss... a father, since two mothers shall / Make that up to him".

Barrett Browning, therefore, imagines prior to the last book of Aurora Leigh a muse who is a silent other over whom she has power. The male poet separates the muse from the precursor, supplanting the father in her affections, reenacting thereby the oedipal struggle. Barrett Browning separates from the father/ precursor by maintaining the privileged preoedipal affectional bond of mother and infant. Once that silent boy individuates into adult manhood, the danger is that he will assume the "master-right," become the composite precursor, and silence the woman poet with his inhibiting glory. It is this finally that Barrett Browning confronts in Aurora Leigh. Initially she rejects Romney who, disdaining her poetry, assumes the inhibiting role. She finds her woman's voice through the agency of Marian Erle and is confident of her maternal role in relation to the muse (a reversal of Wordsworth's throwing himself on nature's bosom). However, she rejects such gender/power arrangements as ultimately inadequate.

The problematic nature of the ending—beyond its conventional narrative resolution—lies in the fact that when the blinded Romney becomes dependent on Aurora he will be as a young child, dependent on his mother. Yet in his blindness, evoking the New Jerusalem Aurora is to write, he is also the authoritative precursor—especially the blind Milton writing the old Eden.

He is both infant son and father/lover, the muse both separate from and identified with the father. But when Leigh Hall bums he is exiled from that ancestral home. Although it is discomforting that he tells Aurora she is to write the new Jerusalem, his call for a poetics of how "the old world waits the time to be renewed", for "new oeconomies, new laws, / Admitting freedom, new societies / Excluding falsehood" echoes Thackeray's vision of "new laws, new manners, new politics, vast new expanses of liberties unknown as yet." Romney overrides the muse's conventional role and evokes a Biblical canonical text, but he also leaves to the woman poet's subjectivity the description of those "new societies," "vast new expanses of liberties unknown as yet." If Aurora does not write such a description, she does initiate a recentering of the sex/gender economy such that it can be written with woman as well as man as subject.

As I stated at the outset, Barrett Browning needs to be read on her own liberal humanist terms. As Marian Erle can only finally be conceived in middle-class rhetoric, so Aurora Leigh is limited by Barrett Browning's "traditional humanism [which is] part of patriarchal ideology." Within that ideology, she resolves the dilemma of being woman and poet with a "Romantic rage" and a "discourse with a shattering revolutionary force."

Barrett Browning rejects the composite precursor; finds a poetic authority in a maternal relation to the muse; embraces her woman's passion through her engagement with Marian Erle, on the latter's terms; and renegotiates her authority as poet in relation to Romney as father poet and lover within the gender and canonical terms of patriarchal discourse. Just as Shakespeare's muse in the sonnets, as Joseph Pequigney argues in Such Is My Love, was a young man, and Tennyson acknowledges Hallam as his muse in "In Memoriam", so Barrett Browning confirms the multiple possibilities for the site of poetic authority and inspiration.

Once she is read on her own terms along with the three male high Victorian poets, then the more recent theoretical speculations about gender can be brought to bear on these four poets at this moment of literary history. Dorothy Dinnerstein, Nancy Chodorow, and the French theorists Julia Kristeva, Hélène Cixous, and Luce Irigaray privilege the preoedipal figuration between parent and infant over the triangular oedipal struggle. Barrett Browning's work suggests that this figuration may well also inform the construction of poet and muse, for both female and male poets.

When Barrett Browning wrote to Mrs. Martin about the reception of Aurora Leigh, she addressed the issue of "coarseness" that the reviewers had raised:

You will grant that I don't habitually dabble in the dirt; it's not the way of my mind or life. If, therefore, I move certain subjects in this work, it is because my conscience was first moved in me not to ignore them.

What has given most offence in the book, more than the story of Marian—far more! —has been the reference to the condition of women in our cities, which a woman oughtn't to refer to, by any manner of means, says the conventional tradition. Now I have thought deeply otherwise. If a woman ignores these wrongs, then may women as a sex continue to suffer them; there is no help for any of us—let us be dumb and die. I have spoken therefore, and in speaking have used plain words... which, if blurred or softened, would imperil perhaps the force and righteousness of the moral influence.

To Anna Jameson, the art critic, she addressed herself to another issue raised by reviewers, namely the similarity between the endings of Aurora Leigh and Jane Eyre. She explained the difference; whereas Mr. Rochester was blinded by the fire, If you read over again those pages of my poem, you will find that the only injury received by Romney in the fire was from a blow and from the emotion produced by the circum stances of the fire. Not only did he not lose his eyes in the fire, but he describes the ruin of his house as no blind man could. He was standing there, a spectator. Afterwards he had a fever, and the eyes, the visual nerve, perished, showing no external stain—perished as Milton's did.

In these two letters Barrett Browning engages the poetics that Aurora Leigh dramatized. Her task is to address the wrongs of women so that as a sex they do not "continue to suffer them." As a woman she must speak or be "dumb and die," like Margret, Rosalind, and the page.

Her speech must be in "plain words" that do not disguise the truth. To realise this aesthetic Barrett Browning has to "tame" Milton. The direct analogy she makes between Romney and Milton suggests that Barrett Browning has finally made her peace with her precursor. Aurora Leigh thereby dramatizes those issues that Barrett Browning first addressed in the Preface of Poems of 1844.

Eve will no longer suffer her "alloted grief" passively; women poets must speak out against it. Milton's glory can no longer inhibit Barrett Browning in her realization of this, because her vision has supplanted his. She enacts what she stated in Casa Guidi Windows: "We do not serve the dead... the past is past". Aurora Leigh eats of the tree of knowledge and, while Romney rises as God's and Milton's specter to punish her, she refuses their prohibition and punishment: the "song" she sings with her assertive "I" is quite other than the "innocent distraction" to which Romney had earlier condemned her.

Aurora Leigh not only presents a new reading of *Paradise Lost* in Aurora's insistence on eating of the tree and on usurping the Adamic privilege of naming the world, but, in its treatment of the relationship between Aurora and Romney, it demonstrates how Barrett Browning empowered herself to do so: Milton/Romney (like Browning by the end of the *Sonnets*) becomes lover/ muse, object of woman's passion and vision.

Barrett Browning's importance as a poet lies in this self-conscious demonstration of both the anxiety of influence and the anxiety of authorship as they affect a strong woman poet writing in a tradition which assumes that the poetic voice is male. *Aurora Leigh* provides a gloss for what Barrett Browning's previous work had shown. Initially the woman poet, like any young poet, must identify with her powerful precursors.

This necessitates imagining herself as male, with woman as object of her vision. Eventually this "frustration" yields to a crisis in which she begins to identify herself as female, as she must in order truly to mature. Having no models for such a yoking of woman and poet, she responds by following the cultural models of woman that as a young poet she had rejected; she transforms herself into the object she has been delineating in her work. Saved from such total passivity by writing of self-abnegation even while fully imagining herself enacting it, she realizes her poetic maturity by embracing and recording her own subjectivity with man as object of her gaze.

Barrett Browning offers a paradigm for the study of women poets. The narrative of her work is an inevitable one for strong women poets as long as the male poetic voice is culturally privileged. For confirmation of this paradigm in the career of a contemporary American poet hear Adrienne Rich in "When We Dead Awaken":

A lot is being said today about the influence that the myths and images of women have on all of us who are products of culture. I think it has been a peculiar confusion to the girl or woman who tries to write because she is peculiarly susceptible to language.

She goes to poetry or fiction looking for her way of being in the world, since she too has been putting words and images together; she is looking eagerly for guides, maps, possibilities; and over and over in the "words' masculine persuasive force" of literature she comes up against something that negates everything she is about: she meets the image of Woman in books written by men. She finds a terror and a dream, she finds a beautiful pale face, she finds La Belle Dame Sans Merci, she finds Juliet or Tess or Salome, but precisely what she does not find is that absorbed, drudging, puzzled, sometimes inspired creature, herself, who sits at a desk trying to put words together....

I know that my style was formed first by male poets: by the men I was reading as an undergraduate—Frost, Dylan Thomas, Donne, Auden, MacNeice, Stevens, Yeats....

I finished college, published my first book by a fluke, as it seemed.... by the time my [second] book came out I was already dissatisfied by those poems....

About the time my third child was born, I felt that I had either to consider myself a failed woman and a failed poet, or try to find some synthesis by which to understand what was happening to me....

In the late fifties I was able to write, for the first time, directly about experiencing myself as a woman....

The choice still seemed to be between "love"—womanly, maternal love, altruistic love—a love defined and ruled by the weight of the culture; and egotism—a force directed by men into creation, achievement, ambition, often at the expense of others. We know now that the alternatives are false ones—that the word "love" is itself in need of revision.

The parallels between Elizabeth Barrett Browning's career and Adrienne Rich's are illuminating, confirming, as Showalter says, how every generation of women writers finds itself without a history. The parallels between Elizabeth Barrett Browning's career and Adrienne Rich's are tragic. Had the work of Barrett Browning, Christina Rossetti, Emily Dickinson, H. D., Edith Sitwell, alongside Frost, Dylan Thomas, Donne, Auden, MacNeice, Stevens, and Yeats, been a crucial part of the literary history to which the young Rich turned for "guides, maps, possibilities," maybe she would not have had to repeat the paradigm in her turn. Only by recognizing women poets' struggle to form the synthesis of woman and poet, to make woman and artist both complete, as a crucial and integral part of humanistic literary history, can we move beyond it.

Chapter 8

Poems of 1844

On March 20, 1844, only about two weeks after the appearance of A New Spirit of the Age, Elizabeth sent to her printer material for the first sheet of her two volumes of verse. For two or three years she had enough new poems in manuscript to fill a volume but had been unable to find anyone who would undertake to publish them. In December of 1842 Edward Moxon had told George Barrett that however much he respected his sister's genius, he could not issue any of her work because of the poor market for poetry. Some two or three months later Moxon asked Kenyon to inform Elizabeth that he would very much like to publish her verses. It was Kenyon who seems to have persuaded Moxon to assume some of the risk, and as she composed further poems for her forthcoming publication, Kenyon was her everpresent confidant and adviser in all matters.

Without his help and encouragement the volumes of 1844 would not have appeared in their present form; perhaps they would never have been published. "Dear Mr. Kenyon," she said of him, "has been my friend and helper, and my book's friend and helper! Critic and sympathiser, true friend of all hours!" Late in March Moxon advised her to bring out two volumes instead of the one she had originally planned. As for the title, she suggested they be called "New Poems," but he preferred simply "Poems"; his choice prevailed. He did not think that such a title would imply to readers the idea that they were being republished.

A week before they were due to appear, Moxon noticed that the first volume was about seventy pages shorter than the second, and he proposed to transfer a number of poems from the end of the second volume to the first. Since she did not wish "The Dead Pan," which came at the end of the second volume, removed from that position, she finished a poem which had been lying half completed in her desk, by dashing off nineteen pages in one day. So, when the first volume was printed, the last forty pages comprised the ballad entitled "Lady Geraldine's Courtship."

On August 13, Moxon issued from his establishment at 44 Dover Street Elizabeth's neat octavo volumes in dark green cloth boards. In addition to being a publisher, he was himself a poet and a friend of poets and had produced Monckton Milnes' Memorials of a Tour in Some Parts of Greece, Samuel Rogers' handsomely illustrated Poems, and the first collected editions of Shelley and of Keats; and he had recently published the verse of Wordsworth, Tennyson, Milnes, Sterling, Patmore, and Browning.

The American edition under the title of A Drama of Exile: and Other Poems did not appear until October 5, In the first paragraph of the preface of this edition Elizabeth wrote, "My love and admiration have belonged to the great American people, as long as I have felt proud of being an Englishwoman, and almost as long as I have loved poetry itself." She concluded the paragraph by addressing her "thanks to those sons of the soil, who, if strangers and foreigners, are yet kinsmen and friends, and who, if never seen, nor perhaps to be seen by eyes of mine, have already caused them to glisten by words of kindness and courtesy."

In view of all that Kenyon had done for Elizabeth, it would have been appropriate for her to have dedicated her Poems to him, but instead she gave that honour to her father, just as she had inscribed to him long ago her earliest printed verses. In the passage "To My Father" Elizabeth wrote, "And my desire is that you, who are a witness how if this art of poetry had been a less earnest object to me, it must have fallen from exhausted hands before this day,—that you, who have shared with me in things bitter and sweet., softening or enhancing them, every day,—that you, who hold with me over all sense of loss and transiency, one hope by one Name,—may accept from me the inscription of these volumes, the exponents of a few years of an existence which has been sustained and comforted by you as well as given."

She concluded, "Somewhat more faint-hearted than I used to be, it is my fancy thus to seem to return to a visible personal dependence on you, as if indeed I were a child again; to conjure your beloved image between myself and the public, so as to be sure of one smile,—and to satisfy my heart while I sanctify my ambition, by associating with the great pursuit of my life, its tenderest and holiest affection." In the preface she said that she was offering to the public the poems she had written during the six years since the publication of her volume of The Seraphim and that all, "with the exception of a few contributions to English or American periodicals," were now being printed for the first time. But of the sixty-one poems in the volumes, twenty-five had already been published.

In the last paragraph of the preface she put on the robes of a high priestess and solemnly explained the mysteries of her calling: "If it must be said of me that I have contributed immemoral verses to the many rejected by the age, it cannot at least be said that I have done so in a light and irresponsible spirit. Poetry has been as serious a thing to me as life itself; and life has been a very serious thing: there has been no playing at skittles for me in either. I never mistook pleasure for the final cause of poetry; nor leisure, for the hour of the poet." Finally, she believed that "the reverence and sincerity with which the work was done, should give it some protection with the reverent and sincere."

By far the longest and most ambitious poem in the volumes was "A Drama of Exile." Late in the previous autumn, as Elizabeth was looking over the manuscripts of her verses, she had come upon a fragment of a masque called "The First Day's Exile from Eden." The twenty lines of the original soon grew to somewhat more than two thousand as she put aside everything else and rapidly finished the work, writing "with continuous flow—from fifty to a hundred lines a day, and quite in a glow of pleasure and impulse all through." But after its completion she doubted whether the poem had any merit and hesitated to offer it for publication. At her request, Kenyon took it home. The next day he praised the poem, which he thought "very superior as a whole" to any of her earlier work.

Today, however, much of the blank verse reads like a burlesque of Paradise Lost, and the choral passages sound like a parody of the choruses of Shelley Prometheus Unbound. The subject, as she explained in the preface, was "the new and strange experience of the fallen humanity, as it went forth from Paradise into the wilderness; with a peculiar reference to Eve's allotted grief, which... appeared to me imperfectly apprehended hitherto, and more expressible by a woman than a man." Elizabeth had "attempted, in respect to Milton, what the Greek dramatists achieved lawfully in respect to Homer." By thus associating herself with some of the greatest writers of the drama and epic she made it clear that she wished to be judged by the highest standards.

The opening scene is "the outer gate of Eden shut fast with clouds." Rows and rows of angels cast from their swords a glare which "extends many miles into the wilderness." Adam and Eve are in the distance, and in the foreground Gabriel is speaking with Lucifer and ordering him to depart. The ruined angel, however, prefers to remain and is unmoved by the rhetoric of the divine emissary. While Adam and Eve "fly across the sword-glare," they hear a chorus of "Eden Spirits" who are "chanting from Paradise," with songs from "Spirits of the Trees," "River-Spirits," a "BirdSpirit," and "Flower-Spirits." The first parents stop for a moment at "the extremity of the sword glare," where Eve expresses her contrition and the wish that Adam punish her. But he consoles her and thanks God for allowing Eve to stay with him. After a "faint and tender" chant of invisible angels, Lucifer appears again and mocks at the fallen pair. He vanishes as he hears the "Song of the Morning Star to Lucifer," from which the following lines may show why many critics found it incomprehensible:

Around, around the firmamental ocean,
I swam expanding with delirious fire!
Around, around, around, in blind desire

To be drawn upward to the Infinite—
Ha, ha!

In the following scene, which takes place in "a wild open country seen vaguely in the approaching night," Eve says that she is terrified at the shapes of the Zodiac. Adam reassures her and explains the signs. Then "Two Spirits, of organic and inorganic nature" rise from the ground and bewail their fate of "undeserved perdition" because of the first sin. Their reproach brings tears to the eyes of Eve, who feels herself "Saddest and most defiled" and asks the spirits to pardon her and Adam. Lucifer returns to curse the two exiles and remind them of the "plagues," the "corruptions," and the "hideous forms of life and fears of death" which will afflict them and their descendants.

A choral interlude of "philo sophic voices," "love voices," "revel voices," and many other kinds of voices is followed by a "Vision of Christ" rebuking the earth spirits, reconciling them to Adam and Eve, and telling them of the future Incarnation, Crucifixion, and Redemption. The poem concludes with a long choral passage sung by "Invisible Angels," while Adam and Eve "advance into the desert, hand in hand." Viewed as a whole, "A Drama of Exile" appeared even to Elizabeth's staunch supporters to be a complete failure. As the summary of the plot shows, the work has no central idea, no action, no conflict, no development of character. Elizabeth had only a hazy conception of what she was trying to express.

The review in the Spectator said that most of the drama was nothing but verbiage, that Lucifer, for example, was "a mere talker, and rather a longwinded one, who is more given to railing and reverie than to practical speech." Likewise Blackwood's spoke of the "vague and impalpable conceptions which form the staple of her poem, the dreamy and unpractical character of her style." The reviewer disliked the lyrical passages, which were "frequently so inarticulate, so slovenly, and so defective, both in rhythm and rhyme, that we are really surprised how a person of her powers could have written them." Edgar Allan Poe, who reviewed the Poems in the Broadway Journal, also disapproved of the choral songs: "We have none of us to be told that a medley of metaphysical recitatives sung out of tune, at Adam and Eve, by all manner of inconceivable abstractions, is not exactly the best material for a poem."

Furthermore Poe thought that Elizabeth's Eve was a shadowy character: "She is a mystical something or nothing, enwrapped in a fog of rhapsody about Transfiguration, and the Seed, and the Bruising of the Heel, and other talk of a nature that no man ever pretended to understand in plain prose." As for the appearance of Christ as an interlocutor, an unsigned article in the New Quarterly Review, probably by Chorley, expressed the prevailing consensus that it was "a serious defect in poetic taste." Elizabeth herself feared that some of her readers might think that the time of the drama, which was only one sunset, was insufficient for so much traveling and for so many long conversations. To anticipate their objections she wrote in her preface that very little was known about the length of the evenings before the flood and that for her part she could not "believe in an Eden without the longest of purple twilights."

The shorter poems were more admired by Elizabeth's friends and critics than were "A Drama of Exile" and "A Vision of Poets." Among the verses which appeared for the first time in the volumes of 1844, "Lady Geraldine's Courtship: a Romance of the Age" found favour not only with Carlyle and Miss Martineau but with almost all her readers. Lady Geraldine is similar to Tennyson's Lady Clara Vere de Vere in wealth and social status, but Elizabeth's poem has a romantic conclusion. The story is told from the point of view of Bertram, "a poor poet," who was "born of English peasants." He "could not choose but love" Lady Geraldine, "an earl's daughter," with many "halls" and "castles." She has "resonant steam-eagles" (a term which puzzled several reviewers) and retainers who "bow before her, as her chariot sweeps their doorways." Although she has "lovers in the palace," she becomes interested in the poet and invites him to visit her at one of her country houses.

Among the other guests are "lovely London ladies" and

many high-born suitors. When Geraldine and Bertram are alone together, he reads aloud from Petrarch, Spenser, Wordsworth, Tennyson,

Or from Browning some "Pomegranate," which, if cut deep down the middle,
Shows a heart within blood-tinctured, of a veined humanity!—

He later overhears an earl ask for Geraldine's hand and her reply that the man she marries will be "noble" and "wealthy" and that she will "never blush to think how he was born." Bertram supposes that she is scornful of himself and favors her noble suitor. After the earl leaves, he abuses her with so many "mad words" that when she replies by merely uttering his name, he is "struck down before her" and, unconscious, is taken by the servants to his chamber. At the end of the poem Geraldine comes to his room and declares her love, "While the shining tears ran faster down the blushing of her cheeks." Then Bertram falls on his knees in adoration.

The "Rhyme of the Duchess May" is no less ridden with clichés. In its subject matter and treatment it is similar to such earlier poems as "The Romaunt of the Page" and "The Lay of the BrownRosary," Rosary," both of which were reprinted in the volumes of 1844. The Duchess May, "a Duke's fair orphan-girl," is disdainful of "Lord Leigh, the churl," to whom she had been betrothed by her uncle and protector, the elder Lord Leigh, since the age of twelve "for the sake of dowry gold." She escapes from father and son and elopes with Sir Guy of Linteged to his castle, which is soon afterward attacked by the Leighs. After fourteen days of siege Sir Guy resolves to spare further bloodshed by sacrificing himself. He asks that his horse be led up the winding staircase to the top of the turret. His retainers think him "grief-distraught" to make such a strange request, but they obey without question. When he prepares to ride over the edge, his "noble wife" foresees his mad purpose and leaps into the saddle beside him. His knights catch at the rein, but too late, for both horse and riders topple below.

"Bertha in the Lane" is also a sentimental treatment of the subject of death. It represents the last words of a girl who resolved to die as soon as she learned that her supposed fiancé had transferred his affection to her younger sister. The concluding line has the merit of brevity: "I aspire while I expire!" Two other poems in much the same vein are "Catarina to Camoëns" and "The Mournful Mother." In the former, Catarina on her deathbed recalls the verses in which Camoëns, who is now abroad, had "recorded the sweetness of her eyes." The chief interest in the poem is that it "greatly impressed" Robert Browning before he "became personally acquainted with their writer whose condition in certain respects had, at one time or so I fancied," he wrote long after his wife's death, "resembled those of the Portuguese Caterina." The mournful mother in the poem of that title is weeping because of the recent death of her blind child, but the poet tells her to dry her tears, for he now "walks in light," and to wait

Until ye two give meeting
Where the great Heaven-gate is,
And he shall lead thy feet in,
As once thou leddest his!

In its material and treatment this poem is similar to "Isobel's Child" in the volume of The Seraphim. Although "The Mournful Mother" now seems among the most mawkish of Elizabeth's poems, it had precisely the qualities which appealed to many of her readers. For example, the Examiner thought it the "most perfect" of her poems because of the "exquisite pathos in its beauty" and quoted much of it in its review of Elizabeth's volumes.

The verses entitled "A Portrait" describe Mr. Barrett's ten-yearold cousin and ward, Georgina Elizabeth (Lizzie) Barrett, who was a member of the household at 50 Wimpole Street. Her mother was insane, and her father in the West Indies may not have had the right type of home in which to bring up a daughter. She stayed in her foster home until she married Elizabeth's brother Alfred Barrett in 1855. Another poem with personal associations was "Wine of Cyprus," addressed to H. S. Boyd to acknowledge the gift of a vial of Greek wine, the taste of which "reminded one of oranges and orange flower together, to say nothing of the honey of Mount Hymettus."

Elizabeth recalls the "golden hours" long ago when she read Greek with him in his cottage at the foot of the Malvern Hills:

And I think of those long mornings
Which my Thought goes far to seek,
When, betwixt the folio's turnings,
Solemn flowed the rhythmic Greek.
Past the pane, the mountain spreading,
Swept the sheep-bell's tinkling noise,
While a girlish voice was reading,—
Somewhat low for Qý–s and oý–s!

One of the most successful poems was "The Romance of the Swan's Nest." Blackwood's praised it particularly for its "graceful playfulness of manner and sentiment, which shows how heartily the amiable authoress can enter into the sympathies and enjoyments of a child." At the beginning "Little Ellie sits alone," dreaming of the noble lover who will come riding on a handsome steed, dismount, and kneel at her feet.

Then "soul-tied by one troth," she will take him to her swan's nest. But when on her way home she pays it her daily visit, she sees that "the wild swan had deserted" and "a rat had gnawed the reeds."

Ellie went home sad and slow!
If she found the lover ever,
With his red-roan steed of steeds,
Sooth I know not! but I know
She could show him never-never,
That swan's nest among the reeds!

Among the sonnets, two of the boldest were those addressed to George Sand, whom Elizabeth in a letter to Chorley once called with her usual exaggeration "the first female genius of any country or age."

Kenyon told Elizabeth that she was "a daring person" to publish them and that a guest of his had recently said that "no modest woman would or ought to confess to an acquaintance with the works of George Sand." The sonnet "Past and Future" affected Browning when he first saw it, as he later wrote, "more than any poem I ever read." It expressed the idea she was to reiterate with many variations in her love letters, that she then thought her "life was ended."

My wine hath run
Indeed out of my cup, and there is none
To gather up the bread of my repast
Scattered and trampled!

The poems of 1844 represent the fruit of some six years of intermittent poetical activity. Much had happened in her life since the publication of The Seraphim. She felt that as she matured, she had gained in constructive ability and had eliminated some of her faults of expression. In comparing "A Drama of Exile" with "The Seraphim," she thought the former was "fuller, freer and stronger, and worth the other three times over," and the two volumes as a whole far superior to all she had written before. She forwarded copies to her close friends and to Wordsworth, Landor, Carlyle, Miss Martineau, and Leigh Hunt, to the latter of whom she was especially grateful for his having written of her as "the most imaginative poetess that has appeared in England, perhaps in Europe."

Then she anxiously awaited their replies and the first reviews. "It is awful enough, this looking forward to be reviewed," she wrote to Westwood late in August. She soon heard from everyone who had received the volumes. Carlyle's advice was not helpful: that a person of her " 'insight and veracity' ought to use 'speech' rather than 'song' in these days of crisis." Harriet Martineau wrote of her "immense advance" on her former volume and said that she had greatly improved "in the whole art of utterance." The "predominant impression" of the verse upon Miss Martineau was of its "originality"; it seemed to her as fresh as if no one had ever written poetry before.

Elizabeth heard from Thomas Noon Talfourd in the Lake District that he liked her books and that they had been "the companions of his pleasantest walks in that romantic country." Dante Gabriel Rossetti and his brother William Michael "revelled" in her works "with profuse delight." Such poems as "A Drama of Exile," the "Rhyme of the Duchess May," and "Lady Geraldine's Courtship" held the Rossetti brothers "spellbound," so that they read them "more than half-a-hundred times over" and learned to recite them from memory. From America James Russell Lowell and Lydia Sigourney sent messages of congratulation. The latter wrote, as Elizabeth told Boyd with pride, that "the sound of my poetry is stirring the 'deep green forests of the New World.'"

Early in September, Chorley, who had reviewed her sympathetically in two different journals, thanked her for "the pleasant emotions" her Poems had excited. He wrote that he had followed her career "step by step" ever since she had begun to print and that her recent volumes "were so much better than any preceding them, and were such living books, that they restored to him the impulses of his youth." Chorley was a friend of Miss Mitford, who several times had asked Elizabeth to admit him to her room.

But as she had illogically written to Miss Mitford in explaining why she could see Browning, though not Chorley, "Now a line must be drawn—or my sepulchre must be prepared—do you not see the necessity?" From that decision Miss Mitford could not appeal. Elizabeth exchanged letters with him from time to time as long as she lived, but she did not see him until the summer of 1852, when she and Browning dined one evening at his London home.

Although the volumes brought her little money at first, they had such a steady sale that a new edition was called for six years later. The Poems of 1844 were praised by the leading critical journals and were more widely reviewed than any of her earlier works. Most of the poems now seem diffuse, sentimental, and trite. What qualities did many well-known writers and responsible critics find in her that so delighted them? Although Elizabeth was "without a single personal friend among these critics," she thought herself "singularly happy" in her reviews and had "full reason for gratitude to the profession." On both sides of the Atlantic the most-respected journals published long and thoughtful reviews; and while they mentioned many deficiencies in her verse, they also found much to praise.

The British Quarterly Review said that, "She possesses

genius, a cultivated mind, a truth-loving heart, quick powers of observation, and luxuriance of fancy and expression." Tait's Edinburgh Magazine called her volumes "the out-pourings of a pure and noble spirit, disciplined by study, and by the greater discipline of sorrow, revealed in tones which are musical by the greatness, depth, and music of the thoughts." Blackwood's wrote that her "powers appear to us to extend over a wider and profounder range of thought and feeling, than ever before fell within the intellectual compass of any of the softer sex"; and it declared that she was "gifted with very extraordinary powers of mind" and that "her genius is profound, unsullied, and without a flaw."

It concluded that, "Were the blemishes of her style tenfold more numerous than they are, we should still revere this poetess as one of the noblest of her sex." H. F. Chorley in the Athenaeum added his praise to that of the others by characterizing her volumes as "remarkable manifestations of female power."

Many other journals were even more extravagant in their expressions of approval. The writer in the Atlas experienced a "lively pleasure" in reading her poetry, with its "almost endless variety of subject," its "tuneful harmony," its "supreme sense of beauty," and its "happy thought most happily evolved"; he asserted that her volumes showed "extraordinary power, and... extraordinary genius." The Metropolitan Magazine spoke of her "deep piety," "bold and original thought," "newness of simile," and "suggestive description," and it said that "she seems to us 'one bright particular star,' shining from a firmament of her own."

In his concluding sentence the reviewer held "a bright augury" for Elizabeth's poetical reputation—that she would be, "as she deserves to be, esteemed and admired at once and throughout future generations."

The Monthly Review thought that it "would be difficult to name within the range of the poetry of the last quarter of a century, a publication that presents so much of independent effort, of original power, and of sterling beauties, as do these volumes." And to the Prospective Review, Elizabeth's work represented the "Phoenix of true Poetry," which was rising again from its ashes. The New Monthly, Ainsworth's Magazine, and the London Globe were no less favorable. It is no wonder that after reading such glowing estimates of herself, Elizabeth wrote Cornelius Mathews, "Your kindness will be glad to learn of the prosperity of my poems in my own country. I am more than satisfied in my most sanguine hope for them, and a little surprised besides."

While some of the reviews were uncritically laudatory throughout, the notices appearing in the most influential journals were in agreement that the poems had the same lapses in expression which disfigured her former volumes. The British Quarterly Review, which Elizabeth later wrote to Browning, "has been abusing me so at large, that I can take it to be the achievement of a very particular friend indeed," objected to her "fantastic images and phrases." Although the reviewer had spoken warmly of her poetry in another part of his article, he felt that much of what she had written was unintelligible because her thoughts did not seem to have been clearly conceived. "And the case is rendered more hopeless by her attributing it, not as one would have expected, to her own feeble grasp of her subject, and defective power of expression, but... to her thoughts being too sublime and grand to be spoken out in clear, connected phrase."

An article in the Critic also condemned her style for its obscurity and affectation; it seemed to the writer that she mistook "vagueness for sublimity, and the chaos of a dream for a creation." Yet reviews often cancel each other, for the Eclectic Review named "conciseness as one of Miss Barrett's distinguishing excellencies," and the writer defined "conciseness" as "fulness of meaning, conveyed in few and simple words." The Prospective Review said in her defence, "Those who offer... objections are not in a position to understand her. Our authoress has risen above their horizon, and she must on no account stoop to lift up into it those whom she has left behind."

Almost all the reviewers disliked her false rhymes. In attempting to defend herself against the charge of carelessness, she explained to Boyd that she had used double rhymes with slightly different vowel sounds "after much thoughtful study of the Elizabethan writers," and she added, "If I deal too much in licences, it is not because I am idle, but because I am speculative for freedom's sake. It is possible, you know, to be wrong conscientiously; and I stand up for my conscience only." Nevertheless such rhymes as "shade is" and "Hades," "Hellas" and "tell us," "Niades" and "and breeze," "glories" and "floorwise" can have for most readers only a comic effect.

The Westminster Review, which Elizabeth described as "our most influential quarterly (after the 'Edinburgh' and right 'Quarterly')," commented on the absence of humour in her verses. It attributed her style, which was "not unfrequently, wanting the ease of colloquial expression," to her long seclusion during which she had lived too much in the world of books; thus, in the opinion of the reviewer, the development of her poetical powers had been weakened rather than aided. Yet she herself well understood that her ignorance of many aspects of life beyond the confines of her room was a severe handicap to her art. "How willingly," she later wrote Browning, "I would as a poet exchange some of this lumbering, ponderous, helpless knowledge of books, for some experience of life and man." The Westminster Review pointed out that the defects of many of her poems were "the result of rapidity of composition."

Elizabeth told of the speed with which she wrote "A Drama of Exile" and "Lady Geraldine's Courtship," and no doubt she also finished other poems with equal haste. Yet she always believed that she took great care both in the original composition of her verses and in their revisions. "I have worked at poetry—it has not been with me reverie, but art," she said to Horne. In the same spirit she told Kenyon, "Very few writers... pay more laborious attention than I do habitually to the forms of thought and expression." The John Bull, which Elizabeth learned had cut her up "with sanguinary gashes, for the edification of its Sabbath readers," poked fun at her prolixity. It gave as an example part of a sentence in her preface, in which she wrote that "A Drama of Exile" was the longest poem which she had ever "trusted into the current of publication," instead of the simpler "published."

A review in the Examiner, written probably by John Forster, also censured her for verbosity: "She uses all her thoughts and feelings for whatever she does. The art of knowing what to keep and what to reject, she has not attained." In AMERICA Elizabeth's literary reputation had been steadily increasing for two or three years before the publication in New York of her volumes of 1844. Her poems in Graham's and other American magazines were making her known in the literary circles of New York and Boston. The New York Daily Tribune for July 15, 1844, printed "Pain in Pleasure" from the August issue of Graham's and called the poem "an exquisite thought by Mrs. [sic] E. B. Barrett."

In the same newspaper, on November 27, the writer of a review of Rufus W. Griswold The Poets and Poetry of England, in the Nineteenth Century, which contained a critique on Elizabeth Barrett, mentioned having "read, admired, and copied 'The Romaunt of Margret' from a London magazine, years before we heard that it was written by Elizabeth B. Barrett, and even before we knew there was such a woman." Griswold's critical sketch of Elizabeth, which had been written before he saw A Drama of Exile: and Other Poems, is remarkably full and generous in its praise. He knew about her because he had been an assistant editor of Graham's during the years when it published many of her poems.

Although American readers, he said, had not yet seen many of her verses, she had "already made herself a home in the hearts of the people; a proof that the popular taste does not lie altogether in the direction of sing-song echoes, sickly sentiment, or empty blank verse; a proof, too, in her own case, that the most varied acquirements of learning do not impair the subtlest delicacy of thought and feeling." It is of interest that in contrast to these handsome eulogies in The Poets and Poetry of England, in the Nineteenth Century, Griswold in the same volume disposed of Robert Browning in only one short paragraph, which dealt mainly with his alleged obscurity.

The many American reviews of Elizabeth's volumes

praised and blamed them for much the same reasons which were being expressed in her own country. Cornelius Mathews wrote an article on her poems in the United States Magazine and Democratic Review. Since he had been one of her warmest admirers in America and had recently helped her volumes through the press, he spoke with reverence of the "most exquisite utterances of the divine soul of poetry that glows within her, generated of the sweetest union of womanly tenderness of heart and masculine loftiness and power of intellect.", He praised "A Drama of Exile" for its "lyrical, descriptive, and dramatic forces all in unison" and for the "complete and harmonious impression" it left in the reader's mind; and he declared that "A Vision of Poets" was "one of the finest pieces of criticism in the language."

The Methodist Quarterly Review found "no two qualities more manifest in her than intensity and deep religious feeling" and maintained that among the "spiritual poets" she was "at the very head." The Christian Examiner placed her "in the centre of that constellation of our favourites, Keats, Hood, Sterling, Tennyson, Emerson, Lowell," and it declared that in "bold imagination, beautiful fancy, and tender humanity... she surpasses all other living writers." The author of the article found it "inspiring to meet such lofty genius blended with such meek simplicity of Christian faith-such purity—such peace." His further assertion that "Elizabeth Barrett is herself, and not another or others" is a characteristic example of the reviewing in the literary journals of that period.

The American Whig Review in January 1845 said that there were only two English poets of the new generation who were great: Miss Barrett and Tennyson, and the latter was "certainly not as favorable a representative of the manly character as Miss Barrett is of the feminine." And Margaret Fuller, who was to meet Elizabeth in Florence several years later, did not "hesitate to rank her, in vigour and nobleness of conception, depth of spiritual experience, and command of classic allusion, above any female writer the world has yet known."

Some of the American notices, however, strongly

disapproved of many aspects of her poetry and were surprised that most critics had treated her with such respect. Edwin Percy Whipple in the American Whig Review for July 1845 was offended by her many pedantries, her "barbarous jargon compounded of all languages," and her "elaborately infelicitous style"; and the Knickerbocker felt "ready to despair of Miss Barrett as an artist."

The writer of the critique in Graham's was baffled by much of Elizabeth's poetry, the first reading of which, he thought, "produces pain in the eyes." He added that, "The brain staggers beneath the weight of her compound epithets, or falls back exhausted in striving to follow or unriddle her dark subtlety of fancy. " The harshest criticism came from the Southern Literary Messenger, which expatiated upon all the deficiencies mentioned by other reviews and enumerated many others. The reviewer acknowledged, however, that he was presenting a minority report and concluded that "the more outré and unnatural a writer is, the more lavishly and unscrutinizingly is praise heaped over him."

One of the most comprehensive of the American notices was by the poet Poe. Of his review in the Broadway Journal Elizabeth later said to Browning, "You would have thought that it had been written by a friend and foe, each stark mad with love and hate, and writing the alternate paragraphs." Rather than her long, ambitious pieces, he preferred the simpler poems like "The House of Clouds" and "The Lost Bower," both of which, he believed, were "superlatively lovely, and show the vast powers of the poet in the field best adapted to their legitimate display."

He thought that she was deficient in rhythm, and he disapproved of her inadmissible rhymes, of her overabundant and inappropriate imagery, of her archaic and "quaint" diction (for example, "blé," "'gins," "'las," "'ware," "oftly," "erelong"), of her "excessive reiteration of pet words" (such as "chrism," "nympholeptic," "down," "leaning"), and of her fondness for compound epithets (for example, "dew-pallid," "pale-passioned," "silver-solemn"). Poe was evidently puzzled by Elizabeth's character and personality.

He wrote that her seclusion from the world gave her "a comparative independence of men and opinions" and "a happy audacity of thought and expression never before known in one of her sex"; yet in the following sentence he contradicted himself by saying that her isolation had perhaps "invalidated her original Will—diverted her from proper individuality of purpose—and seduced her into the sin of imitation." The main theme of his article is that Elizabeth had never shown herself capable of any sustained effort, that "her wild and magnificent genius" seemed to exhaust itself in short passages. Yet in spite of his adverse criticisms he declared that she had "done more, in poetry, than any woman, living or dead," and that she had "surpassed all her poetical contemporaries of either sex (with a single exception)."

Only Tennyson, he implied, was a greater poet. Thus Elizabeth had been welcomed by critics on both sides of the Atlantic as one of England's great poets. But she had been given a friendly warning by most of the reviews to express herself with greater simplicity and compression, to restrict herself to more conventional rhymes, and to deal only with subjects close to her own experience. Unfortunately for her artistic development she was never in her later career (with two or three exceptions) to heed their advice.

Chapter 9

Poems of 1850

At Four O'clock in the morning of March 9, 1849, Browning wrote Elizabeth's sisters that "thro' God's infinite goodness our blessed Ba gave birth to a fine, strong boy at a quarter past two: and is doing admirably." After her baby was born, Elizabeth did not sink with exhaustion but "rose up into a state of ecstasy" so that she "could scarcely be kept quiet." She was relieved to see that the child was rosy, fat, healthy, and normal-looking, for she had feared a malformation or "some evil" on account of the morphine she regularly took and also because of a serious fall upon the floor of her apartment in the autumn. The child, who was named Robert Wiedeman Barrett Browning, inherited his mother's oval features; in the long years ahead he was to become in his personality and way of life much more like a Barrett than a Browning.

Soon after the birth of his child, Robert's joy was cut short when he heard from New Cross of his mother's sudden death. He had "loved his mother as such passionate natures only can love"; Elizabeth "never saw a man so bowed down in an extremity of sorrow —never." The Brownings had hoped to go to England in the summer to show their baby to friends and relatives, but Robert told Elizabeth that "it would break his heart to see his mother's roses over the wall, and the place where she used to lay her scissors and gloves." By the middle of May Robert was still "looking very unwell—thinner and paler than usual" and remained depressed in spirits. Early in the summer his loss of appetite and of sleep and his worn, dejected appearance so alarmed Elizabeth that she insisted on his traveling with her to find some place where they, Wilson, the manservant Alessandro, the baby, and his Italian nursemaid might spend the summer away from the heat of Florence. They went along the coast past Carrara to La Spezia, near which, at Lerici, a glance at Shelley's house made her "melancholy... of course."

Then they retraced their steps southward to a mountain village named Seravezza, soon abandoned it because of high prices, proceeded to Bagni di Lucca, rented a house there until the end of October for £12, and returned for the other four members of the household. The road from Lucca to the Baths winds upward along the embankment of the Serchio past great white houses surrounded by vineyards and olive orchards, with steep hills on both sides covered with chestnut forests. About fourteen miles from Lucca the road leaves the Serchio, turns east, and runs for a mile beside the Lima, a rushing mountain stream, to Ponte a Serraglio, the first of the three villages. From there a road winds up the side of a mountain to the second of the villages, Bagni Caldi, where the Brownings spent the rest of that summer in "a sort of eagle's nest" perched high above the valley.

The road from Ponte a Serraglio upward along the Lima comes at the end of a mile to the third of the villages, the Villa, which is mostly a long street of private residences, boarding houses, and shops. In the nineteenth century the Baths of Lucca were a fashionable summer resort for the Anglo-American colony in Italy, who took part in the same social activities which they enjoyed for the rest of the year at Florence and Rome. Now, however, few foreigners spend their holidays there. One of the principal monuments of a vanished era is the simple wooden building of the English Protestant Chapel, which is falling into disrepair and appears to have been empty for several years. Elizabeth wrote from Bagni di Lucca in the summer of 1849 that Stuart was "enlightening the English barbarians at the lower village" with his lectures on Shakespeare and that Lever "presides over the weekly balls at the casino where the English 'do congregate' (all except Robert and me)."

Nor did the Brownings ever attend, either at Lucca or Florence, lectures, amateur theatrical performances, or anyone's "days." Their friends and acquaintances were mostly American and English writers, painters, and sculptors, and visitors who were admirers of their poetry. Even though the Brownings lived for many years in Italy, none of their intimate friends and few of their acquaintances were Italians. The Brownings were attracted to their home high in the Bagni Caldi because of "the coolness, the charm of the mountains, whose very heart you seem to hear beating in the rush of the little river, the green silence of the chestnut forests, and the seclusion which any one may make for himself by keeping clear of the valleyvillages."

Almost every day they would go out and lose themselves "in the woods and mountains, and sit by the waterfalls on the starry and moonlit nights," and in their wanderings they "never met anybody except a monk girt with a rope, now and then, or a barefooted peasant."

One day in the middle of September the entire household, including the baby, made an all-day excursion along the dried-up beds of mountain streams to the top of Prato Fiorito, five miles from the Baths. Elizabeth, Wilson, and the balia rode on donkeys, and Browning and Alessandro on mountain ponies. The scenery was "magnificent," Elizabeth wrote one of her sisters. "At the top you look round on a great world of innumerable mountains, the faint sea beyond them, and not a sign of cultivation—not a cottage—not a hut." There they sat down with their guides to a picnic lunch, during which the baby lay "rolling and laughing" on the shawl Elizabeth had spread on the grass. By the middle of October it had become so cool that they had to cut short their idyllic, carefree way of life in the mountains and return for another season at Casa Guidi, where they arrived on the seventeenth.

During the following autumn and the winter, the Marchesa d'Ossoli, formerly Miss Margaret Fuller, often called on the Brownings. Elizabeth wrote Henrietta that she was "one of the very plainest women I ever saw in my life, and talking fluent Italian with a pure Boston accent. Still she is a woman of a good deal of generous and womanly goodness." Miss Fuller had first achieved recognition in Boston with her series of very successful "conversations" on serious subjects conducted for the young women of that city. Along with Emerson and George Ripley, she was later an editor of the Dial, the organ of the Concord transcendentalists, and then she became a protégée of Horace Greeley and for almost two years wrote reviews and articles for his newspaper, the New York Daily Tribune. In the summer of 1846 she sailed for England, where she hoped to meet, among others, Elizabeth Barrett, to whom she was carrying a letter of introduction from Cornelius Mathews.

Elizabeth's marriage and removal to Italy had prevented their meeting in London. Miss Fuller traveled around the British Isles, France, and Italy, and then settled in Rome for the winter of 1847-48 and astonished her acquaintances by marrying an Italian military officer about a decade younger than she, penniless, and with no pretension to her degree of intellectual culture. Both she and her husband aided the cause of the Roman republic, and when it fell in July 1849 they went with their child to Florence, where she undertook the writing of a history of the Roman revolution.

"Over a great gulf of differing opinion" both of the Brownings "felt drawn strongly to her." Elizabeth was liberal in her political views and much more progressive and broad-minded than many of her acquaintances and relatives, but she was shocked at Madame Ossoli's radical socialism; she later described her guest as a woman "of noble instincts, but a very hampered intellect, and of opinions quite the wildest." When Madame Ossoli paid a farewell call upon the Brownings during her last evening in Italy, she was filled with "gloom" and "sad presentiment" and gave as a parting gift from her child to the Brownings' baby a Bible, with the inscription "In memory of Angelo Eugene Ossoli," which seemed to Elizabeth "a strange, prophetical expression."

On the voyage back to America, the ship (the Elizabeth) carrying Madame Ossoli, her husband, and their child sank, and all three were drowned. Elizabeth was very much depressed when she heard of the tragedy, "affecting in itself," she wrote Miss Mitford, "and also through association with that past, when the arrowhead of anguish was broken too deeply into my life ever to be quite drawn out." Both of the Brownings were busy with their own poetry in the winter of 1849-50. Robert was writing his Christmas-Eve and Easter-Day, and Elizabeth was revising her volumes of 1838 and of 1844 in preparation for a new edition. Browning's poem was not brought out by Moxon, possibly because the poet considered him too slow and too conservative, but by Chapman and Hall. Elizabeth thought that the new work, which was issued on the first of April, was "full of power," but it received few acceptable reviews and the sales were poor.

Indeed, during Elizabeth's lifetime all of Browning's poetry failed to win general recognition, and his reputation was very much overshadowed by that of his wife. For example, when the post of poet laureate became vacant after Wordsworth's death in April 1850 it was Elizabeth, not Robert, whom the Athenaeum recommended to the position. On June first the first paragraph of "Our Weekly Gossip," a column probably written by H. F. Chorley, said that to grant the laureateship "to a female would be at once an honourable testimonial to the individual, a fitting recognition of the remarkable place which the women of England have taken in the literature of the day, and a graceful compliment to the Sovereign herself." The writer added, "There is no living poet of either sex who can prefer a higher claim than Mrs. Elizabeth Barrett Browning."

Three weeks later the Athenaeum reported that Leigh Hunt was being considered for the post. Although the author of the article believed that Hunt had a claim, he thought that it was "not of the kind which can be properly recognized by the laureateship," and again suggested Elizabeth's name. After the position was granted to Tennyson, the writer in the Athenaeum regretted the decision because the award had not gone to a woman and because Tennyson already had a pension. Elizabeth had at first favored Leigh Hunt, who was "a great man and a good man in spite of all," but she later said that Tennyson was "in a sense" worthier of the laureateship than Hunt; "only Tennyson can wait, that is the single difference."

Although Elizabeth had not published much poetry since her volumes of 1844, she had not been altogether forgotten either in America or England before the discussion about the laureateship. An American critic and traveller, Henry Theodore Tuckerman, who had been for a while editor of the Boston Miscellany of Literature and Fashion, in which Elizabeth had published in 1842, wrote an appreciative review of her work in his Thoughts on the Poets, which appeared in New York in 1846. He emphasized her classical scholarship and declared that her poems were "imbued with the spirit of antique models." A Scottish preacher and journalist, George Gilfillan published an article on her poetry in Tait's Edinburgh Magazine in 1847. He praised several of her shorter poems but counseled her to simplify her style, "to sift her diction of whatever is harsh and barbarous," and to write "in the clear articulate language of men." Clarity of expression, he implied, was primarily a masculine characteristic.

An American clergyman, musician, and minor poet, George W. Bethune, wrote in 1848 in his The British Female Poets of Elizabeth's "high religious faith, her love of children, her delight in the graceful and beautiful, her revelations of feminine feeling, her sorrow over the suffering, and her indignation against the oppressor." Thomas Powell, an Englishman who had collaborated with R. H. Horne in The Poems of Geoffrey Chaucer, Modernized and who later became a journalist in New York, published there in 1849 The Living Authors of England, in which he described Elizabeth as "the greatest poetical intellect ever vouchsafed to an English woman." That same year an English editor and author, Frederick Rowton, paid tribute to her genius in his The Female Poets of Great Britain.

He found in her precisely the qualities she seems now to lack: "She is chief amongst the learned poetesses of our land: at least, I know of no British female writer who exhibits so intimate an acquaintance with the spirit of both antique and modern philosophy, or so refined a perception of intellectual purity and beauty. Her poetry is the poetry of pure reason." Elizabeth herself probably did not know of all these flattering articles which had appeared on both sides of the Atlantic, but she was much pleased to have been suggested for the laureateship. While she was awaiting the critical reception of her new volumes, she suffered in the summer of 1850 from her fourth, her last, and by far her worst miscarriage and her most serious setback since she had left England. For six weeks afterward she could not walk and was thin and white and greatly depressed.

Her physician Dr. Harding realized that no amount of medicine could effect a cure and that she would have to move to a cooler place in the country as soon as she was well enough to travel. At seven in the morning of August 31 the Brownings left Florence by railroad for Siena, with Elizabeth "in a miserably helpless state, having to be lifted about like a baby, looking ghostly rather than ghastly, and feeling as if it were a most uncongenial effort."

They spent the month of September about two miles from the city in a small villa which cost only eleven shillings a week. It was in the midst of its own vineyard, olive orchard, and flower garden and was on a hill called poggio dei venti. The villa was cool and had splendid views in all directions. Elizabeth wrote, "From one window you have a view of Siena, with its Duomo and its campanile, and its Italian colouring over all!... From another, the whole country leaps under the sun, alive with verdure and vineyards." Her health soon improved enough so that during the first week of October, which the Brownings spent inside the city of Siena, she was able to walk through the cathedral and the Academy, where she admired "the divine Eve of Sodoma."

Although she was to live in Siena parts of the summers of 1859 and 1860 and to pass through the city many times on her journeys between Florence and Rome, she was never again strong enough to climb the steps into the cathedral. ABOUT the first of November Elizabeth's "new edition" was brought out by Chapman and Hall, who had published Browning

Christmas-Eve and Easter-Day. The Poems were issued in two octavo volumes bound in dark gray-blue cloth boards. Elizabeth included all of the poems in the volumes of 1844 and all but nine of the poems in the volume of The Seraphim (omitting the weakest, such as "The Little Friend," "Victoria's Tears," and "The Weeping Saviour") and all the verses which had appeared in periodicals since 1844, most of them in Blackwood's, two in the Christian Mother's Magazine, and one each in the Liberty Bell of Boston and the Athenaeum; also "A Sabbath Morning at Sea" from an annual in 1839 and "The Claim," which had been published in the Athenaeum in 1842.

She had not been writing for magazines so frequently as before her marriage. Browning strongly disapproved of the publication of poetry in a periodical before it should appear in a book, because he felt the practice was a deception of the future buyers of the book. The most important of her works being published for the first time were the new translation of the Prometheus Bound, a translation of Bion Lament for Adonis, and the "Sonnets from the Portuguese," as well as three short poems which also were inspired by her love for Browning: "Life and Love," "Inclusions," and "Insufficiency."

In the preparation of her new edition she made many revisions among the poems of 1844 and had to rewrite many pages of the volume of 1838. "Oh, such feeble rhymes, and turns of thought —such a dingy mistiness!" she wrote of The Seraphim, and Other Poems. "Even Robert couldn't say a word for much of it. I took great pains with the whole, and made considerable portions new." First of all, she improved many of the rhymes: "shaped" and "heaped" became "deep" and "heap"; "spade" and "led" was changed to "spade" and "laid." Obsolete words such as "een," "eyne," "pleasaunce," "eke," "aye," "erst," "anear," "enow" were eliminated. Dissyllabic past participles like "kneelëd," "laughëd," "lookëd" were revised to "knelt," "her laugh," "did look"; and outmoded words such as "waxëd" and "trancëd" were removed.

She took out adverbs which had been over-used and were sometimes meaningless; for instance, "striking on thy ringlets sheenly." Many adjectives were placed in their normal position: "water colourless" became "the gray water" and "her small feet bare" was changed to "her small bare feet." The indicative form of the verb was substituted for the old-fashioned subjunctive: "There be (later "are") none of England's daughters." Several of her emendations were of words which had done violence to parts of speech; for example, "verduring the hills" became "to beautify thy hills." Occasionally when a passage was filled with archaic diction, she entirely rewrote the lines. To illustrate, the following verses seemed so unpromising that she eliminated them altogether from the revised version of the "Stanzas to Bettine":

I ween, thy smile is graver—
Paler thy cheek, I ween:
For thou the mystic sight hast seen,
Which maketh quail the braver—

She also removed many of the mottoes for individual poems: verses by Beaumont and Fletcher, Burton, Spenser, Habington, Hawes, Gascoigne, Wither, and others; also Latin verses by Milton and passages in Greek by Plato, Orpheus, and St. Chrysostom; and she discarded a long footnote on the derivation of the name of Homer and two shorter footnotes referring to Biblical passages. Her reason for the deletions may have been that she was weary of her reputation as an uncomfortably learned poet. Since her marriage she had no longer been reading Hebrew, Greek, and Latin, and English literature of earlier periods. The only long poem she had written was the first part of Casa Guidi Windows, which was still in manuscript, on current affairs in Italy. After the bleak years at Wimpole Street she had achieved fulfillment as a wife and mother. She therefore may have wished to come before the public in 1850 as a writer who had moved away from the world of books toward "life."

Prometheus Bound had been finished in 1845 and was later sent to William Blackwood in Edinburgh. In 1848 he also had the manuscript of "A Meditation in Tuscany" but later returned both works because of their unsuitability for publication in his magazine. Elizabeth included them in the Poems of 1850. Her translation of the Prometheus Bound, which received Browning's careful attention in the spring of 1845, is a great improvement upon her earlier attempt.

It is a spirited and readable, rather than a pedantically literal, version; although in many passages she does not pretend to convey every idiosyncrasy of the Greek, she nowhere misleads the reader. She did not make Browning's mistake years later in his translation of the Agamemnon, which remained so close to the original that it was generally considered incomprehensible. One example out of many may serve to illustrate her skill in preserving the meaning of the Greek despite the demands of rhyme. Prometheus, hearing the approach of the Chorus of the daughters of Oceanus, says to himself:

Alas, alas, what rustling motion of birds
of prey do I again hear near by? The
air is whirring under the light flutter-
ings of wings.
In Elizabeth's translation, Prometheus says:
Alas me! what a murmur and motion I hear,
As of birds flying near!
And the air undersings
The light stroke of their wings—

Indeed throughout her version Elizabeth happily reproduces many of the original figures of speech. For instance, in the following passage she makes clear the meaning of the verb åõèìéìæù, "to bring into harmony," as one forces words into their appropriate rhythms in verse. Prometheus says to the Chorus that he alone had the courage to make a stand against the tyrant Zeus. Therefore he is suffering fearful tortures; and although he gave mortals first place in his pity, he himself is thought unworthy of pity, But without mercy I have been thus disciplined.

Elizabeth makes Prometheus say:

While I render out Deep rhythms of anguish 'neath the harping hand That strikes me thus!—

At times for the sake of clarity she expands a metaphor which is merely suggested in the Greek. As an example I quote once again from the two versions. When the members of the

Chorus arrive at the scene, they express their compassion for the hero. They well understand the reason for his punishment:

For new helm-directors hold sway in
Olympus; and with new laws Zeus is
lawlessly ruling, and the mighty things
of old he is now annihilating.

The following paraphrase is much more effective than if it had been an exact translation:

For new is the Hand and the rudder that steers
The ship of Olympus through surge and wind—
And of old things passed, no track is behind.

Among the poems in the volumes of 1850 with personal associations are three sonnets to H. S. Boyd: "His Blindness," "His Death," and "Legacies," the latter of which is filled with lachrymose recollections. The copies of Aeschylus and of Gregory Nazianzen which came to her after his death were those I used to read from, thus

Assisting my dear teacher's soul to unlock
The darkness of his eyes: now, mine they mock,
Blinded in turn, by tears: now, murmurous
Sad echoes of my young voice, years agone,
Entoning, from these leaves, the Græcian phrase,
Return and choke my utterance.

Another poem with the background of Herefordshire was "Hector in the Garden," which had been written before she left Italy and published in Blackwood's in October 1846. Elizabeth recalls the pleasure she experienced at the age of nine from tending in the Hope End garden a "huge giant" of many different kinds of flowers—daffodils, violets, lilies, daisies, and others.

In spite of its descriptive charm, the poem is spoiled by the "moral" of the concluding stanzas. The poet will not allow herself "this dreaming" about the past, but she thirsts for action, "Life's heroic ends pursuing."

It was in the new edition of her Poems that Elizabeth first published the sonnet sequence she had composed before her marriage. On July 22 of her last summer in London she had said to Browning, "You shall see some day at Pisa what I will not show you now. Does not Solomon say that 'there is a time to read what is written.'

"Except for that cryptic remark she told him nothing of the sonnets she had been writing on the miracle of her life: her former isolation, ill-health, and sense of deep grief followed by the triumph of love over doubts and fears. Just before the last, the forty-fourth of the sonnets which Elizabeth copied into her small white notebook, she wrote, "50 Wimpole Street 1846, Sept." In this poem she spoke of the many flowers Browning had brought her from his garden, and in return she presented him with her sheaf of sonnets:

So, in the like name of that love of ours,
Take back these thoughts, which here, unfolded too,
And which on warm and cold days I withdrew
From my heart's ground.

But neither at Pisa nor for the next two years at Florence did she show her husband the sonnets written for him. It was not until the Brownings were at Bagni di Lucca in the summer of 1849 that Elizabeth first placed "that wreath of Sonnets" on Robert "one morning unawares, three years after it had been twined." Her reluctance to let him see them all this time may have been due to her shyness or to a chance remark Browning had once made "against putting one's loves into verse."

At Lucca he had suddenly spoken "something else on the other side," and the following morning Elizabeth "said hesitatingly 'Do you know I once wrote some poems about you?'—and then—'There they are, if you care to see them,'—and there was the little Book"—the same one which Browning had beside him when he later wrote these words to Julia Wedgwood three years after Elizabeth's death.

When Robert saw the manuscript, he was "much touched and pleased" and thought so highly of the poetry that he "could not consent," Elizabeth wrote Arabel, "that they should be lost" to her volumes. Browning and she decided "to slip them in under some sort of veil" and chose the title "Sonnets from the Portuguese," which might seem to mean "from the Portuguese language," but which really referred to "Catarina to Camoens," the poem immediately preceding the "Sonnets."

Browning had read this poem before he made Elizabeth's acquaintance, and it "had affected him to tears,.. again and again."

Ever since then he had "in a loving fancy" associated her with the Portuguese Catarina. According to legend she was the girl with whom the Portuguese poet Camoëns fell in love, and she is supposed to have died during his absence abroad and to have left him "the riband from her hair," as Browning said. And so Elizabeth and Robert gave the "Sonnets" their ambiguous name and allowed the public, "who are very little versed in Portuguese literature," as Elizabeth wrote, to interpret the title as they pleased. Forty-three of the "Sonnets" came at the end of the second volume of the new edition. "Future and Past," which was the last poem of the first volume, later became the forty-second of the sonnet sequence in the fourth edition of 1856.

Elizabeth did not place the sonnet with the others in 1850 because of its association with "Past and Future" published in the Poems of 1844, and she thus hoped to preserve the anonymity of the new sequence. In the earliest of the three manuscripts of the "Sonnets" which have been preserved, she gave titles to eight of the poems: "Deathand love" and love", "Love's Obstacles", "Love's New Creation", "Love's Expression", "Love's Causes", "Love's Repetitions", "Love's Refuge", and "Love's Sacrifice". But she wisely decided that forty-three titles all somewhat similar to one another would have a monotonous effect and crossed out the eight she had tentatively chosen so that in the published form the individual poems were designated only by numerals. Elizabeth took more pains in the composition of the "Sonnets" than in any of her former poems.

For once the expression was concise and coherent, the rhymes almost all conventional, the imagery in better taste, the syntax clear, and the diction simple and unaffected. A study of the significant revisions of one of the sonnets will illustrate the great care with which she wrote and later emended them. The "Sonnets" may be seen in five different stages of development: the manuscript in the Pierpont Morgan

Library, the George Murray Smith Memorial Manuscript in the British Museum, the new edition of the Poems, the third edition of 1853 (in which she made only three or four slight revisions of the "Sonnets"), and the fourth edition of the Poems in 1856. The earliest manuscript reading of "Sonnet 16," for example, is as follows:

And yet because thou art above me so,
Because thou art more strong, and like a king,
Thou canst prevail against my fears and fling
Thy purple round me till my heart shall grow
Too close against thy heart to henceforth know
Its separate trembling pulse. Oh, conquering May prove as noble and complete a thing
In lifting upward as in beating low!
And as a soldier, struck down by a sword,
Cries "Here my strife ends", and sinks dead to earth,—
Even so, beloved, I, at last, record.. "My doubt ends here—" If thou invite me forth,
I rise above abasement at the word!—
Make thy love larger to enlarge my worth.

The words "art above me" were given a stronger meaning by the substitution of "overcomest." "Strong" in line 2 was changed to "princely" and later to "noble." The awkward and needless splitting of the infinitive in line 5 was corrected so that the phrase became "henceforth to know." Perhaps since the movement of the first four words in line 6 was hindered by the excessive number of s and t sounds, she eliminated the expression and substituted "How it shook when alone." The word "noble" had been used in the revision of line 2 and was therefore removed from line 7 in favour of "lordly." In line 8 "beating" was replaced by the more vivid "crushing." In the change of the next two lines, the figure became much happier: the wounded soldier raised by his gallant enemy is compared to the poet herself, whose hesitations were conquered by a generous lover.

And as a vanquished soldier yields his sword
To one who lifts him from the bloody earth,—

The first four words of line 12 became in 1850 the more

emphatic sentence, "Here ends my doubt!" and in 1856 the meaning was enlarged by the change: "Here ends my strife." Yet despite Elizabeth's conscientious craftsmanship the freshness of the "Sonnets" has faded, and they no longer evoke the eager response of earlier generations; with all their singing angels, floods of tears, chrisms, lutes, and golden thrones, they are very much in the idiom of the period. But no poems were ever called into being by a love more true and sincere.

SHE received fewer reviews of her new edition than she had in either 1838 or in 1844. The Poems of 1850 were almost unnoticed in the United States, because no separate American edition was issued. A Boston publisher had agreed to reprint her two volumes and to pay for the rights, but he was anticipated by C. S. Francis of New York, who pirated the two volumes of her Poems without any of the alterations or new material. "I don't know when I have been so provoked," Elizabeth wrote to Arabe of the failure of the Boston publisher to honour his agreement because the volumes had already appeared in New York. "So I lose everything—both money and reputation."

A brief, perfunctory notice of one paragraph in the Christian Examiner of Boston referred to Elizabeth's "possession of the richest poetical gifts." An equally short para graph in Harper's Magazine spoke of her "peculiar boldness, originality, and beauty" and said that the new edition would be "thankfully accepted by the wide circle which has learned to venerate Mrs. Browning's genius." In England the most favorable review was in the Athenaeum and was probably written by Elizabeth's friend H. F. Chorley. He quoted from many of her best-known poems, such as "The Cry of the Children" and "Catarina to Camoens" and concluded with handsome praise: "Mrs. Browning is probably, of her sex, the first imaginative writer England has produced in any age:—she is, beyond comparison, the first poetess of her own."

The Eclectic Review, which was also extravagant in its commendation of the Poems, spoke of her "splendid poetry," her "profound thought," and her "pervading spirit so pure and so womanly." The writer thought that the romantic ballad

"Bertha in the Lane" was "unrivalled in its pathetic beauty" and that the carelessly written "Lady Geraldine's Courtship" was "one of the most charming and finely-elaborated poems in the language" and had an effect which was "indescribably delightful." No other woman writer, in the reviewer's opinion, had such a combination of "solemn purpose with large intellect and the same intensity of imagination." But the Guardian, the Examiner, Fraser's Magazine, and the English Review were all more temperate in their praise and believed that even her most recent poetry had the same faults of style mentioned in the reviews of earlier volumes: diffuseness, obscure and affected diction, ungrammatical syntax, inappropriate and absurd images, confusion of the parts of speech, slovenly versification, and faulty rhymes.

Each of the four reviews, however, found something to commend. The Guardian, for example, said that "in melody of verse, in tenderness, in true pathos, in abundant language, command of rhyme, and affluence of imagery, she is quite in the first ranks of living writers. In all her works she evinces marks of a truly poetical mind." The English Review asserted that Elizabeth took "high rank among the bards of England" and that there was perhaps none who surpassed her "in her especial beauties—in the combination of romantic wildness with deep, true tenderness and most singular power." Yet unlike many critics at that time the reviewer considered Browning a greater poet than his wife: "Upon the whole, we think Browning's the higher and the master spirit; hers the more tender, and the more musical also." A remark in the Examiner on "Lady Geraldine's Courtship" and "The Romaunt of the Page" was expressed with the characteristic glibness of reviewers: that both poems "show how delicate, pure, and intense a spirit of womanly love is connected with this masculine and far-reaching intellect."

On the whole the reviewers had curiously little to say about either the new translation of the Prometheus Bound or about the "Sonnets from the Portuguese." It is doubtful whether the writer of the notice in the English Review understood Elizabeth's responsibility as a translator, for he wrote of her Prometheus Bound that the hero's "complaints are rather too rhetorically rendered, without sufficient dramatic earnestness." The Eclectic Review called her version of the drama "a noble achievement" and said that it was one of the many evidences in the volumes of the poet's "solid classical scholarship." None of the reviewers made a close examination of the Prometheus Bound by comparing it with the original, nor did any of them appear to know that the new translation was her second of the same drama.

The reviewers were equally imperceptive in their comments on the "Sonnets from the Portuguese." They mostly ignored these new poems, and the two or three which mentioned them failed to grasp their significance. The writer in Fraser's Magazine did not understand that the sonnets were a revelation of the poet's own love, but he suggested that they were more than translations: "From the Portuguese they may be: but their life and earnestness must prove Mrs. Browning either to be the most perfect of all known translators, or to have quickened with her own spirit the framework of another's thoughts, and then modestly declined the honour which was really her own." The Examiner described the themes of the "Sonnets," which it thought a "remarkable series," but it gave no hint that they might have been based upon Elizabeth's personal experiences.

The Spectator was the only important journal which found almost nothing of merit in the new edition. The reviewer believed that although Elizabeth had shown great promise in her earlier volumes, she had made almost no progress in her art: "Mrs. Brown ing has given no single instance of her ability to compose finished works. Diffuseness, obscurity, and exaggeration, mar even the happiest efforts of her genius." It seemed to the writer that most of her poems were only "rough sketches, thrown off, it is to be supposed, in one or two sittings." Elizabeth was not exhilarated by the notices of her volumes of 1850, as she had been in 1844, probably because copies of the reviews did not arrive in Italy until months after they had been published. Since many of the reviews had been kind to her, she could not have been disappointed (for example, the article in the Guardian, which she read early in May 1851, just as she was beginning her journey to England, gave her great pleasure).

But the authors of the articles had mostly read her poems with the same carelessness and haste they had imputed to her writing, and they had expressed themselves superficially and in clichés. In November and December a young American paid a number of calls at Casa Guidi. Charles Eliot Norton, who was later to be the first professor of fine arts at Harvard, was on a leisurely tour of the East and of Europe. At their apartment in Florence he found the Brownings "sitting in a pleasant home-like room, surrounded with pictures and books, with an open fire shedding a genial light through it." Browning, as Norton described him, had "a pleasant open expression and manner" and seemed in his looks and conversation quite unlike the idea of him he had received from his poems. Elizabeth's appearance was also altogether different from what he had expected after reading her works. He noticed her slight and delicate figure, her "reserved and timid" manner, her quiet plaintive voice.

At first she had little to say, and Norton felt "as if she were so distrustful of herself that she kept back the expression of her sentiments and thoughts from all but those with whom she was familiar." Her face, like her voice, was "melancholy" and "full of sensibility" so that she looked like "the most delicate and sensitive of poets," rather than the author of poems of "very great intellectual strength and power of expression." The more he saw of the Brownings, the more he liked them. Browning's conversation he thought extraordinary, with its quick flow of ideas and its inexhaustible fund of anecdotes told "with such entire straightforward earnestness that one cannot but like him." Norton continued, "He is quite unconscious and never even in the slightest way claims any regard for himself as a poet, or shows that he expects you to remember that he is one. Indeed one of the most charming characteristics of both him and his wife is their self-forgetfulness."

IT WAS during the winter of 1850-51 that Elizabeth wrote

the second half of Casa Guidi Windows on the events which had taken place two years before. Early in the spring she sent the manuscript to London, and the work was published as a slender octavo volume by Chapman and Hall on the last day of May. Later in the year C. S. Francis in New York pirated the poem in a volume which included the revised Prometheus Bound and the other new poems of Elizabeth's edition of 1850. The American Whig Review, which was one of the few journals in the United States to notice it, was unsympathetic and made fun of almost all the poems because of their unconventional diction, syntax, and rhyme. The writer of the article, which was a joint review with Browning Sordello and the series of Bells and Pomegranates, believed, however, that the Brownings had "two of the greatest poetical minds of the day" and were "possibly the most interesting married couple on record."

Elizabeth knew that her sharp criticism of British foreign policy in Casa Guidi Windows would offend many English critics. Nor was she mistaken; a number of journals ignored the poem, and those which reviewed it were mostly unfriendly.

To many English people the Italian situation seemed remote, and the war of 184849 was all but forgotten. None of the reviewers was interested enough in the work to discuss in detail Elizabeth's attitude toward Pius IX, Duke Leopold, Guerrazzi, and Garibaldi, and her reasons for the failure of the liberal movement. The Athenaeum, the Guardian, and the Prospective Review condemned the poem for its diffuseness, its excessively colloquial style, and its poor choice of subject matter. According to the Prospective Review, one of the chief defects of the work was "its limitation in scope and topic"; it was "too truly and too literally described by its title." But Elizabeth had already explained in the introductory "Advertisement" in her volume that she was attempting "no continous narrative, or exposition of political philosophy" and was presenting only "a simple story of personal impressions."

The Guardian called the poem "an unmistakeable and complete failure," filled with "a great deal of diffuse and rather commonplace reflection and regret." Miss Mitford, who had always preferred Elizabeth's romantic ballads to her other types of poems, described her recent work as "a dull tirade on Italian politics" and added that the treatment of the material was "so unreal that it excites no sympathy." The Eclectic Review, on the other hand, considered that the poem was "perhaps, the finest which she has produced, and is certainly one of the noblest productions of female genius. The language is singularly eloquent and strong; the feeling which pervades it is in the highest tone of humanity." The writer was surprised, however, at her "crying so coldly and cruelly for war" after advocating in the first part of the same volume that England should remain at peace.

The Literary Gazette, which found in the poem "all the charm which might be expected from Mrs. Browning's fine and original perceptions and ardent style," praised her for having "systematically adopted a chaster and severer style." The reviewer thought that many passages were "dashed off with a fiery energy and a picturesque brevity which are almost Dantesque." Although the Spectator had spoken harshly of her new edition of the Poems, it said that Casa Guidi Windows was a great improvement and admired Elizabeth for her "womanly faith and trust" which had remained firm in the face of many disappointments. Unlike almost all the other journals, it approved of her writing on the politics of the hour and strongly recommended the book "as a proof of the feminine warmth of heart that may coexist with a vivid sympathy with the public affairs of nations."

But whether the notices were laudatory or censorious, Elizabeth paid less attention to them than she had to the reviews of some of her earlier books, for she was making her first trip back to England. Except for a few remarks in the letters which she received at Lucerne and at Paris from Arabel, she heard little about the reception of the volume. The Brownings had not been able to return to England in the summer of 1849 because of the death of Robert's mother, or in 1850 because of Elizabeth's pregnancy and severe illness. By the winter and spring of the following year she had fully regained her health and was stronger than she had been at any time since her childhood.

Once she even walked up the long steep hill to the ancient Basilica of San Miniato al Monte. Several years after Elizabeth's death, Browning referred to this period as the time when she "was at the very height of her health, so far as she ever recovered it: but we returned for the first time to England, and there was fatigue, and afterward, other troubles began, and she never touched that height again." It was probably on May 3, 1851, that Elizabeth, Browning, the baby, and Wilson left Casa Guidi for a tour of northern Italy and Switzerland on their journey to England. They planned to settle in Paris for the winter and to visit Rome in the following spring, but they were not to see Italy again until the autumn of 1852.

Chapter 10

Poems before Congress

Aurora Leigh was Elizabeth's last major poetical work. The effort of composition had exhausted her; afterward she had almost nothing new to say, and for the remaining four and one-half years of her life she produced only a few short poems, most of which were written to express her sympathy with the Italian cause after the outbreak of fighting in 1859. Her loss of creative energy was due partly to a series of bereavements which depressed her spirits and sapped her strength. First of all, Kenyon, who had been a kind and generous friend of the Brownings and more than a father to Elizabeth, died at his home on the Isle of Wight on December 3, 1856, only a few weeks after the publication of the poem which had been dedicated to him. "It has been a sad, sad Christmas to me," wrote Elizabeth, who could scarcely imagine England "without that bright face and sympathetic hand, that princely nature."

The Brownings heard that they had received a legacy from Kenyon of £11,000, of which the sum of 6,500 was left to Robert, "marking delicately a sense of trust" for which Elizabeth acknowledged that she was especially grateful. They invested most of the amount in Tuscan bonds, which brought them an annual income of about £550, and they also continued to receive small royalties from the sale of Elizabeth's books and about £175 a year from her investments in British government bonds. Henceforth their total income was to be more than enough for their needs; "altogether, we want nothing," Elizabeth wrote Henrietta. The next death which saddened Elizabeth was that of her old friend G. B. Hunter, who had never resumed his correspondence with her after she had left her home on Wimpole Street. "So our dear friend, dear Mr. Hunter, with all his morbid sensitiveness and many high qualities, is at rest from the turbulence of this world at last,", she wrote Arabel in February 1857.

In the same letter she said that for two or three days before she heard the news, her thoughts had strangely gone back to her days at Sidmouth and to her friendship there with "poor dearest Mr. Hunter." When she first learned of his death, she was deeply shocked and spent a sleepless night thinking "of all that past at Sidmouth." Although she realized that life would have continued to separate them more completely than death, the certainty that Hunter and she would never see or write to each other again was "painful, painful." She sustained a much severer blow soon afterwards when she received word from England of her father's death on April 17, within a month of his seventy-second birthday. He was buried beside his wife in the Parish Church of St. Michael and All Angels in Ledbury.

On May 3 Browning informed Mrs. Martin that Elizabeth had been sadly affected and that she was still weak and prostrated. "So it is all over now," he wrote, "all hope of better things, or a kind answers to entreaties such as I have seen Ba write in the bitterness of her heart. There must have been something in the organisation, or education, at least, that would account for and extenuate all this; but it has caused grief enough, I know; and now here is a new grief not likely to subside very soon." A few days later he wrote that he thought that the death had been "very strange and sudden and mournful." Early in the summer Elizabeth described in a letter to Mrs. Martin the great bitterness she had felt within her and the recoil against herself. Long ago she had lost hope of reconciliation; yet strangely enough, what she had for many years called "unkindness" had left within her, now that it was gone, "such a sudden desolation!"

During the previous summer both Mrs. Martin and Mrs. Hedley (Aunt Jane) had made a last attempt to persuade Mr. Barret to "forgive" the three of his children who had married and to treat them no differently from the other members of his family. That Mrs. Hedley failed in her effort may be seen from three sentences in Elizabeth's letter to Henrietta postmarked at Florence January 11, 1857: "I am glad that dear Aunt Jane is to be received in W. St. after all. It would have been too painful if her solicitude and kind feeling toward us had been visited on her unpleasantly. Now it is all over (hope lessly for us, Henrietta) she will be held in higher esteem for it even by the person whom she irritated for the moment."

Just before Mr. Barrett's death, Elizabeth heard from Mrs. Martin that in reply to her letter of intercession, he had written her that he "had forgiven" and that he even prayed for the "well being and well doing" of the three families he had never recognized. "Those were his words," Elizabeth wrote a few weeks after her father's death. "Let us hold them fast beloved Henrietta. He prayed for us. Our poor little children had so much from him. And we when we pray, may thank God for so much comfort." What Mr. Barrett wished to signify by the word "forgive" is not clear, for he refused to tell Kenyon's executor the address of Henrietta, who had been willed £100. He never communicated with Elizabeth, Henrietta, or Alfred after their marriages, nor did he leave them anything in his will.

In spite of Elizabeth's distance from England she had never abdicated her right as the eldest of the children to advise her brothers and sisters from time to time how they should arrange their lives. As she acknowledged half in jest, "I am moved in the spirit always to get up and meddle, and put everybody in the place I want them to stand in—which is foolish, and very provoking, I dare say." After her father's death she pleaded with Arabel to visit Robert and her in Italy, thinking that her sister would prefer something more cheerful and less sectarian than her way of life in London, with her devotion to the Chapel and to the Ragged Schools for destitute girls. She seems to have hurt Arabel to the point of tears by assuming that she would leave London immediately.

Even though Arabel had the means and the leisure, she had no desire for a trip to Italy or anywhere else and firmly told Elizabeth that the life she had been living seemed worth while and congenial in all ways and that she had no plans ever to change the pattern. To calm Elizabeth she vaguely promised that some day she would come to Florence, but she never went to see the Brownings in Italy. Then Elizabeth hoped that the Barrett family would remain under one roof and not scatter themselves throughout England. Now that they were financially independent, however, they preferred to live in separate establishments. Elizabeth was distressed to learn that the house at Wimpole Street was soon disposed of and that Arabel, instead of spending some of her money to see Italy, was buying furniture for a home of her own, facing the Paddington Canal at 7 Delamere Terrace.

As soon as the eldest living son, Charles John, heard in the West Indies of his father's death, he sailed immediately to England, where he secured for a time possession of a country estate in Shropshire, near the Welsh border. Some months later Elizabeth wrote both to Henrietta and to Arabel that she thought it was absurd for Charles John, Septimus, and Octavius to go to Jamaica, since she could see no valid reason for their wishing to live on the family plantations far from friends and relatives in England. She disapproved of Alfred's going to a distant country—possibly China—on a government mission and leaving his young and attractive wife in Cheltenham, with all its temptations, and she expressed to Arabel the wish that he return from "that unhealthy climate where he professes to find no overwhelming advantages."

Not long after George Barrett received his share of his father's estate, he bought a house in Devon and gave up his law practice. Elizabeth wrote to him that she was vexed to learn that he was planning to settle in the country, with no specific occupation in view. She reproved him for failing to gain a wider view of the world before burying himself in a place remote from any centre of intellectual activity. In spite of all advice from their eldest sister, the brothers and sisters continued to manage their affairs just as they pleased.

After the publication of Aurora Leigh, Elizabeth's literary reputation far exceeded Robert's. An Irish traveller and writer on many different religious and philanthropical subjects,

Frances Power Cobbe, who knew the Brownings at this time, wrote that she thought that no one of the group which surrounded them in Florence considered Robert as a great poet or in any way equal to his wife, whose long novel in verse had recently appeared. She added that Browning's unselfishness in constantly speaking of Elizabeth's fame, in showing to his friends favorable reviews of the poem, and in referring to the many editions through which the work had run perhaps obscured his own claims.

He himself always maintained "the simple truth" that Elizabeth was "the poet" and he "the clever person by comparison." Miss Cobbe re membered Robert as a kindly man with a pleasant face and cordial manners who had a fund of droll stories to tell. Elizabeth also observed that, "As a sort of lion, Robert has his range in society, and, for the rest, you should see Chapman's returns," which indeed must have been negligible. Although she could scarcely complain on her own account of an unappreciative public, she felt that "the blindness, deafness, and stupidity of the English public to Robert are amazing." It seemed to her that no one in England pretended to do him justice except a small group of Pre-Raphaelite writers and artists.

The most interesting visitor to the Brownings' apartment in the spring of 1857 was Harriet Beecher Stowe, whose Uncle Tom's Cabin—"the most successful book printed by man or woman," Elizabeth called it—had made her one of the best-known women novelists in the English-speaking world. Elizabeth was happy to discover "no rampant Americanisms" and found Mrs. Stowe pleasant appearing, with a mass of dark, wavy hair, and more refined than she had imagined her to be. She wrote to Mrs. Jameson, however, that Mrs. Stowe's "brow has not very large capacity; and the mouth wants something both in frankness and sensitiveness."

Three years later Mrs. Stowe called again on Elizabeth when Browning and she were in Rome, and the two women talked about spiritualism and the French emperor. Since Mrs. Stowe also believed in "the spirits" and was becoming more of a Napoleonist, their conversation must have been harmonious. After this visit Elizabeth wrote Isa Blagden that she liked Mrs. Stowe very much and thought her "surprisingly large and open, considering her antecedents and early associations."

During the winter of 1856-57 and the following spring Elizabeth mostly led a very quiet life at home because of her frail health. One evening, however, she went with Robert to a masked ball at the opera house, which was the last time in her life she ever thus "dissipated." Browning had engaged for £2 5s. a box for the ball at the close of the carnival season, intending to repay a number of people who had entertained him, and had made for himself "a beautiful black silk domino." On the evening of the ball it was so warm that he urged Elizabeth to accompany him. Although she had scarcely left her fireside for three months, she immediately sent out to hire a domino and buy a mask. The Brownings arrived at the theater at half past ten.

Elizabeth felt too adventurous to remain all evening in her box, and so Robert and she went down into the masked dancers below and made their way through the crowd to every corner of the theater. When someone hit her playfully on the shoulder and cried, "Bella mascherina," she replied in the spirit of the occasion, knowing that no one could recognize her under a mask. In all her years in Italy she had never failed to be delighted with the courtesy of the crowds, and this evening not a coarse word or rough gesture came from anyone, with all the social classes enjoying one another's company in a way which would have been impossible in England.

At one o'clock in the morning Ferdinando served for the Brownings and two or three of their friends their supper of gallantina, rolls, cakes, ices, and champagne. Elizabeth was enjoying the party and would have stayed if she were well enough. "The brilliancy and variety of the sight," she later wrote, "were well worth coming for." At two o'clock, however, she felt so much oppression in her chest that she went home by herself in a carriage, leaving the others to come later, "as Robert did at four in the morning."

On July 30, 1857, the Brownings went to Bagni di Lucca,

where they remained until October 7. They rented a pretty house in the Villa, with a great terrace overlooking a private garden surrounded by oleanders and peach trees, only a few doors away from the place where they had spent the summer of 1853. Two or three days after they moved to the Baths, Isa Blagden, her friend Annette Bracken, and Robert Lytton arrived and stayed at a nearby inn. Elizabeth was physically weaker than usual and very much depressed in spirits, having made but slight recovery from the shock of her father's death, and looked forward to the repose of their summer retreat. Lytton, however, soon became ill with a kind of "gastric fever" and had to be nursed day and night by Isa Blagden and Browning.

Pen later caught the same infection and was in bed for two weeks. In the midst of the Brownings' troubles Wilson had to go away because of her pregnancy, and their Italian maid Annunziata was also seized with gastric symptoms. Elizabeth had been "peculiarly brittle" when she left Florence, and Pen's illness, as she later wrote Arabel, "ended by breaking me to pieces." The following winter, therefore, which the Brownings spent in Florence, was no better for Elizabeth. She informed Arabel that the weather, which was colder than usual, had undermined her health, that her nervous apprehensions also kept her unwell, and that her poor physical condition made her ever more uneasy in her mind. Her past griefs hung heavily on her, and she spent much of her time "brooding, brooding, brooding, and reading German, German, and German."

She resolved to take an interest in life once again, to do some writing before the year was over, and to "get out of the cloud if God lets me." In the daytime Robert left the apartment to take drawing lessons, and three or four evenings a week he was at Isa Blagden's villa or at the homes of other friends, while Elizabeth went to bed with a book. With his "enormous superfluity of vital energy," as Elizabeth put it, he felt the need of much more activity than did his invalid wife, and so they were necessarily apart more than during the early years of their marriage.

Elizabeth was not too unwell, however, to receive calls now and then from her friends in Florence and from writers and artists who were passing through the city. The Brownings' most memorable visitors in the spring of 1858 were Nathaniel Hawthorne and his wife, both of whom came to Casa Guidi in the evening of June 8. William Cullen Bryant and his daughter and the Brownings' friends Fanny Haworth and Mr. and Mrs. David Eckley were also present. Hawthorne immediately noticed Pen's strange likeness to his mother. Both seemed to him tiny, fragile, elflike creatures almost without substance, who might fly off some day when Browning least suspected it. The nine-year-old child with his long curls and velvet frock was in Hawthorne's eyes "as un-English a production as if he were native of another planet." During the evening Pen helped to serve the cake and strawberries, conversed with the guests, and meditated by himself on a couch. Hawthorne wondered what would ever become of such a fairy-like being and thought he would look queer if he were to wear boys' trousers.

Browning, who was agreeable and vivacious, appeared to carry on an animated conversation with all groups at the same moment. Hawthorne was more impressed with Elizabeth than when he had seen her at a breakfast party at Monckton Milnes' home in London two years earlier. He thought it wonderful to see how small she was, how bright and dark her eyes, how pale her face, which was framed with her black ringlets. It was marvelous to him how "so extraordinary, so acute, so sensitive" a person could make him feel assured of her benevolence. "There is not such another figure in the world," he wrote in his notebook. Although there were four well-known writers in the room, the conversation in Hawthorne's opinion was dull. It was largely on "that disagreeable and now wearisome" subject of spiritualism, and in particular the Brownings discussed the notorious affair at Ealing.

While Robert in his hearty manner exposed Home as a charlatan, Hawthorne felt that he had dispelled the mystery of the subject, but Elizabeth "ever and anon, put in a gentle word of expostulation." According to Julian Hawthorne, both his father and Browning "abominated" the whole business from the beginning. Late in June, Hawthorne met Browning at Isa Blagden's villa on Bellosguardo. Although both T. A. Trollope and the American composer Francis Boott were in the room, Hawthorne felt that Browning had the most powerful personality of the group. The English poet seemed amiable and filled with energy, as always, and spoke "most rapturously" of Gordigiani's portrait of Elizabeth, which had been commissioned by Mrs. Eckley. Hawthorne recorded that when Browning talked, even his nonsense was "of very genuine and excellent quality, the true babble and effervescence of a bright and powerful mind."

The Eckleys, whom Hawthorne had seen at Casa Guidi, were for two or three years close friends of the Brownings, and the two couples used to see each other almost every day at Florence and at Rome. The Eckleys were wealthy Americans whom the Brownings had first met at Bagni di Lucca in 1857. The British Museum has copies of five books published by Mrs. Eckley, possibly at her own expense; four are slender volumes of verse and of short sermons and meditations for the Lenten season, and the fifth describes a trip to Egypt, Palestine, and Syria. Elizabeth wrote Arabel that Mrs. Eckley (Sophie) had "fallen in love" with her and worshiped her "with a blind passion in all sorts of ways." At this time Elizabeth was convinced that Mrs. Eckley had "a pure, sweet, and noble nature." Almost every day she came to see Elizabeth, who thought her "so delicate and refined" that her visits were never boring or upsetting.

It was a "peculiar and a most delicate affectionateness—more delicacy is impossible." Their common interest was spiritualism, and Mrs. Eckley used to tell Elizabeth such stories as having heard at church sounds which followed her to the communion table and were so loud that she feared the rest of the congregation might have been disturbed. Elizabeth was astonished at the simplicity, enthusiasm, and generosity of both the Eckleys, who were in her opinion characteristically American (though she realized that not all her transatlantic friends were either so naïive or so generous) and could scarcely have been English. It seemed to her that everything and everyone Mrs. Eckley loved her husband also loved "with a sort of child's devotion" and a desire to give away everything in his pockets to show the sincerity of his feelings, "with tears in his eyes and a trembling in his voice." He would lay his head under the Brownings' feet, Elizabeth added, and beg them to walk over him, not because his wife told him to do it, but "because she feels so herself."

When the Eckleys heard that the Brownings had plans to spend the summer of 1858 on the French coast in order that a change of air might help Elizabeth regain her strength, Mrs. Eckley at once hoped that her husband and she might go with them, but she evidently realized the idea would be impracticable because both Robert and Elizabeth would necessarily be with their respective families almost every minute of the day. She then resigned herself to an absence of two or three months from Elizabeth and heaped up parting gifts: a ring, a brooch, a traveler's bag, Damascus slippers, and a rosary from the Holy Sepulchre. "Such floods of tears there have been—floods," Elizabeth wrote of Mrs. Eckley's farewell as the American woman went with her husband to Bagni di Lucca for the summer.

The Brownings traveled by steamer from Leghorn to Marseilles and from thence to Paris by express trains, arriving in the French capital on Tuesday evening, July 6. They stopped there for about a fortnight before going to Le Havre, where they stayed until September 20. In a letter from Paris, Elizabeth told Mrs. Eckley that Charles Sumner visited Robert and her and greatly pleased them by his "frank, generous, simple bearing." Sumner was traveling in Europe for medical treatment to recover from the brutal physical attack he had received on the floor of the United States Senate.

Although Elizabeth became somewhat stronger because of the sea air at Le Havre, she wrote Mrs. Eckley that she detested the section of the city where they were living because it was ugly, dull, and foul smelling. Sarianna and Browning's father were in adjoining apartments, and they all came together for their meals. Also Milsand was with them for a time, as well as Arabel, George, and Henry, who came with his recent bride. Much to Elizabeth's distress, her other brothers did not make the trip to see her, al-v though at the moment the three who had gone to Jamaica were living in England. The longer she stayed at their house on the shore, the more she disliked it. There was no sandy beach, their view of the sea was obliterated by a succession of bathing houses, and the great, flat stretch of sand around them seemed "as dismal as possible." Also Elizabeth had become tired from having too many visitors and from hearing too much conversation, so that she was counting the days until she could return to the silence of Italy.

She wrote to Mrs. Jameson that after the seclusion of her life in Florence she realized that she was no longer "fit for the common everyday life of sensible people here," although she begged Mrs. Jameson not to refer to the subject in any letters to her since she did not wish Robert to think she was not enjoying her holiday. And to Mrs. Eckley she wrote in the same vein that it seemed to her now as if she "must needs go out of the world to get rest." After their sojourn at Le Havre, Elizabeth took Arabel back to Paris with her to "dissipate" for a few weeks by looking at the shops. Arabel then returned to London, and the Brownings left Paris on October 13 for Genoa by way of Chambéry and the Mont Cenis pass, the crossing of which caused Elizabeth much suffering, just as it had six years earlier. From Genoa they went by steamer to Leghorn, where they stayed for a day to recuperate after their rough passage, before returning to their apartment in Florence.

Elizabeth was still in such poor health that she realized another winter in Florence would be impossible. Robert and she leaned toward Rome because of its milder climate. While they were debating whether or not to go, Mrs. Eckley "kept her family for weeks" in a hotel in Florence, waiting to see whether or not the Brownings would travel to Rome or remain at Casa Guidi, because if they did not move away, Mrs. Eckley also wished to stay. As soon as the Eckleys learned of the Brownings' decision to go to Rome, they told them they were also making the trip to that city and had two carriages ready, one of which they asked the Brownings and their servants to use, as a special favour to them. The offer was accepted with thanks, and Mrs. Eckley to show her pleasure later gave Elizabeth a "most expensive pair of fur cuffs."

The party left Florence on Thursday, November 18, 1858, and journeyed about thirty miles a day by way of the scenic route of Arezzo, Perugia, Spoleto, and Terni, arriving at Rome on the afternoon of the twenty-fourth. In the course of the trip "the spirits" several times "made signs" both to Elizabeth and to Mrs. Eckley. But more startling than the supernatural visitations were two events which almost cost several lives. Once during the descent of a mountain, with one side of the road overlooking a precipitous cliff, the horses rebelled and nearly dragged the Brownings' carriage over the edge. Another time, two drivers of the oxen teams who came to pull the carriages up a mountain began to fight each other. When one drew out a knife and was on the point of stabbing the other, Browning rushed forth from the barouche and although successful in disarming the man was thrown on the ground. Pen shrieked "in an agony of fear," as Elizabeth wrote to Arabel, "Oh, that naughty man is killing papa," and then she all but fainted.

The Brownings reached their destination with no further disturbances and once again rented for about £11 a month their former apartment at 43 Via Bocca di Leone. Within a few weeks they had seen many of their old friends, such as the Storys, Charlotte Cushman, Harriet Hosmer, W. C. Cartwright, who was later a member of Parliament in London, the young English artist Frederick Leighton, and the English diplomat Odo Russell. They also met two distinguished Americans from Boston: the historian John Lothrop Motley and Charles Callahan Perkins, who was a wealthy art critic. Even though Elizabeth had many congenial friends in Rome, her increasing frailty made it impossible for her to go out except for short drives in the daytime. On Christmas morning, however, she was strong enough to attend with Robert and the Eckleys the grand mass at St. Peter's, where the blast of the silver trumpets—as she put it—"thrilled" through her bones.

Robert, who appeared more robust than ever before in his life, was "plunged into gaieties of all sorts," Elizabeth wrote Isa Blagden, "caught from one hand to another like a ball, has gone out every night for a fortnight together, and sometimes two or three times deep in a one night's engagements. So plenty of distraction, and no Men and Women. Men and Women from without instead!" If they had an evening together once in several weeks, they called it a holiday. Since Elizabeth was not well enough to receive guests when she was alone, she retired early to conserve her strength. She wrote Henrietta that she was pleased to see Robert thus amused, but it is clear that she did not like Rome as much as he. The climate, she was convinced, was unhealthy for most people, and the members of the foreign colony were filled with "reckless dissipation."

The city seemed to her "like a great roaring watering place. Cheltenham or Baden Baden—nothing thought of but dancing and dining, and crowding in some way or another." She wondered how the Caesars were able to sleep amidst such confusion and confessed to Isa Blagden that the atmosphere was not conducive to work. In February, Field Talfourd made a drawing of Elizabeth which had been commissioned by her English friend now living in Rome, Ellen Heaton, who wished to "have the only portrait in the world of Mrs. Browning." Although it would have been impossible for Miss Heaton to have achieved such an ambition because Gordigiani had already painted Elizabeth in Florence, "dear Sophie Eckley"—as Mrs. Browning wrote her sister Arabel—said that she was wounded by the "slight."

A curious aspect of the last years of Elizabeth's life was the series of petty jealousies to which her women friends gave expression as they vied with one another for first place in her favour. Ellen Heaton "never could bear Mrs. Eckley"; Fanny Haworth thought that Isa Blagden was "cold" to her; Elizabeth reproached Isa for being "as cold as ice" to Mrs. Eckley at Casa Guidi; Isa used to speak to Elizabeth of "those horrid Kinneys," and she never cared for Mrs. Story; and Mrs. Jameson was rather cool toward Elizabeth after a visit in Florence during the summer of 1857, possibly, as Elizabeth explained to Henrietta, because Isa was such a frequent visitor at Casa Guidi.

It was also in February that Elizabeth first spoke of the subject with which she was to be obsessed from now until the last hours of her life—the last phase of the Italian Risorgimento. Early in the month she wrote Sarianna of the "ignoble way" in which the English were treating Italy, in contrast to the "generous and magnanimous" action of Napoleon III, the "only great-hearted politician in Europe." In a letter to Arabel in March she told of the pleasure she had received from a visit by one of the greatest of Italian statesmen and patriots, Massimo d'Azeglio, who was then the Piedmontese ambassador in Rome. Elizabeth's attention was drawn to his "chivalrous, noble head," and she felt the "moral grandeur of the man, in a moment." Elizabeth's comment that he was "one of the very noblest men in Italy" was scarcely an exaggeration; without doubt he was the most important figure in Italian politics whom she met in Italy.

In the same letter to Arabel she again spoke in disparagement of English policy, which she believed too narrow and based on unfounded jealousies. After Orsini's attempt in Paris on the life of the emperor and the empress in January 1858, Napoleon had resolved to do something for Italy, and in his obscure, tortuous fashion he had been working steadily toward war with Austria.

In the following July he had secretly met Cavour at Plombières, where the two men conspired to bring about the freedom of Italy. Napoleon promised to liberate Italy from the Alps to the Adriatic and to make war at the right moment against Austria with 200,000 troops, if the Italians would also provide 100,000 men. He envisioned a kingdom of upper Italy in which Lombardy, Venetia, Parma, Modena, Bologna, and possibly the Marches were to be fused with Piedmont; and a kingdom of central Italy, uniting Tuscany and Umbria under the Duchess of Parma. The Pope was to retain Rome and King Ferdinand Naples. The four states thus constituted were to form a loose confederation under the presidency of the Pope.

The price Italy would have to pay for its freedom was the cession to France of Savoy and possibly of Nice. Napoleon fixed the late spring of 1859 for the outbreak of the war and left it to Cavour to find a plausible casus belli in which Austria was the aggressor. By the end of the year the treaty informally discussed at Plombières was officially signed. In January 1859, when Victor Emmanuel in his address to the Sardinian Parliament in Turin said that he could not remain insensible to the "cry of grief" which had reached him from many parts of Italy, a phrase which had been approved by Napoleon, all Europe realized that France and Italy were intending to make war within a few months.

The British government, with Derby as Prime Minister and Malmesbury in the Foreign Office, was against any change in the Vienna Settlement of 1815 and in particular did not want to see the balance of power in the Mediterranean upset; nor did it wish to weaken Austria, which was England's traditional ally. Malmesbury, hoping that the matter might be settled by Austria's reforms in Italy, had no understanding of the desire for independence throughout the length and breadth of the peninsula. The Derby government was not prepared, however, to intervene on the reactionary side to maintain the status quo, because the English people as a whole were friendly to Italian aspirations. Malmesbury determined to keep the peace if he could and hoped that the Italian question might be solved not by war but by a congress of the five powers, which was proposed in March by the Russians.

Although Napoleon had promised to come to Piedmont's aid if it were attacked by Austria, he was in a difficult position because most of his ministers and the business interests were opposed to the idea of a war against Austria, and Roman Catholic Frenchmen had no enthusiasm for military action which would diminish the Pope's temporal power. The emperor secretly instructed Cavour to continue his preparations for war, hoping, however, for delay in the outbreak of hostilities to give him time to win the approval of official Europe to the French-Italian point of view.

When Napoleon finally yielded to Malmesbury's proposal

of simultaneous disarmament by France, Piedmont, and Austria as a preliminary step to the congress, a joint English-French demand was sent to Turin. Cavour was on the verge of suicide after receiving this note on April 18. He supposed that the war would not take place, and he knew that a congress would never sanction Italian independence and an enlarged kingdom of northern Italy. Since the emperor had apparently deserted him by succumbing to English pressure, he had no choice but to telegraph his acceptance of the note from Paris and agree to disarm along with France and Austria. But the intransigence of Vienna in scorning the French-English offers of conciliation saved the day for Cavour.

On the twenty-third an ultimatum from Vienna that Piedmont disarm within three days was presented at Turin. If the Italians failed to comply, they would be immediately attacked. Cavour's policy had triumphed; he had provoked Austria into the war he had long desired. Napoleon, faithful to his word, entered the struggle late in April and began to transport to Italy the troops he had promised. On May 12 he arrived at Genoa and prepared for the advance. The first of the two principal battles of the campaign was fought on June 4 on the plain of Lombardy a few miles to the west of Milan, at Magenta, from which the Allies expelled the enemy after two hours of severest fighting.

The Austrians then evacuated Milan and retreated eastward across Lombardy to the Mincio, along which the final battle took place at Solferino, south of Lake Garda. Again the Allies under the leadership of Napoleon, Victor Emmanuel, and the French general MacMahon gained a decisive victory. A few days later Napoleon's forces crossed the Mincio and established their headquarters at Villafranca and Sommacampagna and were about to undertake the siege of the Austrian fortress at Peschiera. An Allied fleet was stationed in the Adriatic and was ready to attack the coastal forts of Venice. Just when everyone supposed Napoleon was on the point of taking the last step toward the fulfillment of his promise to free northern Italy, the Italians suddenly had their hopes dashed.

On July 6 Napoleon asked for an armistice, which was signed on the eighth, and on the eleventh he met Franz Joseph at Villafranca, where the emperors agreed upon the following terms: Austria was to cede Lombardy—except for the fortresses at Mantua and Peschiera—to Napoleon, who in turn would hand it over to Piedmont; Venice was to remain in the possession of Austria; and the Grand Duke of Tuscany and the Duke of Modena were to be restored to their states, though apparently without the use of force. Why did the French emperor disappoint the Italian people by bringing the war to an inconclusive end when ultimate victory against Austria seemed within his grasp? First of all, Prussia had 400,000 armed men along the Rhine, and Napoleon had to protect his country against this threat.

He had suffered casualties of 17,000 troops at Solferino, about 10 per cent of his army, and was horrified at the prospect of further bloodshed. In spite of the popular enthusiasm of the Italians for their cause, the response to the appeal for recruits had been disappointing; not many more than 12,000 men out of Italy's millions had joined the colors. The Austrians could draw upon vast reinforcements and might well win another battle. Besides the military situation, Napoleon realized that Cavour had seized the political initiative and was using his influence to make northern and central Italy one great kingdom under Victor Emmanuel.

Cavour's policy was directly opposed to Napoleon's, for the emperor did not wish Italy to become united, strong, and independent of France. Napoleon had hoped the Italians would gain their freedom, but his plan was for them to become a confederation of small, autonomous states, looking to France for their protection. Another reason for making peace was his reluctance to offend the clerical party in France by giving too much help to the Italians in their struggle against the Pope. In The meantime Robert Browning was following the situation with friendly interest, and Elizabeth had become a violent partisan of the movement. She wrote Arabel from Rome in April 1859 that there was "one unity of burning enthusiasm" from the north to the south of Italy, that if war had not come, there would have been a revolution, and that Piedmont would have been crushed by Austria but for Napoleon's noble act.

In May she expressed her conviction that the emperor was acting sublimely; his generos ity, she said, touched her to the heart. The faith and constancy of the Italians and the prospect that their land would soon be free and united seemed to her "like a beautiful dream,—too beautiful to be other than a dream!" She thought it "a holy cause" and a war on which she might "lawfully ask God's blessing." The "lies" in The Times, which Elizabeth believed had for two years been "a tool of Austria," and the cautious, neutral policy of the Derby régime filled her with rage, so that she wrote again and again to relatives and friends in England that the British government, press, and people had all covered themselves with dishonor.

The Brownings left Rome late in May, making the trip by carriage with the Eckleys, and arrived at Florence in the midst of the excitement over the war. The Grand Duke had fled from the Pitti Palace in April, and the government of Florence was now in the hands of three men, of whom Ricasoli was fast becoming the dictator as he led Tuscany toward a fusion with Piedmont, which was a step toward the creation of a strong constitutional kingdom. The Tuscan cabinet voted for Victor Emmanuel's sovereignty, and the communes declared themselves in favour of annexation by an overwhelming majority. In August a representative assembly met in the Palazzo Vecchio and passed a resolution that it was the firm intention of Tuscany to become a part of an Italian kingdom under Victor Emmanuel.

Elizabeth was delighted that her hopes were being realized much faster than she had thought possible, but she became so tense that she could not write, eat, or sleep and spent much of her time talking with friends about Italian politics. As she read in the newspapers of Napoleon's military victories and of the success of the cause which mattered more to her than almost anything else in her life, she lived "in a glow of triumph and gratitude"; it seemed to her as if she "walked among the angels of a new-created world." After the peace of Villafranca she wrote to Mrs. Martin about this period of ecstasy before her disillusionment: "All faces at Florence shone with one thought and one love. You can scarcely realise to yourself what it was at that time. Friends were more than friends, and strangers were friends." Almost never before had she been so happy, she wrote, and she was happy not only for Italy but also for the world because she thought "that this great deed would beat under its feet all enmities, and lift up England itself (at last) above its selfish and base policy." She was emotionally involved with the issues of the moment and owing to her physical weakness had less control over herself than during her first period of excitement when the Italians fought in 1848-49. She wrote Arabel that she had "literal physical palpitations" after reading the newspapers, which tears came into her eyes and sobs to her throat.

She was especially upset when she heard of such events as the attack on Perugia, where the Papal Swiss Guard put down a revolt with the greatest brutality, killing women and children in the streets. Also she wept with vexation when she read Tennyson's verses "Riflemen Form!" which had appeared in The Times, May 9:

True we have got—such a faithful ally
That only the Devil can tell what he means.
Form, Form, Riflemen Form!
Ready, be ready to meet the storm!

She was offended at Tennyson's scornful reference to the French emperor and wrote her relatives that the British fear of Napoleon was hysterical, for the French were not going to attack the English. Besides the excitement of a war and a new government in Tuscany, Elizabeth had upon her return to Florence another cause for anxiety. Her former maid Wilson, who through the years had been on the whole reliable and possessed of common sense, had become partially insane and appeared to have wasted away as though by an inner fire.

She told Elizabeth that from much reading of the Bible she was convinced that the world was soon coming to an end and that she could not live with her husband Ferdinando any longer, for they were "too near in blood" and their two children Orestes and Pilades were the "first fruit of the first resurrection." A few weeks later she said to Elizabeth that she had seen an angel carrying Orestes past her house in Florence. As Elizabeth looked at Wilson's mad expression and heard her uttering such nonsense with a strange intensity, it was all she could do, she wrote her sister Arabel, to keep from screaming and fainting away. Wilson had a rooming house in Florence, and Elizabeth realized that if it were known that the proprietor was mad, the business would be doomed and Wilson would have to be sent back to her relatives in England.

While Elizabeth was thus worrying about her maid and about the Italian cause, she heard without any warning the news of the cessation of hostilities and of the terms to which the emperors had agreed at Villafranca. At first she could not believe the re port was true:

Peace, peace, peace, do you say?
What!—with the enemy's guns in our ears?
With the country's wrong not rendered back?
What!—while Austria stands at bay
In Mantua, and our Venice bears
The cursed flag of the yellow and black?...
No, not Napoleon!—he who mused
At Paris, and at Milan spake,
And at Solferino led the fight:
Not he we trusted, honoured, used
Our hopes and hearts for.. till they break—
Even so, you tell us.. in his sight.

The Italian people were sullen and felt aggrieved with the emperor for not having won Venetia for them. Elizabeth, however, after her momentary reaction of incredulity and despair, was convinced that Napoleon had behaved magnificently and had been true to the cause from first to last. In a letter to Henrietta she blamed England for frustrating Napoleon's generous impulses: "I never will forgiveEngland for her part in these things—never —in helping Prussia and confederated Germany, by a league of most inhuman selfishness, to prevent the perfecting of the greatest Deed given to men to do in these latter days."

But she was misinformed, because the new British

government which had come into power in June had three members of the cabinet who were friendly to the Italian cause and helped it in countless ways: Palmerston, who was the Prime Minister, Lord John Russell, the Secretary for Foreign Affairs, and Gladstone the Chancellor of the Exchequer. Russell understood that the agreement at Villa franca left Austria the virtual ruler of Italy, and he brought pressure upon Napoleon to revise the treaty in favour of the Italians. Also he warned that his country would protest the restoration of the Dukes by force. Elizabeth, however, had no faith in England's good intentions toward Italy and did not realise that it was Palmerston's régime, not Napoleon's, which was sympathetic to the idea of a strong Italian kingdom independent of France. She wrote Fanny Haworth that she still believed in the emperor: "He did at Villafranca what he could not help but do. Since then, he has simply changed the arena of the struggle; he is walking under the earth instead of on the earth, but straight and to unchanged ends."

After living among the stars for months, Elizabeth was struck down by the sudden announcement from Villafranca. "It was as if a thunderbolt fell," she wrote. She was filled with grief and "impotent rage against all the nations of the earth," which had, as she believed, forced Napoleon's hand. Her nerves were so agitated that she suffered from a severe cough, "the worst attack on the chest" she had ever experienced in Italy. For two days it seemed as though she had been stricken with angina pectoris, so that Browning must have feared the worst, and for somewhat more than two weeks afterward her health was scarcely better. When her physician prescribed an immediate change of air and warned that failure to leave Florence might have fatal consequences, she decided to risk the journey to Siena, where Browning and she planned to remain until the arrival of cooler weather.

On July 30, looking like "a dark shadow," she was taken downstairs into a carriage, from which she was lifted into a train compartment, and at Siena was carried to her bed in the hotel where the Brownings stopped for two days before they moved into the Villa Alberti. Her physician E. G. F.

Grisanowsky was so much concerned over her health that he followed them to Siena by the next train and stayed at their hotel to be near his patient. It was he who selected for the Brownings' summer residence the Villa Alberti, a large, cool house in the low hills about two miles from the centre of the city. After they had been there a week, Robert wrote Mrs. Eckley that Elizabeth had not yet been able to walk three steps without help and that she had been too un well to write anything or to see anyone except her family. Every day, however, she was dressed and seated in a large, airy room and was slowly recovering strength.

In the Villa Belvedere nearby lived the Storys, who had been "most kind in every way," and their guest Walter Savage Landor. Early in August, Story had written Charles Eliot Norton of the recent arrival of the Brownings and of Landor's having come to stay with him three weeks earlier. Landor, who had been living for almost a year with his wife and children in a most unhappy and stormy relationship at the family villa in Fiesole, was turned out of the house one noon early in the summer of 1859 "with some fifteen pauls in his pocket" and was told "to be off and never to come back." Tired and ill, the eighty-four-year-old man walked along the burning streets to Florence, where after wandering around aimlessly he saw Browning, who took him back to Casa Guidi. In Story's words, "It was the case of old Lear over again."

Browning and Kirkup went to Fiesole to try to persuade the family to take him back, but their trip accomplished nothing. Then Mrs. Landor came to Casa Guili, and the aged poet, hearing that his wife was at the door, cried, "Let her come in, and I throw myself out of the window." The wife replied to Browning, "The best thing he could do." In writing of the episode to Henrietta, Elizabeth said that Landor's daughter had told Robert that "to save her father's life, she wouldn't give him a glass of water." Browning, who had "always said that he owed more as a writer to Landor than to any contemporary," showed his gratitude by becoming his guardian and the trustee of his funds. He placed Landor in a hotel for a short time, since Elizabeth's poor health would not permit his living at Casa Guidi, and in the middle of July he accompanied him to the Storys' villa in Siena.

One sultry morning Landor arrived with his benefactor, "looking very old, and almost as shabby and dusty and miserable as a beggar." Three weeks later, when the Brownings came, Robert arranged for Landor to move from the Storys' house to a cottage near the Brownings' villa. It was probably not until her last few weeks at Siena that Elizabeth was well enough to sit on the lawn in the evening under the ilexes and cypresses and talk with Landor and the Storys.

In view of his strong antipathy against Napoleon III, he must at times have seemed to her a most unsympathetic conversationalist. Story's daughter Edith remembered how "Mrs. Browning, with her face hidden under her large hat and curls, would be stirred past endurance by these assaults on her hero who was her 'Emperor evermore,' and would raise her treble voice even to a shrill pitch in protest, until Mr. Browning would come into the fray as mediator."

Emelyn Story, however, recalled that the many anecdotes narrated by Landor were amusing and full of charm and that "Mrs. Browning was often convulsed with laughter at his scorching invective and his extraordinary quick ejaculations, perpetual God-bless-my-souls, &c.!" In the middle of September, Elizabeth wrote Henrietta that she was well enough to go for a drive every day but that she would not be strong enough to stay for more than a few weeks in Florence after their return early in October.

Robert and she were thinking of Palermo because of its warm climate, but since she did not look with pleasure upon the prospect of passing "a winter without civilization," she supposed they would once again go to Rome. Meanwhile she was taking great pleasure in her quiet, comfortable house: "Our villa is really enjoyable—great rooms, with beautiful views.

Sunsets red as blood, seen every evening over deep purple hills, with intermediate tracts of green vineyards. And the silence, the repose. I drink them from this full 'beaker of the warm south.'" After the Brownings went back to their apartment in Florence, they planned to stay only a few weeks before proceeding toward Rome.

They were delayed in their departure, however, by a cold wind which kept Elizabeth confined to two or three rooms and also by the arrangements which Robert was making to settle Landor in his apartment at Wilson's lodging house on Via Nunziatina, not far from Casa Guidi. Wilson was to receive £30 a year for taking care of him, "which sounds a good deal," Elizabeth wrote; "but it is a difficult position." She added that he had excellent, generous, affectionate impulses, but the impulses of the tiger every now and then." When the Brownings went away, they left Landor "in great comfort." Elizabeth visited his suite of a sitting room, bedroom, and dining room and found that though they were small, they were quiet and cheerful and looked into a pretty garden.

Now that Landor had been settled for the winter and the weather had become milder, the Brownings were able to leave. As they set forth in their carriage on November 28, 1859, toward Perugia, Foligno, Terni, and Rome, they had with them, in addition to Ferdinando and the maidservant Annunziata, a second manservant who had recently been hired to take care of the pony which Robert had bought for Pen. The pony was fastened by a rein to the other horses, and although the Brownings feared they might have to leave him on the road with his groom, the animal surprised them by coming in fresh at every stage, and Elizabeth was convinced that it "would have travelled to the end of the world on the same terms."

After a pleasant excursion of six days, during which Elizabeth suffered no more fatigue than was usual on such trips, they arrived at Rome on Saturday, December 3, and were met at the outskirts of the city by the carriage of the Storys, who for several days had been driving out to greet them. The Storys escorted them to a hotel and then found them an apartment at 28 Via del Tritone in a building which has long since been destroyed when a wide, modern thoroughfare was built from the Piazza Barberini to the Corso. Owing to the war scare which kept all but a few English and Americans from visiting Rome, the Brownings were able to rent for only £11 a month a large and elegant suite, beautifully furnished and carpeted, with two salons besides the dining room, all with full exposure to the sun.

Although Elizabeth was careful of herself, she was less well that winter than ever before in Rome. One evening at about five o'clock Robert and she went in a carriage from their apartment to the shop of Castellani the jeweler to see the display of swords presented by the grateful Romans to Napoleon III and Victor Emmanuel. The Brownings were received "most flatteringly as poets and lovers of Italy; were asked for autographs; and returned in a blaze of glory and satisfaction, to collapse [as far as Elizabeth was concerned] in a near approach to mortality." As she wrote to Fanny Haworth, she could not catch just a simple cold: "All my bad symptoms came back. Suffocations, singular heart action, cough tearing one to atoms." Although she partially recovered from the attack, she felt herself "brittle" afterward and said that she had become "aware of increased susceptibility" and had to live for a while on a diet of ass's milk.

In the same letter to Fanny Haworth she also said that she was "going into the fire" for Louis Napoleon by issuing "a little 'brochure' of political poems." Her book, which was called Poems before Congress, was a slender octavo volume published in London by Chapman and Hall on March 12, 1860, and in New York by C. S. Francis under the title of Napoleon III in Italy, and Other Poems. The Brownings had Chapman sent complimentary copies to their close relatives and to many of their friends, such as Forster, Chorley, W. J. Fox, Monckton Milnes, Ruskin, the Rossetti brothers, Thomas Woolner, William Allingham, and Francis Sylvester Mahony. The congress to which Elizabeth referred in the title of her English edition was supposed to have taken place in January at Paris. When the peace treaty had been signed at Zurich on November 10, invitations for a congress of the leading powers had been issued and accepted.

On December 22 an anonymous pamphlet was published in Paris entitled Le Pape et le congrès, which, though not written by the emperor, was inspired by his ideas. The aim of the work was to urge that the congress reduce the Pope's territory and leave him only Rome. Napoleon had decided that the Romagna, which had already secured a de facto separation from the Papal State, must not again return to the domain of the Church. Austria asked if the French emperor intended to advocate at the congress the principles enunciated in the pamphlet, and on being given an affirmative answer withdrew early in January. Thereafter the congress was indefinitely postponed. Thus when Elizabeth's volume appeared in March, the title of the Engish edition was somewhat misleading.

In the preface of her book she expressed with her characteristic idealism the doctrine that truth and justice must transcend national boundaries and that even at the risk of being called unpatriotic she could not approve England's policy of nonintervention. Patriotism, she felt, did not mean "an exclusive devotion to one's country's interests," which would be a narrow and selfish attitude. "Let us put away the little Pedlingtonism unworthy of a great nation," she continued, "and too prevalent among us. If the man who does not look beyond this natural life is of a somewhat narrow order, what must be the man who does not look beyond his own frontier or his own sea?" She hoped that some day an English statesman would have the courage to propose a policy which would be of more benefit to the peoples of the world than to British trade.

Of the eight poems in the volume, one had no connection with the Italian cause: "A Curse for a Nation," which had been published in the Liberty Bell in Boston, 1856. It was unfortunate that Elizabeth included these verses against Negro slavery in the United States because a number of critics thought, after a superficial reading of the lines, that she was cursing her own country for its failure to enter the war on the side of Italy. The other seven poems all dealt with the Italian situation in 1859. "A Court Lady" tells of a beautiful and aristocratic woman in Milan who, after putting on a robe of silk and covering herself with diamonds, goes in an open carriage to a hospital where she comforts the wounded Italian and French soldiers.

Elizabeth does not explain in the poem why the heroine thought it appropriate to display all her jewelry while she was on this errand of mercy, but she informed a number of correspondents that the idea of the verses was based "on the general fact that the ladies of Milan went in full dress through the streets to the hospitals." "The Dance," which is somewhat similar, relates the story of a titled Florentine woman asking the French soldiers stationed in the Cascine park to dance with her and the other Italian women who are present. When the dancing is finished, the Frenchmen take their partners back to their Italian husbands, who thereupon "kissed the martial strangers mouth to mouth."

Then a great cry of gratitude for "the gallant sons of France" went up from all the Italians who participated in the episode. "Christmas Gifts" describes the fear of the Pope and Cardinals at the growing power of the Kingdom of Northern Italy; the joyful people, however, have been given the present they have long desired: the prospect that within a year or two their land would be free and united. One of the poems on Italian affairs, "A Tale of Villafranca," was already familiar to many English readers because it had appeared in the Athenaeum several weeks after the announcement of the armistice. In these verses the poet tells her Florentine son why his native city is in mourning:

A great man (who was crowned one day)
Imagined a great Deed:
He shaped it out of cloud and clay,
He touched it finely till the seed
Possessed the flower: from heart and brain
He fed it with large thoughts humane,
To help a people's need.

But sovereigns and statesmen were angry and fearful that the doer of the deed threatened the right of the great powers to bully the weaker nations and destroy all which aimed at independence. Thus Napoleon's noble aims were "truncated and traduced" by men who were too narrow and mean to understand him. "An August Voice" also deals with Napoleon's action and represents him in August 1859 ironically urging the Florentines to take back their worthless Grand Duke.

The longest poem in the volume is "Napoleon III in Italy," which is a glorification of the "Sublime Deliverer," the man "who has done it all." The emperor is greater than "All common kingborn kings" because he represents the will of the people. All his policies are unselfish and straightforward; he would never "barter and cheat" or act from base motives, as "vulgar diplomates" do. Thanks to him, Italy lives anew, and patriots are swarming from every province to enlist. The poet is sure that historians will always say of him,

That he might have had the world with him,
But chose to side with suffering men,
And had the world against him when
He came to deliver Italy.
Emperor
Evermore.

This portrait indeed flatters its subject almost beyond recognition. Yet in spite of all the faults which liberal historians have seen in the main figure of the Second Empire, it is none the less true that he was genuinely interested in the cause of Italian freedom, though not of its political unity, and that as a result of the contribution of the French army in the spring of 1859, the country achieved independence years earlier than it would have without that help.

Elizabeth was grateful to the emperor for his deed of knight-errantry in behalf of her adopted country, in the struggles of which she had taken an almost personal interest. She saw a great, liberal movement taking place around her, and she assumed that the chief actors on the scene, the French emperor and the brilliant, wily first minister of Piedmont, were honest and without blemish in both motive and deed. In thus oversimplifying issues and recognizing only the best qualities in people, she remained true to character.

The most idealistic poem in the volume is "Italy and the World," in which Elizabeth rejoices that, thanks to France, the provinces of central Italy—"Florence, Bologna, Parma, Modena" —have risen from their graves to become the nucleus of a free and united kingdom. As for England, the poet is angry because of its refusal to go to war alongside the Italians, and she wonders at the hysterical efforts of her native country to defend itself against a nonexistent aggressor:

I cry aloud in my poet-passion,
Viewing my England o'er Alp and sea.
I loved her more in her ancient fashion:
She carries her rifles too thick for me,
Who spares them so in the cause of a brother.

She urges the central Italian provinces to extinguish their separate lives and to merge themselves in the newly created kingdom, which, in its turn, she hopes, will some day become an integral part of a world community based on Christian ideals, a brotherhood far above "earth's municipal, insular schisms." With the coming of this era of universal benevolence, there will be

No more Jew nor Greek then,—taunting
Nor taunted;—no more England nor France!
But one confederate brotherhood planting
One flag only, to mark the advance,
Onward and upward, of all humanity.

Elizabeth wrote Fanny Haworth that she expected "to be torn to pieces by English critics"; her prophecy was fulfilled. Almost all the reviews objected to her point of view and felt that contemporary political events were not fitting material for poetry. The two critical notices which were strongest in their condemnation appeared in Blackwood's and the Saturday Review, both of which irritated Elizabeth because of their virulent and unfair attacks.

In a letter to Mrs. Jameson she referred to "that mob of 'Saturday Reviewers,' who take their mud and their morals from the same place, and use voices hoarse with hooting down un-English poetesses, to cheer on the English champion, Tom Sayers," —a popular prize-fighter. The tone of the article in the Saturday Review was so ill-tempered that it seemed as though the writer had a personal grudge against the poet because of her disapproval of British neutrality.

The notice was probably written by G. S. Venables, who

was a wealthy lawyer and a well-known writer for the Saturday Review and The Times. Since the Saturday Review was insular in its point of view, hostile toward Napoleon III and indifferent to the Italian cause, the reviewer's unfriendly treatment of the volume is not surprising. In order that he might not appear to be condemning Elizabeth herself, he pretended that the opinions in the book were expressed not by its author but by a fictitious character conceived to be a "bearded exile" from England who was also a poet and a long-time resident of Florence.

The main theme of the article was that this "illogical renegade" had lived away from England so long that he had forgotten the meaning of liberty and of constitutional government. The reviewer scoffed at the "cosmopolitan English exile" who frittered away his time between "dilettante Liberalism and dilettante art."

He spoke of the "delirium of imbecile one-sidedness" with which this "denationalized fanatic" protested against the Volunteer movement in England, and he referred to the "servile and seditious platitudes" uttered by the "poor prattler" who praised the emperor in "Napoleon III in Italy." According to the review, the speaker of the poems had no ideas of his own except for the ones heard in "Liberal Italian casinos," all of which were influenced by French thought, and thus the English convert "echoes their ignorant calumnies in the shape of unauthorized apologies." Throughout the article the author ridiculed ideas which were "democratic," "liberal," "cosmopolitan," and "Continental."

He particularly objected to the abolitionist poem: "When an angel enjoins her [the speaker of the poem] to indite her superfluous execration, she endeavours, with more than the perversity of Balaam, to express by preference that hysterical antipathy to England which Mrs. Browning attributes in turn to almost all her characters."

He then quoted some twelve lines from the "Curse" in which the poet spoke of the "sins" she believed were still characteristic features of English life: "little feet / Of children bleeding along the street," the House of Parliament representing the few rather than the many, and the widespread system of bribery.

The reviewer replied contemptuously to her allegations of British injustice: "This is the kind of stuff which ignorant foreigners delight to repeat; and their pleasure is multiplied tenfold when English renegades can be found to vent calumnies against a land which they have forgotten. There are more barefooted children and rough pavements, and a greater amount of neglected poverty in any Italian village than in an English town of thrice the population." This article was perhaps the most harshly expressed and unjust review of Elizabeth's poems which came from any critical journal during her lifetime.

In a notice entitled "Poetic Aberrations," Blackwood's was almost as unfriendly as the Saturday Review. The writer was pained that "one of England's most gifted daughters" had published a volume which was "so ineffably bad" in its poetical composition, "so strangely blind" in its political principles, and "so utterly unfair to England and English feeling." In the eyes of the reviewer, the principal fault of the poems was that they were composed by a woman.

He believed that women ought not to write about controversial issues of the day but should confine themselves to their household duties and that if they had to go out of their homes, they should become nurses, like Florence Nightingale: "We are strongly of opinion [the article began] that, for the peace and welfare of society, it is a good and wholesome rule that women should not interfere with politics.

We love the fair sex too well, to desire that they should be withdrawn from their own sphere, which is that of adorning the domestic circle, and tempering by their gentleness the asperities of our ruder nature, to figure in the public arena, or involve themselves in party contests." The reviewer continued that women were like angels when they visited the sick, provided food for the hungry, and prayed at lonely deathbeds; when they discussed politics, however, they "overstepped the pale of propriety" and no longer resembled angels but "so many tricoteuses in the gallery of the National Convention."

He implied that a sensible person would not have written on Italian nationalism but that the poet might be forgiven her choice of subject because of her long residence in Italy. It also seemed to him that the Treaty of Vienna, which in 1815 placed Italy under Austrian rule, was in many respects a satisfactory arrangement, since it procured for Europe a long period of peace; he thought that the Italians were now somewhat unreasonable in asking for the control of their country. The writer had a strong aversion to the French emperor, rebuked Palmerston and Russell for having been sympathetic to the French expedition in Italy, and maintained that Elizabeth in writing her "Napoleon III in Italy" had been "seized with a... fit of insanity."

The review concluded with a meaningless and unfair comparison between two greathearted Englishwomen: "To bless and not to curse is woman's function; and if Mrs. Browning, in her calmer moments, will but contrast the spirit which has prompted her to such melancholy aberrations with that which animated Florence Nightingale, she can hardly fail to derive a profitable lesson for the future."

Fraser's Magazine was also unfavorable, but it was more temperate in its language than Blackwood's and the Saturday Review. It disagreed with her high estimate of the French emperor and thought that her portrait of him was "a monstrous caricature of history." The writer of the notice believed that Napoleon's reign was based on fraud and force, and he maintained that the sense of insecurity which then paralyzed the commerce and arts of Europe "might convince the most incredulous, might convince Mrs. Browning herself, how mischievous to steady progress this disturbing element invariably proves." To the reviewer the most painful feature of the volume was the bitterness with which the poet had spoken of her own country. In his opinion, she had completely misjudged English policy, which seemed to him "upon the whole wise and honourable, prudent and resolute." As far as the poetry was concerned, the reviewer wrote that it was "the weakest, most inchoate, most unmusical, and most ineffective" that he had seen for a long time. The London Globe reminded

Elizabeth that rulers had to work hopefully with mixed evil and good and that instead of impatiently scolding and vilifying people, she should try to convert them.

More than all the other vituperative notices, H. F. Chorley's remarks in the Athenaeum gave Elizabeth the greatest pain. He wrote that her art suffered from the violence of her temper and that in this political pamphlet of sixty pages he found "not so much of lute as of marrow-bone and cleaver." Elizabeth was especially irritated that Chorley, who had followed her career with sympathetic interest longer than any other Engish critic and who was a close friend of both Robert and herself, should have supposed that the last poem of the volume was a curse against England.

Yet he was not greatly to blame, for it is not immediately clear against whom or what country the poet vented her curse. She herself admitted to Isa Blagden that "certain of those quoted stanzas do 'fit' England 'as if they were made for her.'" Furthermore no critic would have supposed that a volume apparently devoted to the Italian movement would contain a poem written for the American abolitionist cause. Elizabeth should not have expected to receive a friendly review from Chorley because in his Roccabella, published in 1859, he had already shown himself to be hostile to the Italian effort. This novel, which was ironically dedicated to Elizabeth, had an Italian patriot for its chief villain. In acknowledging the dedication, she had writen Chorley that she was in complete disagreement with his views, especially with his apparent assumption that "God made only the English."

After a copy of the Athenaeum containing the review of Poems before Congress reached Casa Guidi, both of the Brownings were much upset at the treatment of the volume by the anonymous reviewer whom they supposed to be Chorley. Robert, who was more angry than Elizabeth, expressed in letters both to Edward Chapman the publisher and to Isa Blagden his belief that Chorley had not made a thoughtless error but had intentionally maligned Elizabeth. It was evidently at Browning's insistence that Elizabeth wrote Chorley a letter of protest and explained her "Curse," which she said a more careful reading would have made clear to him. Through no fault of Chorley's, as he later claimed, the Athenaeum did not print this letter but merely said in its weekly gossip column that Mrs. Browning wished the editors to state that her "Curse" was aimed not against England, "as is generally thought," but against the United States, not on account, "she now tells us," of the Italian cause but of the Negro question.

The writer of the paragraph then asked, in extenuation of the reviewer's "hasty and incorrect" reading of the "Curse," why a poem on the issue of Negro slavery should have appeared among Poems before Congress. When Elizabeth saw these words of apology instead of the text of her letter, she was more vexed than she had been at first and wrote Chorley that the wording of the paragraph implied that she had been ungenerous and cowardly, "as if, in haste to escape from the dogs in England," she had thrown them the good name of another country. She emphasized to him that in publishing her volume she had not written to please anyone, not even her husband, and that she had not expected to advance her reputation in England, "but simply to deliver my soul, to get the relief to my conscience and heart, which comes from a pent-up word spoken or a tear shed."

She added, "Whatever I may have ever written of the least worth, has represented a conviction in me, something in me felt as a truth." Her attitude throughout the exchange of these letters with Chorley shows the extent to which her obsession with Italian affairs had destroyed her sense of proportion. A London weekly, the John Bull, found much to praise in the volume, although it did not agree with all her views. It said in her favour that her enthusiasm and sympathy had "lent fire and energy to her verse" and that in many passages she still possessed "her old power in wielding the English language and her wonderful gift of rhythmic melody." The critic believed, however, that she had "some impatience of strict justice and some blindness to historic truth."

The writer quoted her remark in her preface-"Non-intervention in the affairs of neighbouring states is a high political virtue; but non-intervention does not mean, passing by on the other side when your neighbour falls among thieves"—and then he asked, "But which is the neighbour and which is the thief?" The reviewer thought that an ambassador sent from the Court of Turin to Florence who made use of his position in Tuscany to stir up a conspiracy against his own Prince in Piedmont was a thief rather than a neighbour. Likewise he believed that the threats of assassination made publicly by the secret societies at Parma against all who would give any help to the cause of the exiled Duchess were also the devices of thieves.

"In this diversity of opinion and sympathy," the reviewer maintained, "no English Ministry would be likely to interfere on either side. Nor would they, notwithstanding Mrs. Browning's indignation, have been justified in so doing." He also did not share her hope that the steps which were being taken to amalgamate the provinces of northern and central Italy might foreshadow an eventual world community of Christian nations. In his opinion the spirit of 1848 and more recently of 1859 was one of nationalism and should not be confounded with any notion of universal brotherhood. Her idealistic dreams were "flatly contradicted by the instincts of our age." He reminded his readers that "these cants" about international fellowship had been tried and had failed years ago: "One would suppose that Mrs. Browning had gone to sleep in the days of Marat and Danton, and had just now awoke with these specious chimeras fresh in her recollection."

Although almost all newspapers and literary journals were outraged by the book, she received at least two generous and friendly reviews, both of which gave her much pleasure to read after the other hostile criticisms. The London Daily News thought that the volume was "a work of considerable power—rough, wild, savage even in parts, yet all a-glow with enthusiasm, from the first page to the last." It was also welcomed by the Atlas, which said that it had been much interested in the Italian movement and the greatness of the French emperor.

Although in the opinion of the journal the poems were

not without some eccentricity and obscurity of expression, they nevertheless were "luminous with noble thought and nobler feeling—harmonious with a harmony beyond mere sweetness." Elizabeth's relatives and most of the Brownings' English friends apparently did not share her political views. William Michael Rossetti, however, wrote Elizabeth from London within a week or two after receiving his copy of Poems before Congress that he too believed that Louis Napoleon was a great and noble leader and that he honored her for courageously asserting her ideas in the face of a "blatant and intolerant" public opinion in England.

This was Elizabeth's last volume published in her lifetime. Twenty-two years earlier she had issued her first book under her own name. The Seraphim volume was filled with angels, wandering souls, lovelorn maidens, ancient halls, and proud knights; everything was weak, imitative, and sentimental. The reviewers had liked her romantic idiom and had greeted her as a poet of unusual promise but had warned her to come down from the clouds and to write about the world she knew. In her poems of 1860 she dealt earnestly with what she considered the greatest issues of her time and vigorously defended her right to do so, but the change in subject matter from romantic ballads and pseudoreligious dramas to journalism in verse about the politics of the hour was not altogether a gain.

Bibliography

Casa Guidi Windows: A Poem (1851)

Elizabeth Barrett Browning: Hitherto Unpublished Poems and Stories (1914)

Napoleon III in Italy, and Other Poems (1860)

New Poems by Robert and Elizabeth Barrett Browning (1914)

Sonnets from the Portuguese (1850)

The Battle of Marathon: A Poem (1820)

The Complete Poetical Works of Elizabeth Barrett Browning (1900)

The Complete Works of Elizabeth Barrett Browning (1900)

The Poems of Elizabeth Barrett Browning (1850)

The Poetical Works of Elizabeth Barrett Browning (1889)

The Poetical Works of Elizabeth Barrett Browning (1897)

The Seraphim and Other Poems (1838)

Two Poems (1854)

"Queen Annelida and False Arcite;" "The Complaint of Annelida to False Arcite," (1841)

"The Daughters of Pandarus" from the Odyssey (1846)

Diary by E. B. B.: The Unpublished Diary of Elizabeth Barrett Browning, 1831-1832 (1969)

Elizabeth Barrett Browning's Letters to Mrs. David Ogilvy, 1849-1861 (1973)

Elizabeth Barrett Browning: Letters to Her Sister, 1846-1859 (1929)

Letters from Elizabeth Barrett to B. R. Haydon (1939)

Letters of Elizabeth Barrett Browning Addressed to Richard Hengist Horne (1877)

Letters of the Brownings to George Barrett (1958)

Letters to Robert Browning and Other Correspondents by Elizabeth Barrett Browning (1916)

New Letters from Mrs. Browning to Isa Blagden (1951)

The Greek Christian Poets and the English Poets (1863)

The Letters of Elizabeth Barrett Browning (1897)

The Letters of Robert Browning and Elizabeth Barrett Browning, 1845-1846 (1969)

The Unpublished Letters of Elizabeth Barrett Browning to Mary Russell Mitford (1954)

Twenty Unpublished Letters of Elizabeth Barrett to Hugh Stuart Boyd (1950)

Unpublished Letters of Elizabeth Barrett Browning to Hugh Stuart Boyd (1955)